THE ART OF
HIGH-STAKES
DECISION-MAKING

THE ART OF
HIGH-STAKES
DECISION-MAKING

tough calls in a speed-driven world

J. KEITH MURNIGHAN, Kellogg School
of Management, Northwestern University
JOHN C. MOWEN, College of Business
Administration, Oklahoma State University

John Wiley & Sons, Inc.

Published by John Wiley & Sons, Inc., New York
Published simultaneously in Canada.

This publication is designed to provide accurate and authoritative
information in regard to the subject matter covered. It is sold with
the understanding that the publisher is not engaged in rendering
professional services. If professional advice or other expert
assistance is required, the services of a competent professional person should be sought.

Library of Congress Cataloging-in-Publication Data:

Murnighan, John Keith.
    The art of high-stakes decision-making: tough calls in a speed-driven
world / J. Keith Murnighan and John C. Mowen.
        p. cm.
    Includes bibliographical references and index.
ISBN 0-471-41576-6 (cloth : alk. paper)
1. Decision making. I. Mowen, John C. II. Title.

HD30.23 .M865 2001
658.4'03—dc21   2001026751

10 9 8 7 6 5 4 3 2 1

Printed in the United States by Morris Publishing
3212 East Highway 30 • Kearney, NE 68847
1-800-650-7888

Dedicated to

Beth, Kate, Annie, and Will

and

Maryanne, Katherine, and Cara

CONTENTS

PREFACE

Robert F. Kennedy said, "Only those who dare to fail greatly can ever achieve greatly." As we have seen time and again among our students and consulting clients, it is not a lack of talent or effort that keeps professionals from achieving their goals; rather, it is the fear of making high-stakes decisions. Our goal in writing *The Art of High-Stakes Decision-Making* is to provide a guide to help you dare to make the hard choices and to make them with absolutely maximum effectiveness.

We all make hundreds of decisions every day. Most are inconsequential. For instance, it rarely matters if our blouse doesn't quite match our pants or if we choose a longer but more scenic route to get to work. But with surprising frequency, we must make tough calls that can have tremendous consequences—for us as well as for others. When we ignore these opportunities, we often fail to recognize that we have just made a high-stakes decision. (As we all realize, the decision not to make a decision is itself a decision.)

How can we make the right choice under the gun? How can we make sure that we don't miss golden opportunities? And how do we prepare ourselves for a moment that could ultimately lead to a disaster? *The Art of High-Stakes Decision-Making* provides practical guidance for answering these questions. We believe that our book provides three benefits that are jointly offered by no other books on decision-making.

First, we tell compelling stories about real people making real high-stakes decisions. Second, we have distilled our structured approach to decision-making from the findings of hundreds of research studies, including our own. Third, we provide this structured process to help take the fear out of making high-stakes decisions.

In *Poor Richard's Almanac*, Benjamin Franklin said, "Experience is a dear teacher, and only fools will learn from no other." We have been fortunate to know people who have been willing to share the stories of their high-stakes decisions with us so that we can share their experiences with you. By reading these stories, you can follow Ben Franklin's advice and learn from their successes and their failures.

Most of our stories concern tough choices made in the business world, but we recognize that professionals can also learn from broader examples. Some of our vignettes come from high-stakes leisure activities, such as one physician's attempt to climb Mount Everest. Others draw from our particular areas of interest. For example, Keith Murnighan is particularly interested in the decision-making of professionals; thus many of his interviews focus on medical decision-making. John Mowen was once a Ranger-qualified army officer who served a tour of duty in Vietnam; the stories of decisions in the military and in the space program are his.

Many people have contributed to this book. Colleagues whose research findings have influenced us include Linda Babcock, Max Bazerman, Colin Camerer, Robyn Dawes, Baruch Fischoff, Tom Gilovich, Danny Kahneman, Irwin Levin, Sarah Lichtenstein, George Loewenstein, Lola Lopes, Vicki Medvec, Maggie Neale, Jim Shanteau, Paul Slovic, Dick Thaler, Amos Tversky, and others too numerous to mention.

We must also thank all of our friends and colleagues who have shared their stories with us. Many of them must go unnamed. Their willingness to share their intimate experiences has enriched this book, and we will be forever thankful.

Finally, we thank both our extended and our immediate families, who have been consistently and continuously supportive as we wrestled with the many decisions that went into this book. We dedicate this book to them with the hopes that in writing it, we too have become better high-stakes decision-makers.

J. KEITH MURNIGHAN
Evanston, Illinois
JOHN C. MOWEN
Stillwater, Oklahoma

PART I

Introduction

1

TOUGH CALLS
IN A SPEED-DRIVEN WORLD

The value of art is not beauty, but right action
W. Somerset Maugham

Put yourself in the shoes of Jim Bronson. You are 36 years old and have just received the national entrepreneur-of-the-year award. You and your partner have successfully opened 27 Chicago Brew Pubs in the last nine years. It is 1995, and investment bankers are at your door, wanting you to take your company public so that they can make you rich.

In 1986, you left a position as a senior analyst on Wall Street to pursue your dream of successfully developing a restaurant chain. You and your partner, Paul Springfield, make a great team. You favor a conservative approach to growth, whereas Paul, a natural marketer, constantly pushes you to grow faster. Your decisions so far have been phenomenally successful. Your strategy of carefully growing by three pubs a year has really paid off.

Now that you have won this big award, however, the competitive environment in the brewing industry is changing. Investment bankers are interested in other brew pubs, including L. A. Brew Pub, Big Apple, California Brew Pub, Big City Brew Pub, and Simpsons. There is a chance that each company may announce public offerings this year. You realize that within a one-year period, there may be 300 million to 400 million investment dollars flowing into brew pubs.

You now face a classic tough call. Do you continue your strategy of avoiding serious debt and slowly growing your company, or do you go

3

public and exponentially grow your company as the investment bankers propose? You face a soon-to-close window of threat and opportunity. If you continue your present strategy of slow growth, your more highly capitalized competitors could invade your territory and potentially drive you out of business. If you follow the investment bankers' advice and double the number of Chicago Brew Pubs each year for four consecutive years, you could potentially make several million dollars, but it will also place extreme demands on your managerial ability. Either choice could mean great success or dismal failure. You only have a short time to decide. Once your competitors go public, you may not get a second chance.

Jim Bronson and his partner had only a few weeks to make their decision. They worried that if they failed to act, they would fall behind the power curve; that is, their competitors would become so well capitalized that no matter how hard they tried, or how well they made their future decisions, they would be unable to compete effectively. To stay ahead of the curve, they would have to make the investment. Yet there was an incredible downside to the high-growth strategy. They faced a tremendously tough call, a true decision dilemma. If you were Jim Bronson, what would you do?

A CRASHING PLANE

Now change the situation and the time to December 20, 1995. American Airlines flight 965 is running smoothly. You are the pilot. Suddenly, the crash avoidance system barks, "Terrain, terrain … pull up, pull up." You pull up the nose of the Boeing 757 to gain lift. At the same time, you shove the throttle forward to increase air speed. The plane climbs, but not sharply enough. It clips some trees and slams into the side of a mountain ridge in Colombia, South America. Amazingly, 4 of the 163 passengers survive.

Like any airplane crash, it was a tremendous tragedy. In many ways, the aftermath made things even worse, when investigations revealed that any of three different choices could have led to no crash at all. First, analysis of the data by investigators suggested that the cause of the crash was pilot error. Apparently, the pilot had punched the wrong coordinates into the airplane's computer, making its readouts inaccurate and confusing. Subsequent choices that depended on these inaccurate readings placed the plane in great danger. Second, the accident occurred during the early stages of landing when the pilot followed standard operating procedures to extend small spoilers (called speed breaks) from the top of the plane's wings to reduce lift. When the alarm sounded and a steep climb was necessary, the pilot failed to retract the spoilers. As a result, the plane could not climb steeply enough to clear the mountain. The pilot had fallen behind the power curve, and he did not respond quickly enough when his actions determined the fate of everyone on board his plane.

A third factor also contributed to the tragedy. According to *The Wall Street Journal*, executives at Boeing faced a tough call when they designed the plane, and their choice contributed to the tragedy. Unlike Airbus, Boeing actively decided *not* to build a system into the plane that would automatically retract the spoilers when an emergency climb was necessary. As one retired pilot lamented, "They only needed another two hundred feet to make it, and if that plane had automatically retracting spoilers, they would have made it."

TOUGH CALLS DEFINED

Tough calls are high-stakes decisions that must be made when information is ambiguous, values conflict, and experts disagree. By their nature, they never offer a clear-cut, obvious choice. Due to the high risk that accompanies such hard choices, they may result in tremendous coups or dreadful blunders. Some people have jobs that require them to make tough calls all the time. Those who are successful and who can handle the pressure become the leaders of their fields. In today's society, they become the chief executive officers (CEOs), the eminent scientists, the pilots, the entrepreneurs, and the national leaders whose decisions impact the lives of thousands, if not millions, of people every year.

> *Tough calls are high-stakes decisions that must be made when information is ambiguous, values conflict, and experts disagree.*

Over time, the quality of our decisions determines our future. Each day we make dozens of decisions. Do I wear a seatbelt? Do I have five servings of fruits and vegetables? Do I get an hour of physical activity? We call these habitual decisions "multiplay decisions" because over the course of a few years, we make these routine choices thousands of times. Because their effects accumulate, they can have an enormous impact on our lives. If we choose to develop poor habits, we pay the consequences. Hundreds of books have been written on this type of routine decision-making.

In *The Art of High-Stakes Decision-Making*, we focus on the tough calls that occur less often, but with surprising frequency, in either our personal or our professional lives. Do I sell my company? Do I change my career? Do I report the unethical behavior of my boss? Do I fire an employee? How do I approach the need for increased care for my elderly parents? The answers to these questions have one commonality: The results of these decisions will seriously affect your future as well as the lives of other people.

Our goal in writing *The Art of High-Stakes Decision-Making* is to provide you with a structure and a set of guidelines for making tough calls. Peter Volanakis, the executive vice president of Corning Glass Corporation, argued that managers within an organization should share a common decision-making process for making fast, effective judgments. A sound decision-making process will give you the courage to take responsible high-stakes risks. Volanakis argued that this process will both improve and increase risk taking because managers "have no trouble defending their decision when they know they have taken all the important factors into consideration and used an objective, rational system to evaluate the available information."

In *The Art of High-Stakes Decision-Making*, we present a process called SCRIPTS for making tough calls. SCRIPTS identifies seven parameters that will ensure that your high-stakes decisions will stand the test of time. The seven parameters are: **s**earch for signals of threats and opportunities, find the **c**auses, evaluate the **r**isks, apply **i**ntuition and emotion, take different **p**erspectives, consider the **t**ime frame, and **s**olve the problem. Just as Somerset Maugham suggested in the quote introducing this chapter, the benefit of following a tested procedure is not in its elegance or beauty. Rather, it is in the positive outcomes that result.

Our high-stakes decisions determine our long-term happiness and success. Indeed, research tells us that we most frequently second-guess the hard choices that we have *not* made. It is not a lack of motivation that prevents success. Rather, it is the fear of making high-stakes decisions. By developing an in-depth understanding of the SCRIPTS process, you will be able to identify high-stakes decisions and how you can make them with the courage that comes from developing the essential ability to make hard choices. You will also learn how to make tough calls with the velocity that our speed-driven world requires.

> *It is the fear of making tough calls that keeps*
> *us from achieving our dreams.*

ILLUSTRATING THE FOUR CHARACTERISTICS OF TOUGH CALLS

The Chicago Brew Pub case illustrates the four key characteristics of tough calls. First, the stakes were high—the fate of an organization and the jobs of five hundred employees were at stake. Second, the available information was ambiguous. No one could tell with any certainty, in advance, which course of action would result in the most favorable outcome. Third, basic values were in conflict. On the one hand, Jim Bronson wanted to follow his conservative instincts and build the company slowly and prudently. On the other hand, he knew that a failure to grow the company at this critical time could create difficulties that he might not be able to handle. Fourth, experts disagreed as to the most appropriate choice. The investment bankers urged him to act before the window of opportunity closed. In contrast, traditional bankers counseled him to be extremely wary of the siren song of quick riches.

The fate of American Airlines flight 965 also illustrates the characteristics of tough calls. The pilot faced a crisis situation in which many lives were in his hands. He had to react quickly based on his training, intelligence, and ability to handle stress. The case also identifies two additional aspects of tough calls. First, it illustrates the idea that tough calls can be made by both organizations and individuals. At the individual level, the pilot had to react quickly and skillfully to the crisis. At the organizational level, a team of executives had to decide whether to install a software system that automatically retracted the spoilers.

The flight 965 case also shows that decisions made at one time may impact outcomes many years later. Years prior to the crash, aeronautical engineers and company managers made the decision to leave it to pilots to determine whether to retract the spoilers in an emergency. In the design philosophy of building an airplane, managers must decide whether to maximize a pilot's or a computer's control of the plane and its many systems and safety features. Needless to say, computers can malfunction and cause accidents just like pilots can. The two giant airplane manufacturers, Boeing and Airbus, took alternative routes.

Airbus installed software that instructed the computer system to retract the spoilers; Boeing relied on pilots.

The experts at Boeing and the experts at Airbus disagreed in part because of their different organizational value systems. At Boeing, the value system emphasizes allowing pilots to have maximum control of the airplane. At Airbus, the value system focuses to a larger extent on using technology to fly an airplane. Thus experts in each company examined exactly the same data and came to opposite conclusions.

When choices are tough, no absolutely right answer exists. You can consult the most outstanding experts, but they will disagree on what to do. You can use complex computer programs, but they may only add to the confusion when subtle changes of an assumption or estimates of key variables lead to completely different answers. Even though no one "right" answer exists, you must make the decision and you must bear the consequences.

WHY HIGH-STAKES DECISION-MAKING IS AN ART

The characteristics of high-stakes decisions show that the process of making tough calls is more art than science. Whether the art form is painting, sculpture, drama, or modern dance, the same factors that characterize tough calls also appear in the artistic enterprise. Experts may disagree on quality, the art may activate different values, and information or motivations that instill the artwork with its life may be ambiguous. In addition, whether creating art or making tough calls, while we may gather and analyze data, in the end we must make our decisions when we are not completely certain of their outcomes.

There is no scientifically based replicable formula for creating art. Indeed, by its very nature, art involves creativity and innovation. In a similar manner, because tough calls occur infrequently and because information is often ambiguous, it is impossible to employ mathematical equations to make high-stakes decisions with certainty. Just as artists may employ mathematical relationships to create perspective or to compose music, high-stakes decision-makers may use them to evaluate the risks of different action alternatives. In each case, however, the end result is based on the expertise, intuition, and painstaking efforts of the decision-maker.

Finally, both art and high-stakes decision-making activate emotions. While the goal of art is to elicit feelings (see Chapter 5), making high-stakes decisions well means that we must control and understand how emotions affect our choices.

Just as artists follow guidelines and processes for creating their works, master decision-makers follow a structured process for making tough calls. Following a structured procedure, such as the SCRIPTS process that we present here, is particularly important in today's speed-driven world.

> *Just as artists follow guidelines for creating their works, master decision-makers follow a structured process for making tough calls.*

OPERATING ON FAST TIME

While under high levels of stress, Jim Bronson and his partner had to gather information, evaluate it, and make a tough strategic decision within a several-week time period. In contrast, the pilot of American Airlines flight 965 faced a crisis situation that required immediate and correct action. One major theme in our book is that our fast-paced culture often leads us to perceive a need to make decisions more quickly than ever before.

The push to make fast decisions is caused in part by our ever more complex technology. With each new computer and communications advance, our ability to gather and process information increases. As science breaks down time into ever-smaller increments, we want our decisions to match the speed of our computers. We want to do everything faster, including decision-making. As a result, we increasingly conduct our professional and even our personal lives on fast time. Our point of reference has moved from a focus on making decisions within months or weeks to days, minutes, or even seconds. We live in a fast-paced, speed-driven world, and we often feel that our ability to make tough choices needs to keep pace.

Nowhere has the need for fast choices become more important than in e-commerce. As one prominent venture capitalist, Dennis Kleiman, declared, "Four months—that's the narrow window of opportunity that a would-be Internet entrepreneur has to transform an idea into an actual product that's available on the web." This means taking an idea, clarifying it, making it operational, obtaining funding, hiring personnel, and having the web site functional, all within four months.

Even stodgy General Motors Corporation has recognized the need to hasten the process of making tough choices. In the summer of 2000, its new CEO, G. Richard Wagoner Jr., initiated his "go fast" program, which brought employees together to discover ways to speed up everything from purchasing to strategic planning.

The consulting firm Kepner-Tregoe recently completed a large research project investigating decision-making in the digital age. The authors concluded that because of the digital revolution, decision-makers now have access to an almost-limitless amount of data and are required to make judgments that instantaneously span geographic boundaries and time zones. These increased capabilities have necessitated an increase in decision-making speed. Their survey of 479 managers revealed that 77 percent reported that over the last three years they were required to make more decisions than in the past; 43 percent stated that the amount of time given to make each decision had decreased; and 80 percent reported that they had missed opportunities because they could not make decisions quickly enough.

One of the key factors in high-stakes decision-making is being able to identify how much time you have to make the decision. Even in a speed-driven world, the goal is to take the "right" amount of time to make the tough call. Indeed, one of the goals of the master decision-maker is to identify problem signals prior to the development of a crisis. Should you face a crisis, however, through the intensive practice of the SCRIPTS process, you will be able to instinctively apply its parameters to make the tough call.

TYPES OF TOUGH CALLS

We have developed a simple matrix that identifies the types of tough calls that individuals and organizations face. As shown in Figure 1.1, the two dimensions of the matrix are (1) the time available to make the decision and (2) whether the decision is repeated. The time available to make the decision can range from instantaneous (like the pilot on flight 965) to having months to work out a solution. We must make short-fuse decisions quickly and decisively. Long-fuse decisions give us time to think, bring in experts, and even employ computer simulations.

The second dimension of the matrix represents the frequency with which the same decision is repeated. In our terminology, choices that occur infrequently and are rarely replayed are single-play decisions. At an organizational level, the decision by Boeing not to install automatic retracting spoilers was a single-play decision. Once made, it would be

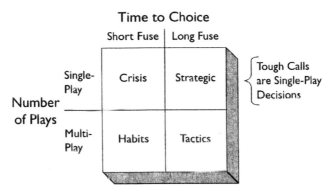

FIGURE 1.1   A Matrix of Decision Types

very hard to change. In contrast, banks replay thousands of times the decision concerning the financial criteria to give credit cards to consumers. The decisions that identify these criteria are strategic decisions. Replaying them over and over again illustrates the tactical application of the tough call. On a personal level, getting married, building a home, and undertaking major elective surgery are all examples of single-play decisions (at least for most people). In contrast, having dessert after dinner, selecting the right outfit to wear, and choosing to drive or use mass transit to get to work are all multiplay decisions.

Tough choices are almost always single-play decisions—whether they have a short or long time fuse. American Airlines flight 965 illustrates both types of single-play decisions. The few seconds that the pilot had to respond to the emergency represent the ultimate in crisis decision-making. Thus **crisis choices** are single-play decisions with a short time fuse, and **strategic decisions** are single-play decisions with a long time fuse. The design decision by Boeing to give pilots maximum control over the plane's functions represents a strategic decision. The decision faced by Jim Bronson represents a strategic decision. The selection of a career represents a strategic decision. Similarly, within organizations, the decision to enter an entirely new market represents a strategic choice. Each of these examples is a single-play decision with an outcome that has the potential of being a horrible blunder. By their very nature, then, tough choices entail considerable risk.

Multiplay decisions, in contrast, involve the execution of many smaller decisions, often over a long time period. Thus when multiplay decisions have a short time fuse, we think of them as **habitual.** Habitual choices tend to involve low stakes—if only because we get so used to making them. Some personal examples include choosing whether to wear a seat belt in a car, the mechanics of monthly bill paying, and how we choose which phone calls to return. Examples of habitual decisions in corporations include choices to highlight or ignore small defects in a product and the choice of internal e-mail for ordinary announcements.

Any single execution of a multiplay decision is unlikely to cause major problems. Thus not wearing a seatbelt on one trip to the grocery store is unlikely to cause any problems. When repeated many times over a long time period, however, multiplay decisions can have enormous consequences.

When time is available to make a multiplay decision, what would otherwise become habitual decisions can now be made tactically. **Tactical decisions** result from the development of a plan of action that fits within a broader, strategic decision. When acting rationally, we make our strategic decisions first and then move on to the nitty-gritty of tactics; strategic decisions provide the umbrella under which we make our tactical decisions. When we make strategic decisions, we focus on grand goals and big objectives and expect to achieve them over the long haul. We use tactics to implement our strategies. Like habitual choices, we make many tactical decisions. When we have time, we can make them deliberately.

An example of a tactical decision that we might make is choosing what to wear to an important interview or board meeting. An example of a tactical decision by an organization involves the processes it might use to open new restaurants. One large restaurant chain, for example, developed a strategy of purchasing distressed properties at rock-bottom prices and then remodeling and opening their new restaurants under their corporate name. The opening of dozens of restaurants over a several-year period represents the tactical implementation of their bigger strategy. The failure of any single restaurant would *not* sink the corporate boat. If the strategy itself was flawed, however, its multiplay implementation would inevitably have caused the demise of the entire company.

THE LAW OF LARGE NUMBERS
AND MULTIPLAY DECISIONS

We have known people who scoff at the importance of habitual and tactical decisions in their personal and professional lives. They are completely correct in suggesting that the outcome of any single tactical or habitual decision is unlikely to have much of an impact on their organization. Two facts, however, make multiplay decisions extremely important. First, they occur very frequently; one researcher recently estimated that 95 percent of our decisions are not just habitual but automatic. Second, multiplay decisions playing out over time have an inexorable quality: If you get them right, you will invariably win; but if you get them wrong, you will invariably lose. The law of large numbers explains why.

The law of large numbers is simple. If you do the same thing over and over again, the chances of failure and the chances of success will reveal themselves much more clearly than if you did that thing only once. Stated differently, if you replay a bet many times, your outcome will probably be very close to the bet's underlying expected value. Thus, if the odds are 60–40 for you, placing the bet a thousand times means that you will win very close to six hundred and you will lose very close to four hundred of the bets.

The law of large numbers explains why casinos are so incredibly profitable. The house has a small probability advantage on every single bet, whether made at the craps table, at roulette, or at blackjack. It also has a small probability advantage on every pull of every slot machine. (It's no wonder that they call them one-armed bandits.) Because they have this small advantage over many, many bets, the house's profits almost precisely match its edge in the odds. And the more bets that people make in any one casino, the higher the profits and the more certain they are to occur. This is why casinos treat big winners so well (e.g., offering free rooms and liquor). They know that if they can keep people betting, the law of large numbers will ensure that the house will increase its winnings. The law also explains why polling services can give such good estimates of election outcomes. By randomly sampling voters as they leave voting booths on election day, polling services can project with tremendous accuracy what the outcome of the election will be, long before all of the votes are in. (In fact, getting data from about 2,400 people provides a prediction of the total population's view within about three percentage points.) The law of large numbers is very powerful.

We can see the implications of the law of large numbers for decision-making by considering two different gambles. First, imagine that we have asked you to flip a fair coin. Before you see the result, you must choose heads or tails. If you are right, we will give you $10,000. If you are wrong, you give us $5,000. When we do this with managerial and executive groups, most people choose not to make the bet—even though the expected value is positive and considerable. Indeed, the mathematical calculation gives an expected value of $2,500. Suppose, however, that we change the bet. This time we will toss the coin one hundred times. For each bet that you win, we give you $100; for each bet that you lose, you pay us $50. The expected value of these hundred bets is exactly the same as the expected value of our one big bet—$2,500. When we offer this bet to managers and executives, they all choose to play.

The first bet is a large, single-play decision. The second is a series of smaller, identical multiplay decisions. The law of large numbers operates in the second case but not the first. Over the course of a hundred rounds of the multiplay bet, you will almost certainly win about $2,500. When we do the single-play bet, however, you will either win $10,000 or lose $5,000. The fear of losing $5,000 makes taking the bet too risky for most people, even though the prize for winning is twice as big.

It is critical to remember, however, that the underlying odds of multiplay decisions are what determine their final, cumulative outcome. When you make many choices, you will win in the long run only *if* the overall expected value of your choices is positive. If the expected value is negative, the law of large numbers will lead you to a terrible final outcome.

> **The law of large numbers ensures that failure occurs when multiplay decisions are poorly conceived.**

Consider the following example. In the summer of 2000, reports surfaced that over a million Bridgestone and Firestone tires that were original equipment in sports utility vehicles (SUVs) were defective. Evidence showed that the faulty tires, plus SUVs' tendency to roll over in a crash, may have been the cause of 148 fatalities and many other serious accidents. Investigators alleged that Firestone's inspections may not have been diligent, particularly at one plant. For any one tire, a careless inspection would not necessarily cause a problem. For millions of tires, however, the habit of not inspecting diligently may have contributed to a colossal disaster.

Buckling your seat belt when you are in a car provides an example of another habit. On its own, each instance of not buckling up is unlikely to result in any serious consequences because the odds of being in an accident today, tomorrow, or even this year are low. Researchers have found that we have an 8 percent chance of being in an automobile accident in any one year. (That number goes up to 28 percent for people 19 years of age or less.) The risk of dying as an occupant of a car is even less, at 1 in 11,000. Another way to express these risks is that average drivers have traffic accidents about once every 100,000 miles. (For truck drivers, it's once in every million miles; for police officers, it's once in every 25,000 miles.) Over a lifetime, however, the probability is high that you will be in a serious accident—an accident in which wearing a seat belt could save your life. For this reason, it can be extremely important for you to wear those belts and for individuals and organizations to be aware of their habits.

Because tactical decisions have the same multiplay character as habits, we must carefully examine them as well. Tactical decisions often emerge as a result of strategic choices; thus it is critical to develop strategy slowly, prudently, and with attention to detail. If the overall strategy is flawed, the hundreds of tactical decisions made to play it out will inevitably result in failure. In addition, if our tactics don't really match our strategies, we're also likely to be disappointed by our end results. Luckily, time is often available to ensure an appropriate fit between tactics and strategies—if we use that time wisely. For example, one strategy of some universities that are trying to improve their academic status is to hire as many star researchers as they can afford. Each star represents the implementation of a tactic to fulfill the strategy. This overall strategy often backfires, however, when the sitting faculty takes offense at the new recruits' special treatment. And the new recruits may also squabble with each other to see who gets top billing. When these kinds of political problems emerge, it becomes difficult for these universities to do anything other than to be less productive than they were before. The moral of the story here is clear: Strategies and tactics both require careful selection and implementation.

A classic example of how following a flawed strategy inevitably ends in failure occurred a number of years ago to a chain of home-and-auto stores. The firm had survived the Great Depression, and its employees and management were optimistic about its future. During the 1980s, the shadow of Wal-Mart fell on the firm. With the competition heating up, the firm moved from an installment-credit approach to using revolving credit for its customers. Their difficulties increased, however, when they employed the same credit-scoring approach for installment credit as for revolving credit. Customers used installment credit to make relatively large purchases, such as refrigerators, stoves, and washing machines. In contrast, they could use revolving credit for any type of purchase, no matter how small.

The change in approach to giving credit would have worked if the company had used a different scoring system to determine who should receive credit, taking into account that revolving-credit accounts have significantly higher default rates than installment-credit accounts. To compound matters, the company failed to track how many credit accounts a customer had with the firm. Finally, the company allowed its retail managers to make their own credit decisions. Because the managers' pay depended on their sales, they were motivated to give people credit even when it appeared risky. The combination of factors resulted in a flawed strategic plan, and as a result, the company went bankrupt.

SCRIPTING TOUGH CALLS

Our goal in writing this book is to provide you with a guide to the art and science of making tough choices. You can capture the essence of the art by using the acronym SCRIPTS. By considering each of seven SCRIPTS parameters, you will improve your odds of successfully navigating your own tough calls in a timely and confident way.

1. **S**earch for signals of threats and opportunities.
2. Find the **c**auses.
3. Evaluate the **r**isks.
4. Apply **i**ntuition and emotion.
5. Take different **p**erspectives.
6. Consider the **t**ime frame.
7. **S**olve the problem.

By considering each of the seven parameters, you will maximize the chances of successfully navigating tough calls. Perhaps just as important, the SCRIPTing approach will give you the confidence to live with the outcomes of your decisions—whether those outcomes turn out to be good or bad; that is, by knowing that you have followed a rational process for making a high-stakes decision, you can take comfort in knowing that you made the best choice under the circumstances. (It is critical to remember that when making tough calls, even the best decision can turn out poorly.)

In your professional life, understanding the SCRIPTS process is important for several reasons. First, more and more executives want decisions to be made quickly. One important way to hasten organizational decision-making is to let midlevel managers and employees on the front lines make hard choices. By allowing everyone in an organization to make tough calls, companies can substantially increase their responsiveness and their ability to satisfy customers—especially if everyone makes their decisions well.

Second, understanding how to make tough choices is critical for handling crises. What would you do if a major client was about to defect to a competitor, employees of your firm were kidnapped by terrorists, or a fire wiped out the production of the key component in your most profitable product? Knowing the parameters of tough choices will allow you to respond coolly, professionally, and effectively to a crisis.

Third, tough choices are a natural part of the strategic management of organizations in the escalating competition of today's marketplace. Even CEOs like Herb Kelleher of Southwest Airlines who profess not to engage in strategic planning make tough, strategic calls. We can see the evidence of strategic decision-making when they create visions for their companies, when they choose whether to settle a labor dispute, when they decide to take over another company, and when they move into new markets.

Finally, mastering the art of tough calls will give you the confidence to make high-stakes decisions. Although many companies are working toward becoming "learning organizations," the people in these companies still bear the responsibility and suffer the consequences of making risky decisions. Senior managers must have the ability and the confidence to make tough choices when hundreds of jobs, including their own, are on the line. Executives must also pass down the ability to make effective tough calls to their employees so that they in turn can handle increasingly higher stakes both on and off the job. If employees are unable to handle the hard choices in their personal and family lives, they will inevitably perform poorly on the job.

Understanding the SCRIPTS process provides the vocabulary and analytical skills to make better decisions. It will allow you to increase the flexibility and speed of your decisions. By training employees in the SCRIPTS process, organizations can respond more readily and more effectively to critical problems. When the people in an organization have a common understanding of how they will make tough choices, everyone will be better able not only to trust themselves but also to trust their peers and even their bosses. At the same time, employees can have the confidence to take action and know that they will be able to explain their decisions to managers who understand the problems inherent in making tough calls. In our fast-paced, speed-driven world, the hare (if undistracted!) will beat the tortoise.

In the same way, knowing how to make tough calls will also augment your high-stakes personal decisions. You may have to make major financial decisions like buying a home, moving to a distant city, or taking a new job. You may have to consider the tough choice of putting your parents in a nursing home. By using SCRIPTS to improve your high-stakes decision-making at home, you can maximize the effectiveness of your choices in your personal life as well as your professional life. Better decisions at home will also help you to build trust and allow you and your family to live with more confidence and less conflict.

Whenever high stakes are on the line, the kitchen gets hot. But the heat and the pressure are not the real problems. The real problem is fear—the fear of making the wrong choice. By understanding the parameters of tough choices, you can take control of your fears and make the tough calls required on the job and in your life. As you gain confidence in your ability to make tough calls, you may even learn to like the heat.

> *Understanding the SCRIPTS process will*
> *provide you with the confidence and the*
> *courage to make high-stakes decisions.*

SCRIPTing the brew pub case

The Chicago Brew Pub case provides examples for each of the seven SCRIPTS parameters. First, Jim Bronson and his partner had to search for signals of threats and opportunities. They recognized that the competitive environment was about to become much more difficult. But Jim also realized that going public would create its own set of problems.

Jim and Chicago Brew Pub did decide to go public. The days just before their initial public offering, however, provided a clear signal of impending difficulties. For 11 days, Jim traveled to 24 states and appeared at 73 meetings. He recognized that this exhausting experience was a harbinger of the difficulties of doubling the number of restaurants for four consecutive years.

The second parameter of tough calls is to find the causes of threats and opportunities. Jim certainly knew what would cause his opportunities to vanish: Only so much money was available to open brew pubs, and unless he acted quickly, the money would dry up. What he failed to ask, however, was why the opportunities appeared in the first place. He knew that the Chicago Brew Pub was the only profitable brew pub chain at the time. Another key question that needed an answer involved whether the market would support a dramatic increase in the number of brew pubs.

Interestingly, Jim told us that neither he nor his partner took any formal steps to evaluate the risks—the third parameter in the SCRIPTS process. One risk factor, however, did impact his decision. He recognized that by going public, they could immediately pay off the $3 million debt that they had taken on to begin a process of franchising restaurants. Thus on one dimension that was immediately obvious to them, going public would decrease risk.

Next, Jim Bronson and his partner needed to apply intuition and emotion—the fourth SCRIPTS parameter—when they considered their options. When we turn to intuition, it is critical to control the effects of our emotions on our decisions. As we will show in Chapter 5, emotions such as greed and fear can short-circuit an otherwise effective process employing intuition. Emotions do have a role, however, in high-stakes decision-making. They are always present because of the stress that inevitably accompanies the decision process. The key is to employ the energy that emotions create to help implement the decision.

For the fifth parameter of tough calls, take different perspectives, the two partners took different viewpoints. Paul Springfield took a marketing approach and focused on the issue of how to please customers and grow the business. Jim Bronson took a finance perspective that focused on how to hold down costs and make a profit. Their perspectives for making decisions influenced their interpretation of the evidence and the values that they brought to the decision-making process. As in many successful partnerships, the interplay of individuals taking divergent perspectives resulted in a winning strategy for many years.

As we show in Chapter 6, professional training provides people with a particular perspective. The best decision-makers recognize the biases that their own frame of reference creates, so they try to increase the number of perspectives that they use to analyze a problem. By viewing a problem through multiple perceptual lenses, they can select the optimum approach (or approaches) for making tough choices.

The sixth SCRIPTS parameter, consider the time frame, also applies here. Of particular importance is the question of how long the window of opportunity will remain open. In the brew pub case, it appeared that the chance to go public would disappear in less than six months. As a result, the partners needed to make a major strategic decision relatively quickly—but not immediately. As we show in Chapter 7, time pressure can dramatically affect the quality of our decisions. Master decision-makers can still function extremely well even in such stressful situations. In addition, they recognize that even in our fast-paced world, not all of their decisions need to be made quickly. Indeed, some of the worst disasters result from taking a "ready, fire, aim" approach to making tough choices and acting more quickly than is really necessary.

After considering the first six SCRIPTS parameters, decision-makers have the information that they need to take the final step, solve the problem, and make the tough call. In Chapter 8, we provide a three-step procedure for making the final decision. When time is available, the procedure can be more formal and employ explicit calculations. When time is short, the procedure will need to be less formal and seriously abbreviated. Having more time will allow you to make better decisions, but the SCRIPTS process will still facilitate quick decisions in important ways.

The SCRIPTS process can handle both long- and short-fuse decision situations. By first identifying and understanding the problem, you will immediately know whether your problem is a crisis or a strategic decision. If you are in a crisis, you must truncate lengthier procedures and use your experience, training, and intuition to make the tough call. If your problem is strategic, you can afford to use the more formal three-step procedure. By practicing the three-step procedure on numerous problems, you will begin to equip yourself to make crisis decisions. The rational decision-making procedures that we provide can thus be hard-wired so that your reactions become almost reflexive. In essence, you will begin to develop the kind of experienced intuition that will allow you to cope with crises quickly and effectively.

THE CONCLUSION

You may be wondering what happened to Jim Bronson and his partner and Chicago Brew Pub. After making a small public offering of stock, they paid the investment bankers and retired their debt of $3 million, leaving them with $15 million for expansion. They began opening pubs but quickly realized that it was extremely difficult to find suitable properties in the fast-growing industry. Over the next three years, they opened as many pubs as their experience and sound judgment indicated. By 1998, they had 67 locations.

Early in 1999, however, the industry started collapsing as competitor after competitor entered the market. In Dallas, for example, the number of brew pubs increased from 3 to 40 in two-and-a-half years.

We interviewed Janice Kline, who was the chief financial officer (CFO) for a company that owned 80 restaurant franchises. Beginning in 1996, she carefully watched the explosion of brew pubs because they were competitors of her firm. For her, the growth of the brew pub industry also represented an opportunity. As the competing brew pub companies sought to spend the $400 million in new capital that they had to expand, they needed to purchase existing properties. Janice was more than happy to sell her company's worst properties for inflated prices. Big Apple, for instance, paid handsomely for properties because of their investment bankers' requirement to grow. Janice told us that she simply waited for the inevitable collapse.

It didn't take long. Every analyst employed by the investment bankers failed the tough call as each company that had gone public lost money. In the end, every publicly traded brew pub company either went bankrupt or was purchased at distressed prices by another firm, resulting in almost-complete devastation for what was an emerging brew pub industry. In early 1999, there were about eight thousand brew pubs. By 2000, the number had been cut in half. Unfortunately, Chicago Brew Pub was caught in the carnage. In 2000, the company went bankrupt.

The experience of Jim Bronson, Paul Springfield, and Chicago Brew Pub illustrates two additional features of tough calls. First, because hard choices are made under conditions of great risk and uncertainty, even the best decision can have bad consequences. Only through the 20–20 vision of hindsight can we criticize the decision of these two young entrepreneurs to go public.

Second, the need to make decisions on fast time can be illusory. After being approached to take his company public, Jim Bronson recognized that he had to take sufficient time to formulate an effective strategy. Because of the pressure of the investment bankers, however, he perceived that his window of opportunity for making the decision would remain open for only a few weeks. In hindsight, however, had he waited longer, his outcomes would have been much better. Indeed, had he waited a couple of years to take his company public, he may have been able to buy up the other failed brew pubs at a fraction of their true value. As we discuss in Chapter 7, considering the time frame is a critical step in making successful tough calls. It's all too easy to get caught up with the idea that "I need to make a decision NOW!"

With the Chicago Brew Pub case acting as a reminder of the hazards of making tough calls, we move to the first parameter of the SCRIPTS process—"Search for Signals of Threats and Opportunities."

PART II

The Parameters of Tough Calls

2

SEARCH FOR SIGNALS OF THREATS AND OPPORTUNITIES

*I think of art, at its most significant, as a DEW line —
a Distant Early Warning system that can always be relied on
to tell the old culture what is beginning to happen to it.*

Marshall McLuhan

It was 4:00 P.M., and Jason McWatters was in rush-hour traffic on Lake Hefner Parkway in his Ford Bronco II. He was driving to Quail Springs Mall to visit a friend and look for a part-time job. It was a warm spring day in Oklahoma City, and Jason had the driver's-side window rolled down as he cruised at 75 miles per hour in the left-hand lane.

Suddenly, Jason heard a loud bang, and something hit his left elbow, which was hanging out his driver's-side window. His SUV lurched hard to the left. Reacting quickly, he threw the steering wheel to the right. His vehicle responded—too quickly—and it careened to the right across three lanes of traffic. Frantically looking in his rearview mirror, he saw cars scattering behind him as other drivers attempted to dodge the pieces of rubber that his car had sent flying. The Bronco was vibrating, and as he put his foot on the brake peddle, the SUV careened hard to the left, across the road again. Carefully applying his brakes, he slowed down and pulled on to the grass median.

Gingerly, he opened the door and jumped from the vehicle. The tread on his left-front Firestone tire was completely shredded, the wheel well was torn up, and the side-view mirror was missing. Then he realized that his left arm was hurting. He checked his elbow and found a large welt where the chards of the tire had hit him. A courteous motorist pulled over to help out. Jason declined the offer but said to the

25

bystander, "Damn, it was lucky that I didn't collide with anyone. I wonder what I hit on the road to cause the blowout." Then he changed the tire and was just a few minutes late meeting his friend. Jason never reported the incident to anyone.

The realization that the blowout was probably caused by the tire rather than by running over something in the road did not occur to Jason until three years later, when, in the summer and fall of 2000, the news broke that certain Firestone tires had an alarming tendency to blow out. By the spring of 2001, the National Highway Traffic Safety Administration (NHTSA) attributed 148 deaths and 1,000 accidents to these tires. What could not be determined was how many additional Firestone tires had failed but were not reported. Only through sheer good fortune were no cars in Jason's path as his car lurched across three lanes of rush-hour traffic. Undoubtedly, many other drivers experienced similar situations.

In this chapter we employ a series of cases, including the Firestone/Ford affair, that provide a foundation for identifying opportunities and threats. After presenting the cases, we describe what it means to stay ahead of the power curve. Next, we present the theory of signal detection, which provides a means of identifying the types of errors that can occur if we fail to act when we should, or if we act when we should not. Here, we describe what it means to "set the trigger." The chapter concludes with a description of situation analysis, which is a means for identifying opportunities and threats on an ongoing basis.

SEARCHING FOR SIGNALS: THE FIRST PARAMETER FOR MAKING TOUGH CALLS

In our observations of both people and organizations, we have found that some of the worst blunders occur when people fail to recognize problems or opportunities quickly enough. The ability to identify problems when they are small and manageable is critical in our nanosecond world. Obversely, the capacity to identify opportunities before your competitors provides a lasting market advantage. The skill of recognizing the situation and then acting prior to a window of threat or opportunity closing is one of the characteristics of the master decision-maker. Indeed, we believe that a failure to identify opportunities early will lead to problems in the future (i.e., if you fail to seize the opportunity, a competitor will).

> **The failure to identify opportunities early leads to problems in the future.**

In the quote that opened this chapter, Marshall McLuhan described art as acting like a DEW line to warn the old culture of the coming changes. Similarly, the ongoing search for signals of threats and opportunities will allow you to identify circumstances that may harm or help you. The story of Jason McWatters and the Firestone/Ford debacle illustrates cases in which two important companies failed to identify and respond in a timely fashion to signals of problems.

Numerous other cases illustrate how decision-makers in the military, in business, and in their personal lives failed to identify signals of threats and opportunities. Let's investigate a few of these.

Signal Recognition and Military Blunders

One arena in which the failure to detect problem signals results in the most vivid blunders may be the military. In 1990, for example, prior to initiating the Persian Gulf War, Saddam Hussein failed to correctly read the signals that the United States would attack Iraq if he invaded Kuwait. His assumption that the United States lacked the will to fight resulted in the devastation of his country. As of 2001, Iraq's humiliation continued as the nation remains under the jurisdiction of the United Nations and U.S. combat jets patrol deep inside its borders.

The U.S. military, however, has also suffered from the failure to detect signals of danger. Fifty years prior to the Persian Gulf War, intelligence officers received clear signals that Japan was preparing for war. In 1940, U.S. cryptographers deciphered MAGIC, the top-secret Japanese diplomatic code. Then in November 1941, military intelligence intercepted messages indicating that the Japanese had set a secret deadline of November 28 for concluding ongoing talks to avoid war between Japan and the United States. On the eve of Pearl Harbor, the U.S. secretary of war, Henry Stimson, declared, "I entirely fail to see the dangers [involved in the application of economic sanctions on Japan] by a nation as powerful as ours against another nation as susceptible to them as Japan in her present condition." The signals were there; unfortunately, they were not interpreted properly and acted upon.

Many other such examples can be found in military records. A classic case occurred early in the Civil War. In the spring of 1862, Major General George B. McClellan took the federal army of the Potomac to the gates of Richmond. He and his troops then fought an inconclusive battle in which the Confederacy suffered many casualties. After the battle, McClellan's army, which was guarded by federal gunboats, retreated down the peninsula to Harrison's Landing. During this change of base, they fought six additional battles. Four were inconclusive, and two were outright losses for the Confederates. Historians argue that McClellan had superior forces and, had he taken the opportunity to pursue the Confederate army rather than retreat, the war would have ended, possibly saving 560,000 lives—all the soldiers and civilians who died during the next four years of hostilities. He had a window of opportunity but failed to seize the moment.

Signal Recognition and Business Blunders

The failure to identify signals of problems or opportunities has affected many businesses. A classic example of failing to recognize an opportunity occurred when a very young Bill Gates approached IBM with a proposal for the giant corporation to purchase his fledgling operating system for personal computers. By turning him down, IBM set the stage for the emergence of a particularly rough-and-tumble competitor, Microsoft.

Two additional examples of business blunders involve two great U.S. companies—Motorola and Ford Motor Company.

Motorola's Failure to Act   The failure of Motorola to identify changes in the cellular phone market demonstrates the failure to detect signals of threats. In one of our interviews, we talked with a senior executive at Motorola who was heavily involved in the most profitable division of the company through much of the 1990s. In the cellular phone business, Motorola dominated the competition. In the mid 1990s, it generated roughly $5 billion of the company's revenues. Analog phones were hot, and Motorola ruled the market. As our contact described to us, the dilemma was that when digital phones began to appear, "the top manager acted as if he were invincible, and even after analog started to decline, he invested almost no money in digital."

Top executives at Motorola recognized that the division manager was not responding adequately to the digital challenge, but they took

18 months to fire him. As we describe later in the chapter, the executives had set a sticky trigger for action. Our source described the situation in the following manner: "Given the nature of hi-tech markets [as illustrated by the history of Sony and JVC and the Beta and VCR technologies], it is critically important to cut off investments in a product that is losing market share [e.g., analog] and get on the train to the new product [in this case, digital]. Any kind of delay will give your competitor a tremendous advantage."

In essence, Motorola handed the digital market to Nokia on a silver platter. By 2001, Nokia had the highest market share and was the most profitable player in cellular phones. As recounted by our contact, when the new division manager was finally onboard in July 1999, he told his staff, "We will have digital phones for the public by October 1, or I will have your ass." He monitored their progress and got his phones on time. Now Motorola is far more proactive in searching for threats and opportunities: "In an attempt to get ahead of the curve, they now poll 1,200 of their top customers, 200 of their suppliers, 80 Wall Street analysts, and 1,200 select employees to try to detect shifts in their key markets."

The Firestone/Ford Case   The maelstrom of controversy over alleged defective tires for SUVs and trucks produced by Firestone during the summer and fall of 2000 illustrates an amazing blunder that resulted from a failure to identify problem signals. Plaintiff's attorneys first began to file cases against Firestone and Ford in the early 1990s. Just as in Jason McWatter's experience, the pattern was one in which a tire tread would shred, causing the driver to lose control. For drivers who were either less skilled or less fortunate, the vehicle (often a Ford Explorer) would roll over several times.

The ability to detect problem signals, however, was particularly difficult for Ford. One of the charges made against Ford was that the company should have replaced Firestone tires in the United States when it replaced them in Saudi Arabia in the summer of 1998. A cursory analysis would suggest that if Ford replaced tires in another country, it should have also replaced them on its vehicles in the United States.

Before drawing any final conclusions, however, we should put ourselves in the position of Ford executives. Imagine that you are Jacques Nasser, the newly hired CEO of Ford in the summer of 1998. Based on the following information, which was available to Mr. Nasser at the time, would you initiate a recall of tires in the United States similar to that in Saudi Arabia?

1. Firestone tires on Explorers are blowing out at an alarming rate in Saudi Arabia. However, reliable information from Firestone indicates that many Explorer owners were deflating the tires to less than 20 pounds per square inch (psi) and using the vehicles as dune buggies.
2. Firestone maintains that there are no problems with the tires. Its management attributes the cause of the problem to consumer negligence in maintaining and using the tires.
3. You know that the Explorer has the second-best safety record among all SUVs, as reported by the NHTSA.
4. Your statisticians tell you that the normal failure rate of tires is about 1 in 10,000 and that Firestone Wilderness tires are failing at about 6 in 10,000. This difference is not statistically significant.
5. You know that State Farm Insurance Company has reported unusual numbers of accidents attributed to Firestone-produced tires used on SUVs.
6. You have no information on the number of accidents in Explorers caused by tires in the last six months because the NHTSA takes seven to eight months to produce these reports.

Clearly, Jacques Nasser's information was ambiguous, conflicting, and far from conclusive. No smoking gun said, "Firestone tires used on Ford Explorers in the United States are defective." On the other hand, when consumer safety is at stake, corporations are obligated to identify and solve problems quickly. Had Ford been able to identify the problem and act on it 12 months earlier, the company would have saved the lives of scores of its customers, as well as hundreds of millions of dollars.

Could Mr. Nasser have foreseen the problems that would soon follow? Two of the six points were clear warning signals. First, the State Farm reports are disquieting because the company is an independent organization with no axes to grind. Even more of a signal, however, is a failure rate that is six times normal. Six failures in 10,000 tires may not sound like many, and the number may not be statistically significant, but it has tremendous practical significance. This piece of information should have sent warning bells ringing throughout Ford's executive offices.

Signal Recognition and Personal Decisions

We must also search for signals in our professional lives. One of our most memorable interviews was with Harold Ramis, a Hollywood writer, actor, and director whose films include *Groundhog Day* and *Analyze This*. You may remember him as the character Egon in *Ghostbusters*. We talked to him about the decision-making that goes into directing a movie. He explained that as a director he faces hundreds of problems every day. "For instance," he said, "the prop man will ask me, what kind of car do you want for this scene. I say a big red convertible, an old one. A week later, he shows me two cars, I pick one. He says, what condition do you want it in, good, poor? I say poor. He says, how poor? Peeling paint or roughed up? I say no peeling paint. He says, do you want it to be dirty or clean? I say dirty. He says, brown dirt or black dirt? I say brown. What shade of brown? And this is just one small example. The same kind of thing happens repeatedly, every day."

These kinds of problems necessitate the small choices that solve tactical issues. They are not the strategic or crisis decisions that result in tough choices. An example of a strategic decision is the choice of whether to take on a new movie project. For instance, Harold told us that after directing *Analyze This*, he planned to take a break before making another movie. But a major studio sent him a hot script. He received it on a Friday, and they wanted to know by Monday if he was interested. He liked the script, so he started talking with them more seriously about the movie.

Soon Harold was working with a production team on a very tight schedule—hiring designers, talking about casting, and so forth. What held them up was finding a star. After some delay (and the hopes that that generated), their first choice declined, forcing them to consider other leads. Harold had some clear opinions and strong preferences, which he openly revealed. Discussions went back and forth, as this was a high-stakes problem. Finally, one of the studio's top executives declared, "What are we screwing around for? We'll use so-and-so. He's the guy."

At this point, it would have been very easy for Harold to simply accept the executive's recommendation, sign the contract, and make the movie. But Harold's antennae were up. Even though the person had a hit television show, Harold recognized that working with this person would be a big problem for him—one that could keep him from enjoying the long, intense process of making the movie.

Harold realized that he faced a tough call. He wanted to direct the film, but he did not want to work with the leading actor chosen by the producer, as he had already made clear. The executive would not budge. In the end, Harold walked away. He told us that other members of the crew also left when he did. He said, "It could be a big hit. But I couldn't do it."

Harold described his general approach to decision-making in the following way: "My own decisions tend to be conservative. If they don't work out, I tend not to be worse off. A little embarrassed for making a fool of myself, but you learn that this does not kill you. So most of my decisions lead to either harmless failures or very positive outcomes."

In the case of this movie, someone else directed it, and it became a reasonable financial success. In 1999, its box-office gross was in the bottom half of the top 50 movies, coming in at over $70 million. But Harold Ramis did not look back. He recognized a problem and acted on it. He also moved on to produce, write, and direct *Bedazzled*, which came out to positive reviews.

STAYING AHEAD OF THE POWER CURVE

The fundamental reason for identifying problems as early as possible is that when the stakes are high, problems can quickly compound over time. If you don't handle them early, high-stakes problems can grow at an astounding rate. Mathematicians describe this effect as a power curve. Depending on the circumstances, the effects of compounding can be either wonderful or horrible. Here are four examples of the potent effects of the power curve:

> **Example 1.** You have $10,000 that you would like to put into a mutual fund so that it can accumulate for your retirement. The mutual fund is very well managed and has returned an average of 12 percent annually for many years. If you assume that the fund will continue to return 12 percent annually, at what age should you invest the $10,000, and what will your initial stake become when you retire at 66 years of age?
>
> **Example 2.** You notice a very small irregularly shaped black mole on your shoulder. How long should you wait to see a physician?
>
> **Example 3.** How long do you wait before entering a new market?

Example 4. It is the summer of 1998, and you are Jacques Nasser, CEO of Ford Motor Company. Do you report to NHTSA that you are having difficulties with Firestone tires?

Let's start with Example 1. The compounding of money can produce almost unbelievable gains. If you put $10,000 into a mutual fund that has an average annual growth rate of 12 percent, in 18 years your initial investment will be worth $80,000. If you leave it alone for 42 years, it will grow dramatically higher. A 24-year-old who puts $10,000 away and watches it grow at 12 percent each year will be able to retire at age 66 with a wonderful nest egg of $1,280,000.

Figure 2.1 shows the power curve that depicts the effects of compounding if you place $10,000 in the fund at age 24. During the first six years, the value of the retirement nest egg has not grown much. After 18 years, when you are 42, you are just beginning to see the curve start to turn up. As six-year increments go by, however, the slope of the curve moves from horizontal to nearly vertical. By the time that you are 54, the curve is accelerating upward, and when you are 60, the compounding effect is dramatic.

Figure 2.1 also shows the not-so-positive effects of waiting to save for retirement. For example, suppose that you want to accumulate a million-plus for retirement at age 66, and you wait until you are 48 years old to start saving. Assuming a 12 percent return per year, your initial investment will double in value only three times instead of the seven times that it would have if you had started at age 24. As a result, you will have to invest 16 times more money ($160,000) at age 48 for it to accumulate to $1,280,000 by age 66.

> *The longer you wait to take action, the more difficult it is to get back on top of the power curve.*

The key concept illustrated in Figure 2.1 is that the longer you wait to take action once a problem sequence has begun, the more difficult it is get back on top of the power curve. To illustrate the effects of getting behind the power curve, we draw a line from the point on the graph that represents age 48 upward to the power curve. From this point, we draw a horizontal line to the vertical axis. Here, it crosses the axis at $160,000. Thus it is easy to see that the initial investment of $10,000

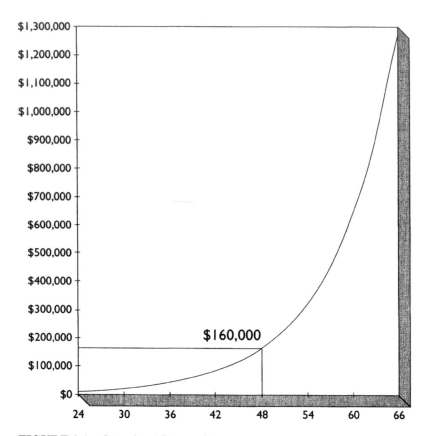

FIGURE 2.1 Standard Power Curve

has increased by 16 times as a result of waiting until age 48 to make the first move.

Now let's consider the second example, in which you notice a small mole on your shoulder. As most of us know, black irregularly shaped moles may be signals of malignant melanoma—a highly virulent skin cancer. Cancer cells multiply exponentially in the same manner as money compounds in a bank account. In the case of melanoma, however, the effects of waiting to respond to the signal can be dire. The reason is that the action taken to cure the disease does not have immediate effects. The impact of the treatment is lagged. Because the positive impact of the treatment is delayed, the disease has a chance to progress even further until the beneficial effects of the treatment take effect.

When the positive effects of an action are delayed and you are in the vertically sloping portion of the power curve, you may not be able to stay ahead of the curve. At this point, you have crossed the tipping point and entered the zone of false hope, where the power curve is accelerating so fast that the lag in the effect of your action means that you can never catch up. As a result, catastrophe occurs.

Figure 2.2 provides a pictorial representation of the zone of false hope. In our example, we will assume that there is a delay of 10 time units before the positive effects of the treatment take effect. If the disease is caught early, say, at 15 time units after it began, the delay has little impact on the outcome because the curve is in its horizontal phase. There is plenty of time for the treatment to have an effect. To cure the disease, a patient must only go through the discomfort of having the mole surgically removed in a simple out-patient procedure. In these early stages, it is easy to stay ahead of the curve.

The danger is that the longer a person waits to start treatment, the harder it is stay on top of the curve. If a person starts treatment late in the progress of the disease, say at time unit 65, the disease is spreading so fast that the 10 unit lag in the positive effects of the treatment gives the disease time to spread at an outstanding rate. By delaying treatment, the patient has crossed the tipping point and entered the zone of false hope, where the power curve is so steep that by the time treatment begins to take effect, at time unit 75, the patient cannot recover.

> ### *In the zone of false hope, no amount effort will allow you to escape disaster.*

We call the area beyond the tipping point the zone of false hope because it will appear to the decision-maker that the problem can be solved. The problem does not seem to be all that bad because it is difficult to recognize that it is compounding so rapidly. Most of us do not have an intuitive understanding of the incredible effects of compounding. We don't often realize that past the tipping point, the effects of the power curve can crush our hopes.

In addition to not understanding the effects of power curves, people also fail to recognize the impact of lag effects. Lag effects are actually very common. Consider the weather. The first day of summer, when the sun can shine the longest in the northern hemisphere, is June 21. Yet the hottest temperatures of the year do not occur until late July

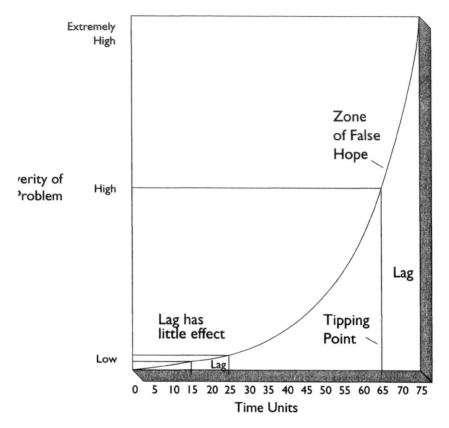

FIGURE 2.2   Zone of False Hope

and August. In the same manner, the effects of a cut in the interest rates by the Federal Reserve are not felt until about six months later. Similarly, the increase in output that results from hiring new employees will be delayed until they are trained and functioning as a team.

For most business decisions, lag effects represent nuisances that can be anticipated. Unfortunately, when the lag in the effects of an action is matched against a power-curve problem, the result can be devastating. It is as though you are swimming against a fast-moving stream.

A classic business example of the lag effect and the zone of false hope is our third example, the company that misses the opportunity to enter a new market before the competition. Once competition becomes entrenched in the market, it is much more difficult to build a presence that is profitable. Because of the lag in the effects of a new entrant's marketing activities, the pioneers only get stronger while the newcomer seeks to gain a toehold. In the mid 1990s, regulations changed to allow banks to open as many branches as they wished, providing an opportunity for big banks to expand. Fast-growing metropolitan areas like Oklahoma City and Tulsa were perfect targets. Two banks—MidFirst and Bank America—seized the opportunity and immediately acquired prime property at low prices and began building dozens of branches in both cities. Competitors that delayed taking action quickly fell behind the power curve. Not only were these two banks able to lock up customers who lived geographically close to their branches, but they also secured the best locations. In addition, the prices of the remaining prime properties quickly escalated. The tipping point had been reached, and any banks that tried to enter the market later faced an extremely difficult situation because they had entered the zone of false hope.

Finally, lets consider our last example of Jacques Nasser and the Ford Motor Company. In the summer of 1998, Mr. Nasser had inconclusive but suggestive information that Firestone tires on Ford Explorers were causing very serious accidents. As the CEO, he should have asked whether he was facing a power curve and ultimately, a zone of false hope. Was Ford in the early (i.e., horizontal) phase or in the false-hope portion of the curve? Would the lag in effects of any action be overwhelmed by the building firestorm of controversy? If Ford was at fault in this affair, the inevitable negative publicity would compound over time and spread through the population like a cancer in a human body. In addition, if Ford had taken aggressive action to make a recall, the positive effects would be delayed while the negative publicity continued to spread.

In the end, Ford waited until the summer of 2000 to make the recall. By that time, the NHTSA had forced Firestone to recall over six million tires. In response, Firestone blamed the affair on defects in the Explorer. In turn, Ford blamed the tire company. While the results are not yet in, it appears that Nasser and Ford may have acted prior to entering the zone of false hope. They were, however, far into the power curve and paid heavily for the delay. Ford had to make a massive effort to help Firestone make the recall. For example, the company temporarily suspended sales of the hot-selling Explorer while it supplied tires to Firestone for the recall, resulting in a huge cost. In subsequent months, sales of Ford Explorers fell dramatically, and Ford's profits plummeted. Although it appears that Ford will eventually get back on top of the power curve, had the company waited much longer to respond, it would have entered the zone of false hope. Indeed, when this book went to press, the outcome for Firestone remained in doubt.

In sum, whether dealing with a corporate crisis or entering a new market, staying ahead of the power curve is mandatory in today's high-velocity business environment. As a final example, consider Intel Corporation, which recently created a Home Products Group. The group's mission is to develop and supply semiconductors for networking and information appliances. The comanager of the group, Jon Bork, declares that achieving first-mover advantage is critical when Intel launches new products. As a result, it is critical for the firm to shorten its product-development cycle. The bottom line is that if Intel fails to provide the semiconductors that manufacturers need when new home appliances are created, the company would be locked out as a supplier. This same urgency for speed is required whether you are in electronics, banking, or the automotive industries.

SIGNAL DETECTION AND TOUGH CALLS

How then does an organization create the processes that help decision-makers to recognize problem signals and then implement decisions so that they can stay ahead of the curve? Similarly, how can we as individuals determine that we need to make a tough choice, now? One good answer lies in understanding signal-detection theory, and the best place to begin is where the theory originated.

The theory of signal detection developed during World War II to explain why soldiers manning radar screens made different types of errors as they went through their shift. Radar operators had the tough task of watching a small screen and determining whether any particular blip represented an enemy plane (i.e., a signal) or a cloud or other innocuous object (i.e., noise). Early in their duty watch, soldiers would more frequently make the error of claiming that a cloud was an enemy aircraft (a needless blunder). As the day went on, their errors would change, and they more frequently made the error of claiming that an enemy aircraft was a cloud (a missed opportunity). After a great deal of research into the problem, psychologists and statisticians realized that the accuracy of the radar operators had not changed. Instead, the criteria that they used to decide that a signal was an enemy plane had changed. Early in the day, their criteria were lower: It took less evidence for them to conclude that a signal was an airplane. Later in the day, after they had been viewing their radar screens for many hours, they relaxed their criteria and only interpreted a signal as indicative of an enemy aircraft if it was particularly clear.

One of the important contributions of signal-detection theory was the recognition that the accuracy of detecting signals is independent of the type of error that may occur. Accuracy refers to the ability to distinguish signal from noise. As accuracy increases, the total number of mistakes decreases. People can increase accuracy by improving the systems they employ to collect and interpret information, by selecting skilled personnel, and by creating high-quality training programs. On the other hand, bias refers to whether a decision-maker more frequently makes the error of a needless blunder or a missed opportunity. Because errors are inevitable when making tough calls, master decision-makers take steps to ensure that when they make an error, it is the least costly.

> *The accuracy of decision-makers is independent of the frequency of needless blunders and missed opportunities.*

Figure 2.3 identifies the four outcomes that occur when we search for signals. There are two correct outcomes in signal-detection analysis. First, when there is a real problem and the person detects the signal and acts, a hit occurs. Second, when there is no real problem and the person accurately recognizes that no signal exists, a correct rejection occurs.

There are also two types of errors. First, when there is a real problem and the person fails to detect the signal and fails to act, it's a missed opportunity. Second, when there is no real problem but the person perceives that a signal exists and acts, it's a needless blunder.

To better describe the two types of signal-detection errors, we present the stories of two notable military errors.

Understanding the Missed Opportunity and the Needless Blunder

In May 1987, the USS *Stark*, a guided-missile frigate, was cruising in the Persian Gulf when its radar operator detected two Iraqi F-1 Mirage

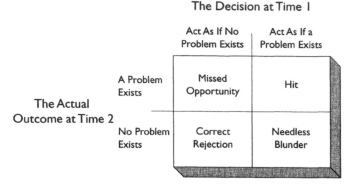

FIGURE 2.3   Possible Outcomes in Signal-Detection Analysis

fighter jets. Iraqi pilots frequently flew missions in the area. At the time, Saddam Hussein was not considered to be hostile to the United States. Even though the *Stark* was patrolling in a potentially dangerous area, its advanced defensive systems were turned off. In addition, a radar receiver that warned the ship of incoming hostile missiles was not functioning. As the situation unfolded, the Iraqis fired two French-made Exocet missiles. Whether the missiles were intentionally fired at the *Stark* or at another unidentified Iranian target is not completely clear. The important point is that they were headed toward the *Stark*.

The first warning that the missiles were honing in on the USS *Stark* came when a lookout saw the missiles seconds before one struck. The results were catastrophic; 37 sailors were killed, and the ship nearly sank. The captain's failure to adequately prepare his ship exemplifies a missed opportunity. He had an early chance to act, with little downside associated with the action and much to support it, and did not. In other words, the captain of the USS *Stark* failed to recognize a potential problem and act on it by deploying its missile defense system, long in advance of the launching of the missiles. As William Crowe, the head of the Joint Chiefs of Staff told us, the Persian Gulf is a dangerous place. Just being there should have been enough for the *Stark* to activate its defense systems. Not doing so was a missed opportunity.

A little over a year later, the USS *Vincennes* was patrolling in the Persian Gulf. The *Vincennes* had just been engaged in a long-distance battle with high-speed Iranian attack boats when radar indicated that an Iranian aircraft had just taken off from an airport in Iran. The plane appeared to be moving toward the ship, and instruments indicated that it was descending from an altitude of 7,500 feet. The crew construed the maneuver as a threatening dive. The aircraft did not respond to three warnings from the *Vincennes* on civilian radio frequencies and four warnings on military frequencies. In addition, it could have been sending out false identification, friend or foe (IFF) signals, which are used by civilian planes to trick the ship's captain into complacency. The captain of the *Vincennes*, Will C. Rogers, issued an order to fire two missiles at the plane. Both reached their target. Unfortunately, the target was an Iranian passenger jet. All 290 passengers died.

This horrible event may have only been the first of two related tragedies. A year later, Pan Am flight 103 was blown up in the skies over Scotland. Some suggest that the deaths of the 270 people aboard were retaliation.

The critical decision to fire on the descending plane is an example of the second type of error, a needless blunder. The captain of the *Vincennes* acted when he should not have; he identified a problem that was in fact not there.

Both of these disasters are associated with the problem of detecting signals early and acting appropriately. Both depended on the decision-makers' thresholds for action. In each of these cases and in many others, decision-makers need to formulate a plan in advance and set their triggers appropriately. Doing so will make their decisions better, particularly in pressure-packed crisis situations in which the time for action is short.

Setting the Trigger

Whether you are searching for problem signals or currently facing a tough choice, setting a trigger for action is critical. The idea of setting a trigger is a metaphor for how much evidence you need before you take action. A "sticky" trigger requires considerable evidence before it is pulled; a "hair" trigger requires much less evidence. The captain of the *Vincennes* set a hair trigger. Indeed, his ship had already established a quick-reaction reputation for itself among seamen, and as a result was nicknamed "Robocruiser" after the movie *Robo-Cop*. In contrast, the captain of the USS *Stark* had a sticky trigger, which almost resulted in the loss of his ship.

How then should we go about setting triggers for action? A particularly effective approach is to imagine that you are starting from the end point; that is, imagine the situation as though the decision has already been made. Then work back to the beginning, where you must make the decision. By imagining that you have the clarity of hindsight, you can often see how to proceed. By starting at your hoped-for end point, you can list all of the things that need to happen for you to get there. The converse also works well. If you imagine everything that could possibly go wrong with your decision, you can do what you can, upfront, to alleviate them. In particular, you can make pointed considerations that address some basic questions: What if you don't act and it's a missed opportunity (i.e., you should have acted)? What if you act and it's a needless blunder (i.e., you should not have acted)? By considering the costs of each type of error, you can set your trigger to avoid the worst-possible outcomes.

For the *Stark*, two pieces of information were key: (1) radar information told the captain that the two approaching aircraft were military, and (2) the ship was operating in a war zone and could justify shooting down military jets. Thus, although acting and potentially committing a needless blunder would have had negative consequences, it could be justified. In addition, the defense systems on the *Stark* would have reacted automatically—and possibly shot down the missiles—if they had been on. Turning them on was a low-cost option that would have avoided an extremely high-cost disaster. The cardinal rule of the U.S. Navy is to defend your ship, and in this instance the captain failed to do so by not activating his defense system early enough.

The normal rules of engagement required ships and aircraft to fire only when they were in imminent danger; that is, they could not fire unless fired upon. In one of our interviews, Admiral William J. Crowe, then head of the Joint Chiefs of Staff, acknowledged that with the increased availability of sophisticated and powerful missiles, the rules of engagement in the Persian Gulf had changed prior to the incident involving the USS *Stark*. Basically, naval officers, their ships, and their personnel were constantly being placed in jeopardy. While noting that the specific rules are classified, he told us that they were "structured so that the commanding officer could shoot before being shot at." Thus, according to Admiral Crowe, the new rules of engagement made the lack of action by the captain of the *Stark* indefensible.

While shooting down the military jets of a country with which you are not at war is bad, having your ship nearly sunk and suffering many casualties because of a missed opportunity is clearly worse. In this case, the cost of a missed opportunity was greater than the cost of committing a needless blunder. Clearly, the military agreed with this assessment: Soon after the incident, the captain of the *Stark* was retired from the navy at a lower rank. Since then, the case has become a standard example in naval training programs of strategic decision-making gone awry.

The *Vincennes* is a perfect example of the second type of mistake, the needless blunder. Hindsight and an investigation of the incident make it clear that a number of signals were present that in combination should have been a warning to the captain. The Iranian aircraft had taken off from an airport used by civilian planes. It was well known that passenger jets often did not respond to radio contacts. It was also clear that destroying a passenger jet would be very costly—infinitely higher than the cost of shooting down a military jet. (On the other hand, military jets are also capable of sending false signals indicating that they are of civilian origin.)

Undoubtedly, the new rules of engagement and the fate of the *Stark* the year before contributed to the accident. In addition, the long-distance battle in which the USS *Vincennes* fired shells at Iranian boats over 15 miles away undoubtedly made the captain wary of additional threats from the Iranians. In our interview, Admiral Crowe noted that both President Reagan and the secretary of defense had participated in the decision to change the rules of engagement. The admiral reported that during their decision-making process, they attempted to identify the worst-possible calamity that could result from changing these rules: "Our greatest fear was accidentally shooting down a passenger jet." (But he also told us that "after we shot down that jet, the Iranians didn't bother us in the Persian Gulf anymore.")

The captain of the *Stark* clearly recognized that the approaching planes were military. One of his problems came from thinking that they were friendly aircraft (which, up until then, they were). The captain of the *Vincennes*, in contrast, did not have clear data. He had threatening data (the plane approaching), information suggesting that the plane might not be military (its place of origin), and no reply from frequent attempts at radio contact. Because his data were not clear, he needed a carefully calibrated trigger. A hair trigger might lead him to respond too quickly. A sticky trigger meant putting his ship at great risk. Because killing innocent civilians in a passenger jet was such a huge cost, the chance that this aircraft carried civilians obligated him to place the *Vincennes* at much greater risk than was true for the *Stark*. The trade-off of possible errors for the *Vincennes* was between a worst-possible "needless blunder" (shooting down a passenger jet) and a very serious "missed opportunity" (putting the *Vincennes* and its crew at risk). In this situation, their inconclusive data should have led them to set a stickier trigger than they did.

> **Set the trigger so as to minimize the likelihood of making the more costly error—whether it's a needless blunder or a missed opportunity.**

When we shift from the realm of armed conflict to the decisions surrounding major motion pictures, Harold Ramis's approach to decision-making provides a clear example of trigger setting. He takes a conservative approach and sets a sticky trigger for himself. He is confident that he can get a job if he needs to. (He always has.) Thus he only acts when he feels that his odds of achieving his goals are high. Although he may feel foolish for refusing to direct a movie that later becomes a hit, he avoids the much higher cost of directing a movie that bombs and damages his reputation.

Three Types of Triggers

From a signal-detection perspective, three kinds of triggers for action can be identified. First, you can set a neutral trigger, which means that needless blunders and missed opportunities will occur with close-to-equal frequency. Second, you can set a sticky trigger, which requires substantial evidence that a signal is present before acting. A sticky trigger reduces the likelihood of a needless blunder but increases the chances of a missed opportunity. Third, you can set a hair trigger, which requires less evidence before acting. A hair trigger increases the likelihood of a needless blunder but decreases the chance of a missed opportunity. In hindsight, we know that the commanders of the *Stark* and the *Vincennes* set the wrong kinds of triggers, thereby paving the way for two serious disasters.

When information is not clear and the level of the signal is ambiguous, master decision-makers avoid making the worst error. They evaluate the relative costs of a missed opportunity and those of a needless blunder and set their triggers appropriately. The key to setting a trigger is to determine the relative costs of potential negative outcomes.

In their book *In Search of Excellence,* Tom Peters and Robert Waterman argued that managers should set a hair trigger. In contrast, Chris Kraft, who ran Missile Control for the National Aeronautics and Space Administration (NASA) during the Apollo moon program, set a sticky trigger for his operations. He used the following rule: "If you don't know what to do, don't do anything." His rationale was that if you do something wrong in space, it can be catastrophic. Similarly, in criminal trials, the U.S. judicial system has explicitly decided that letting the guilty go free is less serious than convicting the innocent. Thus, it avoids many needless blunders by setting a sticky trigger for determining guilt. The judge's instruction, "You must find the defendant guilty beyond a reasonable doubt," sets a sticky trigger and results in more missed opportunities (releasing the guilty) than needless blunders (convicting an innocent person).

In contrast, in civil trials, the jury is instructed to use the criterion of the "preponderance of evidence." Thus, instead of setting a sticky trigger for finding guilt, civil trials have a more neutral trigger. This difference is one factor that contributed to O. J. Simpson being found guilty in his civil trial but not in his criminal trial.

Remember, however, that the setting of a trigger does not affect accuracy. Accuracy depends on your ability to distinguish signal from noise. Strategically sound decision-makers make fewer errors because they realize the possible consequences of their decisions and develop the information systems and the judgment to make correct decisions. Master decision-makers make fewer errors because they are better at obtaining and weighing the evidence for action.

Palm Pilot Sets a Hair Trigger

If there is one phrase that seriously frightens companies, it is "Microsoft has entered our market." Known for its ferocity and no-holds-barred approach to competing, Microsoft has the willpower and resources to bankrupt its opponents. Late in 1999, the executives at Palm, Inc., the maker of the fabulously successful Palm Pilot handheld organizer, discovered that Microsoft was about to bring out its third attempt at a handheld organizer, the Pocket PC. This action threatened Palm's future.

As one Palm executive said at a corporate meeting, "We've got to remember that, with Microsoft, they don't have to get it right—they just have to get it right enough." Making the threat even more serious, in a few months, Palm would be spun off by 3Com as a separate company. It would have to survive on its own.

Soon after the divestiture, Palm's new president, Carl Yankowski, assembled his management team for an important meeting. Using military metaphors, he declared, "Whatever it takes, let's make sure that

Microrsoft doesn't outgun us. We're in a war right now." With these words, he initiated a battle plan called "Operation Rock 'n' Roll." Its goal was to make Microsoft's Pocket PC go down in history as the modern Edsel, last century's famous failure at Ford Motor Company. The result was an aggressive marketing plan that included new print ads, billboards, and direct contact with key retailers.

In April 2000, Microsoft's Pocket PC and the Palm Pilot went head-to-head when Microsoft unveiled its new device at a gala event at Grand Central Station in New York City. In the months that followed, the Palm Pilot organizer outsold the Pocket PC by nine to one. Palm, Inc., had won that round, but it was just the first skirmish of a long-term war.

How did Palm win this first battle with Microsoft? Furthermore, how can they stay ahead? The answer is that Palm constantly searched for problem signals and is continuing the search process to this day. As described by its chief competitive officer, Michael Mace, Palm had to "create palpable fear about Microsoft." In fact, the hiring of a corporate competitive officer was the first in this industry. He was hired for the sole purpose of gathering information about Microsoft's plans. In military terms, Mr. Mace was an intelligence officer. He was searching for problem signals. To perform his job, he scoured web sites and chat rooms, purchased Microsoft's products and minutely analyzed them, attended trade conferences, cultivated contacts in the industry, visited electronics vendors, and conducted meetings with Palm's executives. He even produced a thick report entitled "The Zen of Kicking Microsoft's Butt."

Mr. Mace successfully motivated Palm's executives to be constantly searching for intelligence on Microsoft. At one meeting with a hardware maker, Palm's sales manager heard a rumor that none other than Bill Gates had spent a half hour talking to a sales clerk at an electronics store. Inferring that Mr. Gates was now taking a personal interest in the Pocket PC, executives at Palm launched Operation Rock 'n' Roll.

Is the self-described paranoia of Palm, Inc., justified? Absolutely! By constantly monitoring the actions of its most important competitor, Palm has set a hair trigger for identifying problem signals. If the company grows complacent for even a few months and drops its guard, it could fall behind the power curve and become another of Microsoft's casualties.

The Overconfidence Bias

When weighing the evidence, decision-makers implicitly estimate the probability that they will be correct if they act. However, we often overestimate our probabilities of success; that is, we tend to be systematically overconfident. Overconfidence afflicts us when we overestimate our abilities, when the difficulty of a task increases faster than our abilities increase, and when we face a new task and have insufficient knowledge to handle it. We are right to be confident when we face simple tasks. The problem is that we are often overconfident when we face moderate to extremely difficult tasks.

Overconfidence can happen to anyone, regardless of their knowledge. With a changing world, there is no way to keep up with everything. In many ways, this has always been true. For instance, in 1892, Thomas Edison, one of the most accomplished scientists of all time, asserted, "The radio craze.... will die out in time." Clearly, his ability as an inventor did not translate into product forecasting!

Even when scientists make scientific predictions, they can also get it wrong. In 1932, Albert Einstein predicted, "There is not the slightest indication that nuclear energy will ever be attainable. That would mean that the atom would have to be shattered at will." A scant 13 years later, the first atom bomb proved him wrong.

Academics are no less likely to make predictions that they regret. In 1967, David Riesman, the noted Harvard sociologist, declared, "If anything remains more or less unchanged, it will be the role of women."

These amusing quotes highlight the ease with which you can figuratively place your foot securely in your own mouth. Abraham Lincoln expressed the wisdom of silence best when he said, "It is better to keep your mouth shut and be thought a fool than to open it and remove all doubt."

But many decisions depend on predictions that are inherently uncertain. A classic example is the series of decisions that led to the *Challenger* disaster. On January 28, 1986, the space shuttle *Challenger* blew up, killing all seven of its crew. The terrible image of the explosion overwhelmed Americans, causing immense grief and anger. The emotions galvanized the country and led to a series of investigations. In addition, the entire space program was in shock and put on hold as engineers redesigned the booster rockets for future shuttles. Before the launch of the *Challenger*, however, decisions had already been made to change its design. The problem was that the decisions had simply not been implemented.

In the case of the *Challenger*, it is important to remember first and foremost that the decision-makers were smart people—just like the authors of our funny quotes—who had made similar high-stakes decisions many times before. For this particular launch, however, they were under intense time pressure (due to previous delays) and considerable public scrutiny. As Diane Vaughan notes in *The Challenger Launch Decision*, the inclusion of a schoolteacher, Christa McAuliffe, as a member of the crew "gave the Challenger a special aura."

At that time, NASA's shuttle program had a string of 24 successes and no failures. They were used to being successful. In fact, NASA officials were well aware of the O-ring problems that caused the disaster long before this launch. The presidential commission stated that "NASA had ample warning, beginning with an internal memo, in 1977; these warnings failed to reach the agency's senior management and enthusiasm for the repairs was continually short-circuited." In addition, officials discussed the exact problem of potential O-ring failure due to cold temperatures the day before the launch. On January 27, the temperature predicted for launch time was 26 to 29 degrees Fahrenheit. Engineers at Morton Thiokol, the *Challenger*'s designers and manufacturers, recommended that the launch be canceled—their first recommendation not to launch in 12 years. They faxed NASA 13 charts in support of their recommendation. The charts, however, were far from convincing, leading Thiokol managers to reconsider and conclude that the evidence linking cool temperatures to O-ring failure was inconclusive.

Other decision biases also fueled the managers' overconfidence. For instance, some of Thiokol's managers viewed another delay as a financial loss. One said, "This shuttle thing will cost us 10 cents a share this year." As we show in Chapter 4, framing the decision as one that would avoid a potential loss may have made them more prone to taking a risk. Also, they had postponed the launch three times already, and this particular launch was tied to a presidential address. They were committed to launching. The thought of calling it off became increasingly difficult.

Thiokol's managers were also afflicted by a confirmation bias; when they looked at the engineers' data, they interpreted it as confirmation of their decision to launch, viewing what was actually ambiguous information as supportive of what they wanted to do. Rather than seeing the information as equivocal, they felt that it helped confirm their previous inclinations. They also failed to seek information that might disconfirm their initial tendency to launch. Finally, they were afflicted by the preference for action that many managers have. Waiting and inaction are too passive to fit the effective role that many managers see themselves playing. They have a need for control (don't we all?) that can only be satisfied with action.

All these elements contribute to feelings of overconfidence that can blind us to problem signals. For instance, the presidential commission reported that "as tests and then flights confirmed damage to the sealing rings, the reaction by NASA and Thiokol was to increase the amount of damage considered 'acceptable.'" In our terms, they were changing their thresholds for action such that over time they moved from a neutral to a sticky trigger for action. They stayed their original course, even in the face of evidence that we can now see should have been a major red flag. In other words, they failed to act on clear problem signals.

The overconfidence bias influences our decisions in two ways. First, extreme overconfidence can cause us to fail to gather the information that we need to make the best decision. With insufficient information, our accuracy in detecting signals decreases. As a result, we make more mistakes. There are indications that this is what happened to Firestone. The company's management appears to have been overly confident in the design and production of their tires. As a result, early in the process, its managers failed to collect and analyze data that would have identified the problem. This failure made it extremely difficult for managers to detect the signals of threat and stay ahead of the power curve.

The second way that overconfidence influences decisions is by influencing how we set our triggers. When we consider new courses of action, overconfidence can result in a hair trigger, which increases the likelihood of a needless blunder. That is, overconfidence can cause us to focus on only the positive outcomes that may result, while simultaneously limiting our consideration of the possible negative outcomes. In contrast, once we are committed to a course of action, overconfidence can cause us to set a sticky trigger for changing our course of action. Knowing when to quit is just as important as knowing when to begin a course of action.

> **The overconfidence bias can blind us to signals of threats.**

Managers are taught to present their findings and recommendations with confidence. Most of us realize that to inspire confidence in others, we need to make and present our decisions confidently. Problems arise, however, when we let our need to be confident influence our efforts to obtain critical information. It is all too tempting to believe in ourselves to the point where we fail to do the homework necessary to make sure that we can be confident. This is particularly true when we have been very successful in the past.

One simple solution to the overconfidence bias is to enlist the assistance of unbiased outsiders to evaluate our evidence. Moving away from a completely independent decision-making process can help avoid the disasters that can come from overconfidence. Paradoxically, however, such changes require the kind of wariness that often disappears when we've been repeatedly successful. Nevertheless, if we can allow ourselves to depend on others by asking for their opinions, we can avoid the tunnel vision that confidence, and particularly overconfidence, inspires.

If we uniformly consult people who are outside our inner circle before we make high-stakes decisions, we should also try to maximize the diversity within our groups so that many perspectives come into play before we act. Finally, if we are aware of and understand some of the many systematic biases that can affect our decisions (and we will discuss many others in subsequent chapters), we can be better at guarding our own minds and treading more carefully. Although it pays to appear confident following a decision, we want to be sure in advance that our confidence is adequately justified.

SITUATION ANALYSIS AND SIGNAL DETECTION

The important role of situation analysis in making high-quality decisions was first investigated by researchers assessing the performance of skilled fighter pilots. Their inquiry was prompted by the recognition that traditional approaches to decision-making failed to capture the process through which highly skilled individuals make tough calls. Based on this research, U.S. Air Force researchers proposed the following definition of situation analysis: Situational assessment is "a pilot's continuous perception of self and aircraft in relation to the dynamic environment of flight, threats, and perception." While satisfactory for describing the actions of fighter pilots, this definition is too narrow for our broader goal of helping you to make tough calls. As a result, we define situation analysis as the holistic assessment of the dynamic, changing environment and of the ongoing search for signals of problems and opportunities that impact our progress toward reaching our goals.

There are three basic requirements for performing an effective situation analysis. First, you must know your goals. Second, you must have an information-gathering system that provides continuous data on the environment relevant to your goals. Third, you must have the expertise and knowledge required to interpret the environment and recognize any changes that may represent problem signals or opportunities.

Situation Analysis and Our Four Examples

Situation analysis has application to the examples that we discussed previously in the chapter: investing $10,000, finding an irregularly shaped black mole, entering a new market, and deciding whether to report a product recall to the NHTSA. A 24-year-old who puts $10,000 into a mutual fund must first have a goal of retiring into a comfortable lifestyle. She must also have an information system that provides the data required to make the decision. Does she have adequate financial records and a well-formulated budget so that she knows whether she can afford to put $10,000 away? She should also calculate the opportunity costs of putting the money in a mutual fund (e.g., foregoing further education). Finally, she must have the knowledge of the effects of compounding to recognize the benefits of placing the money in a solid mutual fund as early as possible.

While identifying cancer and finding new market and product opportunities may appear to be dissimilar activities, situation analysis can contribute to improving both of these critical decision processes. Situation analysis requires attention to the environment, information gathering, and knowledge of what to look for. The goal of staying healthy will cause people to pay attention to their bodies and to know each bump, mole, and pain. By keeping track of their bodies and how they change, people gather the information necessary to recognize something new that could represent a problem. Third, people must have the knowledge required to know the meaning of a small, irregularly shaped black mole. Similarly, in the context of identifying new product and market opportunities, decision-makers can improve their decisions by using situation analysis to gather information on competitors' activities, on new technologies, and on changes in laws and regulations.

Finally, situation analysis was critical for Jacques Nasser in determining whether to report the tire recall in Saudi Arabia to the NHTSA. In this case, his goal was to protect and enhance the market position and profitability of Ford Motor Company by selling high-quality vehicles. To achieve this goal, he had to have an information system that tracked the regulatory, economic, political, and competitive environments of the United States and other nations in which Ford products are sold. In addition, he had to have the information systems necessary to track problems with Ford's vehicles. Finally, he had to have the knowledge himself, or depend on people who possessed such knowledge, to be able to interpret and draw accurate conclusions from the information gathered.

In sum, engaging in thorough situation analysis on an ongoing basis is important in our personal lives as well as in our professional lives. We show just how important situation analysis can be in the next chapter.

SUMMARY

The first step in making tough calls is to identify signals of threats and opportunities. Unless threats are identified early, they can compound, sometimes rapidly. According to the law of the power curve, the longer we wait to address a problem, the more severe it will become. Master decision-makers employ situation analysis to monitor their environment and detect problem signals. To perform effective situation analysis, we must know our goals, have outstanding information systems, and have the expertise necessary to interpret the data and recognize the presence of problem signals.

Signal-detection analysis can help us determine whether to respond to a possible problem. In this approach, the decision-maker determines the strength of the signal for action and compares it to a trigger for how much evidence is required before taking action. The trigger for action is based on the relative costs of making the two types of possible errors—a needless blunder or a missed opportunity. As exemplified by the USS *Vincennes*, a needless blunder occurs when an action is taken when it should not have been. As exemplified by the USS *Stark* and by Firestone, a missed opportunity occurs when an action is not taken when it should have been. If a missed opportunity will be more negative than a needless blunder, we should set a hair trigger for action. If a needless blunder will be more negative, we should set a sticky trigger for action.

Decision-makers must be aware of the various biases that impact their detection of signals. In particular, the overconfidence bias may cause a person to set a hair trigger when charting an initial course of action. A hair trigger, however, increases the likelihood of a needless blunder. On the other hand, a previous choice of action allows over-confidence to lead to a sticky trigger. As a result, the decision-maker may have difficulty abandoning a losing course of action.

If we identify a signal of a threat or opportunity, it is critical to determine whether the situation has a short or a long fuse. For short-fuse crises, we truncate the SCRIPTS process and employ guided intuition to solve the problem. For long-fuse problems, we can activate the entire SCRIPTS process. Prior to moving to the second stage of the SCRIPTS process, we summarize the seven principles of signal detection.

The Signal-Detection Principles

1. Employ situation analysis to identify signals of threats and opportunities.
2. Avoid the zone of false hope by identifying problem signals early.
3. Set your trigger so that a mistake will lead to the least-negative outcome.
4. Strive for accuracy in detecting signals by creating outstanding systems for gathering and interpreting data.
5. Recognize that the overconfidence bias can decrease accuracy and influence trigger setting.
6. If you are facing a short-fuse situation, truncate the SCRIPTS process by going directly to guided intuition.
7. Be realistic when making a decision, and be confident when implementing it.

3

FIND THE CAUSES

The difference between fiction and reality is that fiction must
make sense.

Tom Clancy

Katherine Williams has been the managing partner of a regional
accounting firm, CKM Partners, for four years. The firm's
primary clients are three large pension funds. Each of the
funds owns significant parts of a number of companies that are reor-
ganizing and emerging from bankruptcy. CKM's primary task—its specialty—is to audit these rebuilding companies. The funds trust CKM
not only because it can paint an accurate picture of their financial picture but also because it can supply needed managerial assistance on a
short-term basis.

It is October, and Katherine is looking at her firm's workload com-
mitments for the next six months. She has 65 accountants working for
her. Their experience ranges from 1 year to over 40 years in the field.
She and her colleagues are currently evaluating eight bankrupt firms,
all connected to one of the three large pension funds. Katherine real-
izes that CKM is taking a risk by failing to diversify and spreading its
business across many clients. So far, though, CKM's relationships with
the pension funds have been extremely profitable.

Since Katherine has become managing partner, her firm has
helped revive 24 companies consecutively and has not been responsible for a material error in any of its assessments. She is justifiably proud
of her record. She is feeling stressed, however, from the pressures of her
job. The pension funds set stringent time lines for evaluating the com-

panies. If CKM misses a deadline, she knows that her company may lose its business with the firms, which would be catastrophic. Nonetheless, she is highly confident of the professionalism of her colleagues.

Her immediate tough call concerns the largest of the three pension funds, which has just asked her to audit a new company on a rush basis. Although about the same size as previous firms, this particular company has a much higher profile than others because its CEO is a well-known actor. Any problems will therefore be magnified by the inevitable scrutiny of the press. Katherine's dilemma is that the work for CKM's other clients is well underway. As a result, her firm's resources are almost fully committed.

In the past, Katherine has assigned between 4 and 12 accountants to clients of this size. Currently, all 65 of her auditors are tied up. She recognizes that she can pull four accountants from other cases. In addition, if she also works on the case, she would have a five-person team. The question is whether a team of this size is adequate to the task.

To make the decision, she decides to collect some data on her firm's past performance and samples its last 24 major cases. Fortunately, on a routine basis, she requires her auditors to do postmortems on their projects. Although almost unheard of in the accounting profession, the postmortem, which occurs one year after the close of the audit, has proven invaluable to her firm. Katherine has the teams focus their analyses on how assets and revenues are calculated because this is the area in which it is easiest to miss problems and overstate earnings. For each case, she works with the team to identify whether there was any evidence of a near failure to accurately describe earnings.

Among the 24 recent cases, Katherine found evidence of 10 "near failures," which are defined as overestimating earnings by more than 5 percent. Next, she compared the near failures to the number of auditors assigned to the project. Figure 3.1 shows the relationship.

As indicated in Figure 3.1, there were three near failures with three auditors on the case, two near failures with four auditors on the case, one near failure with five on the case, two near failures with six on the case, and two near failures with seven on the case. Williams took the data to the group of five accountants that form her firm's executive committee. After looking at the patterns of the numbers, the oldest of her partners, Knox Ramsey, stated that although there was no apparent correlation between the number of people assigned to the case, he still had reservations about putting only five accountants on this particular client's case. He was especially concerned about the ability of the auditors to assess whether the client's costs were being correctly calculated.

Number	Number of Auditors						
of Failures	3	4	5	6	7	8	9
Three	X						
Two	X	X		X	X		
One	X	X	X	X	X		

FIGURE 3.1   Number of Near Failures and Number of Auditors

Another member of the executive team, Jay Wynn, a 20-something male who graduated from a prestigious university with an accounting degree and a master of business administration (MBA), represents the employees who are not partners in the firm. He argued that even though the company is just emerging from bankruptcy, its potential is enormous. He suggested that if CKM would do the audit, the company had a good chance of becoming the client's full-time accountants, which could mean millions of dollars over the next 10 years.

Katherine knew that she had the swing vote on the issue. She also knew that if the company passed on the opportunity, the pension fund that made the request might well go to another accounting firm in the future. But she also knew that if they took the job and made a material mistake, the consequences would be dire because of the inevitable publicity that the case would receive.

Katherine did not anticipate any unusual difficulties; she had put together a good team for the project. Besides, because of the short time fuse of the project, she could charge extra for it, which would mean a nice bonus at the end of the year. The additional bonus would be welcomed because she had a son starting college at an Ivy League school, at a cost of $35,000 a year. Finally, she wondered if there were any more issues that she should be considering in making the decision.

FIND THE CAUSE:
THE SECOND SCRIPTS PARAMETER

Before proceeding with our story, we first provide a brief road map for this chapter. After identifying a threat or opportunity, the next step in the SCRIPTS process is to find the cause, or causes, of the situation and to begin identifying alternative solutions. We have three broad goals for this chapter. First, we develop the concept that multiple factors combine to cause an event having high-stakes implications. As a result, a systems approach is required to find the cause or causes of the situation. Second, we identify and show the implications of a set of information-processing biases that can lead decision-makers to make incorrect causal attributions. Third, we provide a set of creativity techniques that can be used to identify multiple solutions to a problem or opportunity.

Prior to launching into a full discussion of these processes, we return to the CKM case, which illustrates both the systems approach and the effects of causal biases.

The Systems Approach to Causality

The cause of a threat or opportunity can range dramatically in complexity. On the one hand, a threat or opportunity may arise from a single factor. Usually, however, when high-stakes decisions are involved, multiple factors converge to create the quandary. As a result, it is critical to take a systems approach to understanding causation.

Consider the tragedy of the French Concorde crash in the summer of 2000 as it took off from Charles DeGaulle Airport outside of Paris. The proximate cause of the crash was a piece of metal on the runway. When the plane ran over the object, one of its tires shredded. In turn, the debris from the tire punctured the fuel system, which caught fire and engulfed the plane in flames. A simple analysis suggests that the cause of the accident was the piece of metal, which had fallen from another jet as it took off from the same runway. Looking deeper, however, we must ask the question, "How did a piece of metal get on the runway?" We must then assess the procedures in place to monitor the state of the runway and the maintenance of commercial jets. Going even further, we need to ask whether the design of the Concorde made it particularly vulnerable if a tire should blow out. In essence, the systems approach requires an assessment of the entire structure of the environment surrounding the incident.

The use of a systems approach often reveals that the cause of a serious incident is overdetermined; that is, a number of factors have come together to produce the problem. Had the Concorde been designed differently, had the maintenance of the jet that took off been better, or had the airport had better procedures to identify and remove debris, the accident would not have happened.

The concept that high-stakes outcomes result from multiple causes relates to the quote we used to open this chapter, in which Tom Clancy suggested that the requirement to entertain and avoid overwhelming readers with complexity means that the plots of novels must be simple. Thus, compared with reality, fiction makes more sense. Unfortunately, in the world of high-stakes decision-making, reality is extremely complex because it is marked by multiple factors coming together to cause threats and opportunities.

> **High stakes problems usually result from multiple causes.**

Think back to the problem faced by Katherine Williams. Would you have taken on the new client? To answer the question, you may have sought additional information. Certainly, it would be important to develop a greater understanding of the complexity of the client's case. For example, you would want to know the quality of the accounting system that the client had in place. If it was an outstanding accounting system, your job would be relatively easy. Indeed, this is the viewpoint taken by auditors in the Big Five accounting firms. Their focus is on assessing the accounting systems of their clients. Similarly, when the Federal Reserve evaluates the financial stability of banks, rather than investigating the worthiness of individual bank loans, it focuses on the quality of the bank's systems in making loan decisions. In sum, by taking a systems approach, it is possible to identify the full range of causes of an event.

Biases in Determining Causality

One additional piece of information, however, is absolutely critical to Williams's tough choice. Recall that she had data describing the relationship between the number of near failures and the number of individuals assigned to the audit. Also recall that Knox Ramsey interpreted the data to indicate that there was no relationship between the number of auditors assigned to a case and the likelihood of a near miss. Did you stop to question his statement?

As it turns out, all of the information that we provided here, is exactly the same as that given to NASA just prior to the ill-fated flight of the *Challenger* space shuttle in 1986. Just as you were given information on the relationship between the number of auditors and the number of cases of *failure*, the flight-control managers considered the relationship between temperature and the number of cases in which the O-rings showed indications of failure as a result of burn-through from the rocket fuel. What the flight-control managers at NASA failed to consider was the other half of the cause-effect matrix; that is, what was the relationship between temperature and cases in which no evidence of burn-through was found? Figure 3.2 gives the complete cause-effect matrix.

With all four cells of the cause-effect matrix clearly displayed, the pattern reveals itself dramatically. When the temperature at launch was above 65 degrees, damage to O-rings occurred in less than 30 percent of the flights, and none of the damage was serious. In contrast, when the temperature was below 65 degrees, the O-rings always experienced serious damage.

What was your decision in the CKM case? If you decided to go forward and take on the new project, your decision matched that of the flight managers of NASA in 1986. When we give another version of this case to our MBA students, almost everyone, both individually and in groups, decides to go for it. A key error in our students' decision process is not asking for the other half of the cause-effect matrix: They forget about looking at the data relating to successful flights and temperature.

The failure to employ all four cells in the cause-effect matrix occurs frequently in business settings. For example, consider reports of success in the stock market. How often do you see advertisements for brokerage firms that talk about their gigantic gains between 1982 and 2000? What the advertisers are doing is providing only one-half of the matrix, only giving you information about their gains in an up market. Unless they give you information on gains as well as losses in down markets, you have insufficient information to determine whether there really is a correlation between their stock-picking abilities and their performance.

Our students and NASA's engineers do not lack brainpower. Rather, their failures result from a lack of understanding of correlation. Although correlation is not a sufficient condition to show causality, it is a necessary condition. Without correlation, one factor cannot cause another. As shown in Figure 3.2, all four cells of the matrix are needed before we can clearly and accurately determine a relationship between temperature and O-ring damage (i.e., cause and effect). Understanding the factors that influence the presence or absence of correlations is essential in finding the cause.

THE TIPPING POINT

As illustrated by the French Concorde crash, multiple factors may combine to create an accident waiting to happen. Indeed, in many cases the situation is set so that even the most innocuous factor (even a loud

	Launch temperature less than 65°	Launch temperature greater than 65°
No burn-through	0	14
Clear signs of burn-through	6	4

FIGURE 3.2   The Cause-Effect Matrix Showing the Relationship between Temperature at Launch and O-Ring Burn-Through

sound) can cause disaster. At this point, the system is said to have reached a tipping point.

Consider the following problem. In the mid 1990s, Baltimore, Maryland, was besieged by an epidemic of syphilis. In the course of only one year, the number of babies born with the disease increased 500 percent. The causal mechanism for the dramatic increase identified by the Centers for Disease Control was crack cocaine. Researchers at Johns Hopkins University identified another cause. According to their theory, a breakdown in medical services in the city's poor neighborhoods resulted from a reduction in the budget of the city's sexually transmitted disease clinics. When the number of patients being treated for the disease fell to a threshold level, the epidemic ignited. Finally, a leading epidemiologist identified a third possible cause. He suggested that the crisis resulted from the city dynamiting many of the large public housing projects in the city. As a result of the demolitions, the people who had been most prone to contracting syphilis moved out of a confined geographical area and lived throughout the city. The effect was to place the carriers of syphilis into contact with many new people, which caused the epidemic to spread.

Each causal explanation of the epidemic had its own proponent. None of the physicians, social scientists, or epidemiologists, however, seemed to consider the possibility that the epidemic resulted from multiple causes. Think back to the Chicago Brew Pub case from Chapter 1. No single cause can be identified that accounts for the demise of the entire industry. Instead, a peculiar combination of circumstances came together to create the conditions for failure. When making tough calls, the key is to understand the causal network of factors that account for success or failure.

As it turns out, one individual did suggest that multiple factors may have caused Baltimore's syphilis epidemic. In his wonderful book *The Tipping Point*, Malcom Gladwell defined a tipping point as a moment of critical mass, as a threshold, or as the boiling point at which a sudden change occurs. He proposed that tipping points have three characteristics. First, at the tipping point, little changes can produce big effects. Second, the change occurs in one dramatic moment, such as when the number of syphilis cases in Baltimore increased by 500 percent in one year. Third, the effects are contagious and multiply in a geometric progression, which takes the form of a power curve (see Chapter 2).

We use the tipping-point concept broadly. For example, consider a pile of sand. If we create a very large pile of sand by pouring it from a funnel onto a single spot, the sand will naturally take on a conical shape. The steepness of the cone of sand represents what is called the angle of repose. At this angle, the friction of the sand particles on each other exactly matches the force of gravity, and the sand pile is stable. The addition of one particle of sand, however, increases the mass of the sand to a point that leads to movement, and the effect can be a large sand slide, the dramatic movement of millions of particles of sand. Was the single particle of sand the cause of the mass movement? In reality, any outside force could have caused the sand slide. A gust of wind, a bird landing, even a loud noise could have moved a single grain, which in turn would have resulted in the mass movement.

If an avalanche occurs, what is the cause? Certainly, the proximate cause was a single event, such as a skier traversing a slope. In reality, however, the entire infrastructure of snow and ice is in a critical state. To say that the proximate event was the cause is to greatly oversimplify the situation.

In a similar manner, the causes of great opportunities or threats tend to be overspecified. If the system of cause-effect relationships reaches a critical point, a single action can set in motion a chain reaction of events that progress according to the power curve. The Three Mile Island nuclear incident provides a particularly sobering illustration.

Overspecification and the Three Mile Island Incident

On March 28, 1979, nuclear reactor number 2 at the Three Mile Island plant near Harrisburg, Pennsylvania, experienced an "incident." Here is the sequence of events that forever changed the public's view of nuclear power in the United States:

~ A blockage occurred in a water filter—an event that had previously occurred 15 times at other plants.

~ Moisture leaked into the plant's air-conditioning system.

~ Two valves are tripped, causing the flow of cold water into the plant's steam generator to shut down.

~ Inexplicably, the valves for the backup water system were closed.

~ The view of an indicator showing that the backup valves were closed was blocked by a repair tag hanging from a switch.

~ The relief valve in a second backup system stuck open when it should have closed.

~ A gauge monitoring the relief valve did not work.

~ Confusion in the control room inhibited the ability of personnel to diagnose the problem. New mistakes occurred, and the water level fell below the reactor core, causing it to partially melt.

The Three Mile Island (TMI) incident was not caused by evil people who had a disdain for human life. Rather, in the words of the Yale University sociologist Charles Perrow, TMI was a "normal accident." By this, he meant that, a nuclear plant consists of thousands of complex parts, each of which must function properly. Normal accidents happen when a small malfunction occurs somewhere in the system and an unanticipated interaction of minor events creates a crisis. Because it is impossible to anticipate the millions of possible combinations of events that may occur, we should expect normal accidents in complex technological systems.

Nonetheless, the concept of the normal accident does not excuse the managers of TMI. If the problem had been diagnosed earlier, if any one of the failed mechanical devices had worked as planned, or if operator mistakes had not occurred, the incident would never have happened. The TMI incident teaches us that in complex systems, accidents are waiting to happen. Managers and operators must therefore have a complete understanding of the cause-effect relationships in the system. Finally, problems must be caught early because they can multiply geometrically, following a power curve. Indeed, the situation at TMI was not brought under control until operators finally recognized that the valves in the backup system were closed.

As part of our research on the TMI event, we corresponded with Scott Johnson, who created a nuclear powerplant simulation program. He told us that based on his research and interviews, "Operators at TMI-2 were not trained to understand the causes of reactor casualties; they were trained to respond to any given symptom in a prearranged, rote fashion." To make matters worse, the alarm systems in the plant were poorly designed. Scott supplied us with the following quote from one of the operators of the plant. In a letter to the plant superintendent, the operator stated, "The alarm system in the control room is so poorly designed that it contributes little in the analysis of a causality."

Scott also suggested that the operators were not trained to think; they did not have a good global understanding of the intricate systems that they were charged to operate. For example, according to Scott, "They learned that in a closed system, temperature and pressure tend in the same direction, and since they had a rising water level in the reactor and rapidly falling pressure, they were in completely unfamiliar territory." The two readings were totally inconsistent, and the operators could not think through the implications. As a result, they fell back on the procedures and sought to treat symptoms. The net effect was that it was nearly impossible for them to make sense of the confluence of seemingly impossible readings coming from the monitoring instruments.

In sum, TMI was an accident waiting to happen because the cause was overspecified. No single cause can be identified for the situation. Although the blockage in the water filter was the proximate event that caused a cascade of problems, like a sonic boom starting an avalanche, the conditions were set for an accident. The combination of a poorly designed warning system, failures in mechanical systems, and human error all contributed to the incident. Fortunately, no lives were lost. Individuals in the surrounding community received less radiation than in a chest X ray. For these reasons, we have described Three Mile Island as an incident rather than a disaster.

The outcome, however, could have been far worse. Operators were working against a steep power curve. Had the reactor core been exposed for only a couple more hours, heat would have surpassed the 5,000-degree melting point of the nuclear fuel. A China syndrome would have occurred, and the hot liquid fuel would have melted through the floor of the building. Had the incident moved beyond the tipping point, no amount of human intervention could have contained its geometric progression.

In cooperation with the Nuclear Regulatory Commission (NRC), the owners of TMI (Commonwealth Edison) have implemented a host of changes in how they train their personnel. In particular, each nuclear plant goes through a full-blown, daylong exercise once a year that is graded by the NRC. In one of our interviews, we spoke with Larry Gerner, who is intimately involved in Commonwealth Edison's emergency preparedness programs. According to Larry, the exercises take months of preparation, proceed under conditions of intense time pressure, and push personnel to develop a complete understanding of the plant's systems. They even do a pre-exercise run-through in preparation for the full-scale exercise. Larry told us that the exercises "need to push the bounds of what is credible but be believable enough that people stay committed to them. You want people to realize that if they can handle a complicated and extensive accident scenario, they can handle anything less. Practice doesn't make perfect, but perfect practice makes perfect." "At the conclusion of the exercise," Larry reported, "everyone is completely exhausted."

Root-Cause Analysis

To this point in the chapter, we have shown that catastrophes are often overspecified. We have not, however, described how to find causes. If you are an engineer or work for a hospital, you will know the answer— root-cause analysis. The field of root-cause analysis is huge; we counted over 8,500 web pages devoted to it.

There are many definitions of root-cause analysis. One of our favorites was developed at Cisco Systems. Managers in this high-tech company define root-cause analysis as the "process of analyzing cause-effect relationships between events in complex systems." Our definition is a little more elaborate. We think of root-cause analysis as a structured process for assessing the cause-effect relationships in a system and identifying which component, or components, are responsible for an event. Root-cause analysts engage in a repeated hypotheses-testing process to eliminate alternative explanations. A number of principles apply to root-cause analysis. They include the following:

1. Begin by determining the sequence of events that has led to the incident.
2. Constantly seek answers to the "why" question.
3. Carefully examine human decision-making as well as physical systems.

4. Recognize that a single cause can generate many symptoms and may share symptoms with other causes.
5. Understand that there may be more than one root cause.

The application of these five principles are illustrated in the aftermath of a tragedy that occurred on the campus of Texas A&M University. Each year since 1909, students have celebrated the annual football game against the University of Texas by constructing a huge bonfire. On November 18, 1999, however, their massive layer cake of logs collapsed and killed 12 college students, injuring dozens more. Put yourself in the place of Ray Bowen, the president of Texas A&M. How do you deal with the bonfire tragedy? Do you allow the 90-year-old tradition to continue? When Ray Bowen was the provost at Oklahoma State University, he worked with one of the authors of this book. John Mowen knew Dr. Bowen as an amiable and scholarly man who dislikes conflict. Unfortunately, the heat of the bonfire tragedy landed squarely on Ray Bowen's shoulders.

Quite appropriately, one of Dr. Bowen's first acts was to create an independent task force to identify the cause of the accident and to make recommendations on the future of the bonfire tradition. Members of the commission performed a root-cause analysis to determine why the 8,000-log structure collapsed. They began by reconstructing the exact sequence of events that led up to the tragedy. They considered a series of different causes, including a fracture of the center pole, unstable soil, earthquakes, and sabotage. The commission analyzed the complicated structure with a sophisticated computer-modeling program and also considered behavioral factors. In the end, the commission concluded that "several causes acted together to both trigger the event sequence and to fail all of the barriers provided to prevent the event."

In its final report, the commission identified nine factors, five physical and four behavioral, that caused the tragedy. The physical factors included the following:

1. The bonfire was built on slightly sloping ground.
2. The logs were more crooked than usual.
3. The upper-tier logs were wedged between lower-tier logs.
4. The upper-tier logs were built out farther than in past years.
5. Steel cables were not wrapped around the lowest logs.

From a structural standpoint, the bonfire had an unstable foundation. The ground-level stack of logs was constructed like a barrel without barrel hoops. As a result, the weight of the top tiers, when combined with logs being wedged between the logs of the lower tiers, caused the bottom tier to burst apart at the seams.

When performing a root-cause analysis, we must constantly ask "why?" It is particularly important to go beyond the physical cause of accidents and ask how the decision-making process influenced the outcome. In this case, for example, a key question was why the management system allowed such an unstable structure to be built. The commission identified four decision-making factors that contributed to the accident:

1. The bonfire was designed without adequate engineering analysis.
2. Crucial details of the bonfire were not documented.
3. The university did not acknowledge the magnitude of the danger.
4. Student organizations did not heed warnings that the bonfire was unsafe.

The final report did not blame any specific individual for the calamity. It stated that "The 1999 Bonfire Structure Collapse is a classic example of an organizational accident with failure causes that existed for many years before the event. No one person in Bonfire performed at such a substandard level to directly cause the collapse."

Dr. Henry Petroski of Duke University compared this incident to other colossal structural failures. For example, the ancient Egyptian bent pyramid in Dahshur resulted from an overambitious effort to construct it at a 54-degree angle, which resulted in a massive landslide of stone. After the landslide, the pyramid's builders set the angle in the upper half at a more conservative 43 degrees. Dr. Petroski argued that if the bonfire "had not collapsed last year and had been allowed to continue in the laissez-faire manner of the 1990s, some future Bonfire likely would have led to a tragedy." He continued by concluding, "Had anyone pointed out before the fact the dangers of the individual acts of abandon identified after the fact, they would have no doubt been scoffed at, for the Bonfire had been such a successful tradition. . . . In that regard, the 1999 Bonfire collapse repeats the pattern of a great number of other colossal failures that have plagued amateur and professional builders alike throughout history."

Applications to Business Decisions

Do the situations involving Three Mile Island, the French Concorde, the space shuttle *Challenger*, and the Texas A&M bonfire have anything to do with the tough calls that you must make in your business career? We certainly think so. Regardless of how small or large your organization, it will have systems in place for accounting, for marketing, for managing employees, and for responding to crises. The procedures that run the systems may not be written down, but they are there nonetheless. For the Concorde, a system failure resulted in a small piece of metal lying on a runway, which in turn caused the crash. In your organization, do you have systems in place that will prevent some type of stray debris from injuring a customer or employee? Similarly, a failure of a filter and a series of human errors caused the near nuclear meltdown at Three Mile Island. Are your systems for paying bills and billing customers good enough, and are your employees trained well enough, to deal with a computer breakdown? How much revenue would be lost, along with customer good will, if a serious malfunction occurred? Do you have a crisis-management plan in place that will be able to handle a major accident effectively and expeditiously? Most of all, remember that serious failures are usually overspecified. By paying attention to the details of the system, you can seriously reduce the likelihood of it reaching a critical point.

In the process of interpreting the information from your systems, you need to recognize that a series of illusions can negatively impact the determination of causality. Behavioral-decision-theory researchers have identified a number of human biases that create illusions of causality. We next turn to these.

ILLUSIONS OF CAUSALITY

Several different processes can create illusions of causality, by which decision-makers believe that A causes B when it does not, or that A does not cause B when it does. We investigate seven of these biases here: illusory correlation, the illusion of control, the illusion of the run, the availability bias, illusions of performance, the fundamental attribution error, and the hindsight bias.

Illusory Correlation

Illusory correlation occurs when a decision-maker focuses almost exclusively on the cell in the contingency matrix that represents a "hit." A classic case of this is when a stock-market guru makes a prediction and it comes true. Because investors focus on this hit, the predictions of the guru incorrectly become associated with successful investing. This pattern gives the illusion that a strong correlation exists between the guru's predictions and the ultimate outcomes. What gurus rarely do, however, is include their "needless blunders," disclosing how often they made a prediction that didn't pan out. Similarly, they avoid giving us information on their "missed opportunities," or the times when the market changed when they made *no* forecast. As we discussed earlier in this chapter, to calculate a correlation, we must look at the overall pattern of hits, needless blunders, and missed opportunities. The problem is that most people, even highly educated people, often use only the frequency of hits to mentally determine the causes of events. Thus, we can be "set up" to believe the prognostications of stock-market gurus.

These ideas well describe the incredible bubble in the dot-com stocks in 1999 and the first half of 2000. For example, Abby Joseph Cohen (of Goldman Sachs) made 259 television appearances and Joseph Gruntal (of Gruntal Corporation) made 238 during this time period. Another guru was Mary G. Meeker, who made her name by backing Amazon.com in 1993 when no one else believed in the concept. When she placed a "buy" on a stock, it moved the market. In late March 2000, she had a buy on Internet stocks such as Amazon.com, eBay, and AskJeeves. Unfortunately, by late October 2000, the value of these stocks had plummeted by an average of over 84 percent. AskJeeves fell from a high for the year of $190.50 to $9.75 in October 2000. *Business Week* described the situation as one in which the stock-market analyst was "fast becoming less of a researcher than a celebrity pitchman—for both his employer and the stocks he or she follows." As the case of AskJeeves amply illustrated, bubbles are pretty until they burst.

The illusory-correlation phenomenon also explains NASA's failure to identify the relationship between cold weather and the space shuttle's O-ring problems. In this case, however, the apparent lack of hits caused a perception that no correlation existed. Had scientists looked at the full matrix, they would have recognized the relationship between cold weather and O-ring burn-through.

The Illusion of Control

When the illusion of control occurs, people act as though they can influence purely chance events. It is a type of overconfidence that strikes most of us at one time or another. The world of gambling provides many illustrations of this phenomenon. In the realm of dice, slot machines, and roulette wheels, people get the idea that they can control events that are completely governed by pure chance. In fact, researchers have done many experiments on how the illusion of control influences gamblers.

Suppose that you were given a chance to enter a lottery for the next Superbowl. It costs $1 and gives you a chance to win $50. After you agree to enter the contest and pay your money, one of two things happens: (1) You are allowed to reach into a bowl to pick out your ticket or (2) you are just handed a ticket. The next day, someone else comes up to you and asks how much you would charge to sell him the lottery ticket. Would you charge a different price if you had chosen your ticket than if it had been handed to you? Objectively, you should charge the same price to give up your chance to win; whether you personally selected the ticket or the ticket was handed to you should have no relevance for your chance to win. The results of this experiment revealed that people who were handed the ticket charged an average of $1.96 for their stubs. In contrast, people who chose their own tickets charged an average of $8.67. The gamblers who had a choice created an illusion of control for themselves: Because they chose the ticket, they acted as though they had a greater chance of winning.

Buried deep within the human psyche is the unconscious perception that events—even those that we know result from chance—can be controlled. In most cases, this adaptive mechanism is beneficial, causing us to keep trying even in the face of overwhelming odds. Unfortunately, the illusion of control can create real problems when taken to an extreme, as with the aberrant behavior of some gamblers. We also see it in day traders and people who purchase stocks on the basis of statements made in Internet chat rooms. Indeed, in one case in 2000, a high school boy made $285,000 in the stock market by spreading false rumors. His misinformation influenced thousands of people who believed that they could predict a market that in the short-term moves unpredictably. The investors who were duped by his scam fell victim to the illusion of control by believing that they could gain control over essentially chance events.

The Illusion of the Run

Consider this question. If the parents of a child are tall—for example, both six feet, five inches—how likely is it that their children will be over six feet, five inches? It turns out that the chances are actually quite low. The reason is that genetics is a probabilistic, rather than a deterministic, science, meaning that chance accounts for some of the parents' height. Thus, the children of two very tall parents tend to be shorter than their mother and father. Statisticians call this effect regression to the mean. We call this phenomenon the illusion of the run: When chance causes a run of out-of-the-ordinary events to occur, the effects on subsequent occasions tend to move back toward what's ordinary, that is, the mean. Runs of good or bad luck inevitably end. When people attribute the run to nonchance causes, however, the illusion that it should continue is hard to shake.

One reason we succumb to the illusion of the run is that we allow insufficient room for the effects of chance in accounting for our outcomes, implicitly assuming that outcomes are totally determined by people's abilities and motivations or by some hidden process. Thus when we observe several out-of-the-ordinary events in succession, we usually are very good at identifying an underlying cause. In fact, it's rare that we even think of chance as a cause in the process. As a result, we expect the run to continue because of the underlying cause that we've identified for it.

When people fail to recognize the effects of regression to the mean, they frequently assume that something internal to the person caused the change in performance level. For example, one of the major problems for rookie phenoms in major league baseball is the sophomore jinx. According to baseball lore, a great rookie season is frequently followed by a poor sophomore year. The press likes to intimate that the cause for the jinx is that success has gone to the player's head. As a result, he is less motivated and performs worse. But a more likely reason for the sophomore jinx is regression to the mean. The high level of performance in the first year resulted in part from a run of good luck. Because chance factors are unlikely to repeat themselves, the next year's performance falls off.

The same thing is true, in general, for start-up companies. Most companies that do well their first year have a hard time repeating that success in their second year. Note the word most. Unfortunately, due to another bias that afflicts most of us (the availability bias), we are more likely to remember vivid, unusual examples. Thus, we often focus on the companies that actually beat the trend and do well, and we tend to forget the companies that don't follow their smashing first years with a smashing second. For instance, about 85 percent of new restaurants go under. To people who may dream of owning their own restaurant, this data should give great pause. Yet over and over again, people open new restaurants. And out of every 100 or so, 85 continue to fail. Although all of the numbers are not yet in on dot-com start-ups, it is clear that this picture is not much different. For example, in 2000, over 210 Internet companies folded, with most folding in the last quarter. In January and February 2001, another 101 Internet companies shut their doors. The successful founding of a company is a risky endeavor. Keeping it going is even tougher.

It is critical for managers to recognize that chance can be one of the causes of success and failure. Whether evaluating the performance of your company, your employees, or yourself, take into account the effects of good and bad luck. Ask whether a bump up or down in performance is caused by changes in the organization's or person's behavior or by a happy or unhappy run of luck. If you flip a coin one hundred times, there is a high likelihood that somewhere in the sequence of tosses, there will be a run of six or more consecutive heads or tails. This doesn't mean that the coin is not fair; it's just a normal part of a random run. Understanding this can give you a broader, calmer perspective on change. As we discuss later in the chapter, it can also help you to look at the process as well as the outcome when you are making attributions for the causes of performance.

The illusion of the run also accounts for our overreliance on economic forecasts. Economic forecasts assume that future changes in the economy will be caused by the same factors that influenced the economy in the past. The difficulty in making economic forecasts is that the future is inherently unpredictable. As one critic said, "It's easy to forecast when times are stable. It's just the past year, plus 5 percent, plus a small error factor. No big deal." What economists cannot do is predict dramatic changes in the economy because catastrophes are by their very definition unpredictable. For example, in the late spring of 1990, the price of oil had fallen to $16 a barrel. Economic forecasters saw no hint of a recession in sight. In August, Iraq invaded Kuwait, the price of oil doubled, and the U.S. economy headed into a recession. Ten years later, in the spring of 2000, economic forecasters uniformly predicted a strong economy. The next year, however, the economic expansion had stopped, the manufacturing sector of the economy had seriously slowed, and Nasdaq stocks had lost over 60 percent of their value.

The moral of the story is this: Although decision-makers often seek to gain control by hiring forecasters, they would be well advised to keep an old saying in mind—"Forecasters are like light posts. They're used more for support than for illumination."

The Availability Bias

When we search for causes, we sometimes encounter a villain known as the availability bias. Consider the following question: Which factor causes more deaths in the United States—colon cancer or motor vehicle accidents? In one study, the authors found that 86 percent of the respondents judged motor vehicle accidents to be the more frequent cause. In reality, more deaths result from colon cancer. Why does such an enormous misperception occur? One answer lies in newspaper reports. One informal study indicated that for each mention of colon cancer in a newspaper story as the cause of a death, there were 137 mentions of deaths in newspapers for auto accidents. Because of their greater publicity, instances in which auto accidents lead to death are far more available in our memories.

Not surprisingly, we tend to remember more recent information better than older information. For example, one chemical company found that its engineers had a 15 to 50 percent greater tendency to identify problems that had recently occurred as the causes of present problems. A series of these misdiagnoses led to losses averaging about $2.5 million a year.

Other examples of the availability bias include researchers' tendency to cite studies they have recently read. Similarly, sales personnel push products for which they have most recently received training. The Internal Revenue Service slyly uses this recency effect to discourage tax fraud by indicting several highly visible tax cheaters each March, thus making the potential consequences of cheating highly available in memory just prior to the due date for tax filing.

Using our memories to identify causes is a chancy proposition. One key to avoiding the availability bias is to recognize its existence. A second is to search for enough information to ensure that we have the correct facts on paper *and* in our heads.

Illusions of Performance

As human beings, we have a strong desire to identify the causes for our outcomes. Fortunately, the reasons things happen to us are limited to a few general sources. First, we can attribute our outcomes to ourselves: Because of our abilities and efforts, or lack thereof, good and bad things happen to us. Second, we can attribute outcomes to external factors such as luck, other people, the supernatural, or the difficulty of the problem. When we want to determine the cause of what happens to other people, we use the same internal-versus-external dichotomy: People's good or bad outcomes may come from inside them or from external factors.

How we attribute outcomes influences not only our actions but also our psychological well-being. Most of us have a strong desire to put our best face forward. To protect self-esteem, people often make defensive attributions. These self-serving biases are ubiquitous and afflict decision-makers whether they are in the boardroom or writing for the sports page. When negative events occur, we attribute blame so as to minimize our connections to what happened. And when positive events occur, we can be quick to take the credit!

This pattern of attribution happens even in the seemingly objective realm of annual reports. The Financial Accounting Standards Board (FASB), through its statements of "generally accepted accounting principles," specifies what information goes into them. The Securities and Exchange Commission controls the whole process. With this much regulation, there should be little chance for anything other than the facts, right? A study of the pattern of attributions made in the "Letters to Shareholders" portion of the annual report, however, shows how slanted these documents can be. These letters give management an opportunity to describe what happened in the previous year and explain the company's performance. Research results have revealed a regular pattern of defensive attributions, with favorable outcomes attributed more frequently to internal than to external causes (61 versus 39 percent). For example, it might read, "During the fourth quarter, our management lowered production costs substantially and recorded a strong operating profit." Here, the cause for the outcome is attributed internally, to the actions of management.

The study also found that unfavorable outcomes were attributed more frequently to external than to internal causes (59 versus 41 percent)—for example, "With the marked slowdown in building activity, there was a drastic decline in orders." Thus, the decline in orders was attributed externally (a building slowdown) to factors outside of management's control.

The idea that corporate management is free of human desires to protect its image is a myth. Corporations want to protect their institutional egos just as individuals seek to maintain their own self-images. These defensive attributions can result in real harm to an organization if management believes its own publicity and fails to identify the root cause of a problem.

The Fundamental Attribution Error

The fundamental attribution error describes the propensity of people to place the cause for a person's outcomes in the person. Thus, rather than recognizing that situational forces such as bad luck or an outside factor caused an outcome, they assume that the person's action, or lack of action, caused the problem.

The fundamental attribution error is manifested in the view of test pilots, race-car drivers, and society in general that accidents "don't just happen" and that someone must be at fault. We act as though we believe in a "just world." Such a belief allows us to make plans and to invest in ourselves as we seek to achieve our long-range goals. In a purely whimsical world, it would not make sense to commit to long-term projects. In a completely predictable world, we could gather good information, make sound judgments, and commit for a long period of time. We often act like the latter is true, as though we will always reap the rewards of our efforts. When erroneously applied, however, our belief in a just world gives us false psychological comfort and can lead to highly dysfunctional decisions and actions.

Believing in a just world, for instance, leads many people to blame victims. In a larger sense, the fundamental attribution error indicates that when we observe and evaluate others (particularly people we don't know), we see the cause of their misfortunes as the people themselves. The consequences can be particularly odious. Racists can justify discrimination against impoverished groups by believing that its members lack the ability or motivation to succeed. And uninformed people can think that women are raped because they asked for it. In both instances, external, nonpersonal forces are ignored as causes. More generally, people too often focus on the outcome and blame others for the result.

In one of our interviews, we talked with Steve Badyna, the manager of an industrial plant. Running an industrial manufacturing operation is a lot like the task faced by a ship's captain. In each case, the actions of numerous individuals must be coordinated and a complex set of mechanical, electrical, and human systems must be kept functioning. The leader can make the best possible decisions but still have bad outcomes. In addition, if the outcomes are bad enough, the leader is punished—whether the leader's actions were appropriate or not.

This is the leader's fate. If bad things occur, leaders get blamed, sometimes without regard for the quality of their decision processes. In the U.S. Navy, the failure to protect your ship inevitably leads to demotions. In an industrial setting, the failure to protect your employees from serious injury results in the same fate. As Steve Badyna told us, "If a worker is killed on your watch, your career is finished with that company." For this reason, he always sets a hair trigger for identifying safety problems in his company's manufacturing operations.

It is particularly important for managers to recognize that the fundamental attribution error will influence the public's perception of the cause of events that impact corporations. When a catastrophe occurs to a firm, the public will tend to blame the company. The problems encountered by Ford Motor Company with the Firestone tires is a classic example. Despite the fact that Firestone tires contributed substantially to their rollover accidents, the Explorer still had an excellent safety record as compared with other SUVs. Yet Ford was pilloried in the press for not acting sooner.

The Hindsight Bias

A final reason we sometimes misidentify the causes of events is the hindsight bias. The hindsight bias occurs when we evaluate decisions only after we know the outcomes of those decisions, when evaluators act as though the outcomes were preordained. The hindsight bias is subtle but powerful. Once we know the outcome of a decision or the result of a particular set of circumstances, our belief that we would have anticipated this outcome (even if the actual decision-makers didn't) increases. In other words, in hindsight, we revise our beliefs of what we had thought would happen.

The hindsight bias was readily apparent in the aftermath of severe flooding in Tulsa, Oklahoma. In early October of 1986, massive rains struck Oklahoma, and water began to back up behind the Keystone Dam. Run by the Army Corps of Engineers, the dam acts to control flooding, provide recreation, and provide the correct amount of water for an inland waterway. As the rains continued, the managers had to decide whether to begin releasing water; if the rain continued, they might have to release massive amounts to save the dam.

This was a classic tough call. Releasing extra water would cause minor flooding for certain; on the other hand, holding the excess water would risk major flooding if the rains continued. If managers released water and the rain stopped, they would look like idiots (because they needlessly blundered) for causing unnecessary flooding. If they held water and the rains continued, they would have missed an opportunity to alleviate the problem, and they would be criticized for causing massive flooding.

The managers decided to delay the release of the water. Unexpectedly, the rains not only continued but worsened. Ultimately, they were forced to release huge quantities of water, and a major flood resulted.

Citizens, newspapers, and elected officials were incensed. The investigations that followed put the dam's managers through the wringer. After months and months of critiques of their judgment, competency, and general worth, however, the engineers were vindicated. The investigation revealed that based on the information available at the time, they had made a reasonable decision.

The hindsight bias comes from creeping determinism and our need for control. Once an outcome has occurred, we often believe that it was inevitable. In hindsight, we exaggerate what we could not anticipate in foresight. Researchers have found, for instance, that people misremember their predictions. In fact, after learning of an outcome, people often change their story as to why it occurred so that their predictions actually coincide with the outcome.

The hindsight bias also illustrates how we ignore chance as a causal factor. Bad luck can turn good decisions into bad outcomes. Good luck can transform bad decisions into good outcomes. Because of chance, we should evaluate decision processes rather than decision outcomes. If decision-makers collect the appropriate information, analyze it properly, and reach a logical conclusion, they have made a good decision—regardless of the outcome.

Outcomes are only valuable for evaluating decision-makers who make the same kinds of decisions repeatedly, like CEOs, coaches, bank loan officers, and weather forecasters. When a single person makes many decisions, chance effects cancel themselves out and a performance record tells an important tale, due to the law of large numbers. When people make big decisions intermittently, their outcomes are more susceptible to random, chance events. So we shouldn't judge them as much by their outcomes as by their decision processes.

> **Use root cause analysis to minimize the biases**
> **and illusions of casuality.**

While identifying the cause, or causes, of the threat or opportunity, master decision-makers are continuously aware of the various illusions and biases that can make their decision process run amuck. After the causal sequence has been identified, the next step is to begin seeking alternative solutions.

FINDING ALTERNATIVE SOLUTIONS

Research by the late Charles Gettys, a past president of the Society for Judgment and Decision-Making, identified a common shortcoming in the search for alternative solutions: Decision-makers tend to stop too quickly in their quest for solutions. They will identify two or three possible answers and then stop. But Professor Gettys found that the best resolutions to problems are frequently not obvious. As a general rule of thumb, the more solutions we identify, the more likely we will be to discover one that will be truly superior. As a result, you must dig deep and use creativity to identify a large set of possible solutions.

While a full discussion of creativity is beyond the scope of this book, we can offer five techniques that will assist you in identifying multiple solutions to a threat or opportunity: Identify the inverse, add a feature, change the scale, control the variance, and use metaphors. Think of these techniques as heuristic devices for helping you to generate as many solutions as possible.

To provide a foil for the discussion of the five heuristics, we tell the story of an ongoing real-world case that simultaneously involves a threat and opportunity. After describing the case, we present the five heuristics and discuss how they can be employed to identify possible solutions to the problem.

Identifying New Bank Products

During the latter half of the 1990s, banks in the United States faced an interesting problem. Due to the skyrocketing stock market, competition from insurance companies and brokerage houses, and the increased financial sophistication of consumers, less money was being placed into checking accounts, savings accounts, and certificates of deposit. Called demand deposits in the banking industry, this money is critical to the profitability of banks because it provides a low-cost means of obtaining funds that can then be loaned to consumers and businesses at substantially higher interest rates than banks had to pay to get them.

To maintain and improve their profitability, banks needed to identify new products for consumers that generate either demand deposits or fee income. An example is the use of automatic teller machines (ATMs) that charge consumers a fee when a withdrawal is made from another bank. The quest for new products continued even as the stock market plunged in 2000 and 2001. The problem for banks and for us in this exercise is to identify as many new product possibilities for banks as possible.

The Creativity Heuristics

Let's consider how we can use the five creativity heuristics to find solutions to a threat or opportunity. Remember that in this initial foray into solutions identification, we should not evaluate the quality of the ideas. The goal is to generate as many ideas as possible. This list can be narrowed in a later stage of the SCRIPTS process. In the following sections, we briefly discuss each heuristic and then show how it can be applied to identify new banking products.

Identify the Inverse   A basic tenet of creativity is to identify the inverse, or the opposite, of something. A common approach is to undo what has been done. For example, erasers are added to pencils, and hammers have claws to take out nails. Another example is the emergency ejection seats in fighter aircraft, which help the pilot do the opposite of flying—get to the ground quickly.

How can the inverse heuristic apply to new product development? The answer comes if we ask what banks do and then look for the opposite. What do banks do? They allow people to save and protect their money. The opposite of saving money is spending money. Can a way be developed for banks to help people spend money? This is already occurring with the entire process of loaning money and issuing credit cards. But can we go beyond that? Could banks actually sell goods to consumers? As it turns out, Wal-Mart and other retailers are already doing this by placing branches in their huge retail stores, allowing customers to buy and bank at the same location. Could other banks that target different customer segments also do this? For example, could a bank that targets upscale professionals put a tastefully decorated bank in higher-end department stores?

Add or Combine Features The concept of adding and combining features is a second basic creativity device. For example, consider the fork. It combines three features to create a very useful tool: A handle combines with a spear, and the spear is then repeated three or four times to create the tongs. Another example is the personal computer (PC), to which a host of features have been added. Among its many capabilities, the PC can do word processing, play video games, provide two-way communications between far-away people, provide background music via radio or compact disc, and help you buy products over the Internet.

We already see banks using the adding-a-feature heuristic. For example, the money-market fund combines a checking account with a savings account. What new products might this heuristic suggest? How about adding accounting services or legal services to a bank's portfolio of services? Accountants perform many tasks, including tracking budgets, disbursing funds, and calculating tax liabilities. These accounting services may blend well with banking services. Similarly, attorneys are frequently involved in evaluating and putting together financial deals. Why not have attorneys on a bank's staff to assist in arranging deals?

Change the Scale By changing the scale, we ask whether we can do what we are doing at a much smaller or much larger scale. For example, Wal-Mart revolutionized the department-store industry by opening stores in small towns throughout the United States. It broke the rules by thinking small to grow large.

Could a bank offer its portfolio of products to fewer but much larger sized customers or to many smaller sized customers? Another option is to build alliances with larger banks so that a smaller bank can do deals with corporations whose financial requirements are bigger than the smaller bank can handle alone. Through these means, the smaller bank can act as a marketing arm of the larger bank. Conversely, could a larger bank build alliances with many smaller banks?

Control the Variance Inventors often create new products to control the variance of outcomes. Two classic examples are the cruise-control device on automobiles and the thermostat on heating and air-conditioning systems. The regulation of information is another example.

The Internet provides so much information that it is impossible to process all of it. As a result, web sites have been created that act as filters to regulate information. Web sites such as those maintained by *The Wall Street Journal* or *The New York Times* exemplify this function.

To apply the variance heuristic to the banking industry, we must determine what flows occur and how they can be regulated. One critical flow is the return obtained from the stock market. As we discovered in 2000, the returns from stocks can vary dramatically. There are already products, such as bonds and certificates of deposit, that have lower variance than stocks. Unfortunately, their total returns are usually quite low. Is it possible, however, to develop products that obtain returns closer to that of stocks but protect people on the downside? For example, could a bank develop a product that would appreciate at 80 percent of a basket of stocks (e.g., the S&P 500) but which would guarantee that the consumer would not lose any principle, shifting the downside risk from the consumer to the bank? At the same time, the bank would receive a 20 percent return on any gains in the basket of stocks. (This still entails considerable risk for the bank. Hedged funds are an attempt to alleviate this problem, but we can always ask whether these financial tools are as safe as they advertise.)

Use Metaphors   A metaphor provides meaning by comparing one thing to something else. For example, describing a woman as a Georgia Peach is a compliment in the southeast region of the United States. Using metaphors, similes, and analogies is an important creativity tool because it helps us to break set and get outside of the box.

Can the use of metaphors help us to identify some new product opportunities for banks? Let's try a few. How about—a bank is a hospital. What do hospitals do? They take in seriously ill people and cure them. Could a bank take in consumers who are seriously ill with financial problems and cure them? The answer is "yes." Organizations such as Consumer Credit Counseling Services already do it. So could a bank.

Let's try another example—a bank is a university. What do universities do? They educate people by providing them with the latest thinking on important topics. Could a bank provide seminars and white papers that would encourage customers to use more of their services? Could a bank collect information that is so important that other banks would be willing to pay for it?

The list of metaphors for banks is virtually endless. We could describe banks as orchestras, military units, churches, prisons, or athletic teams. Or we could describe a bank as an animal, such as a dog; that is, it is faithful, warns you of danger, and keeps you warm at night. How many of us think of our banks in these terms?

> **Use creativity heuristics to identify multiple solutions for high-stakes problems.**

Certainly, some of the ideas that we've outlined here may be too far out to be truly effective. But that is the idea of the creativity exercise. The goal is to break set, think divergently, and develop new ideas. There are many more creativity devices than the five that we have identified here to give you a sense of the possibilities. Most people use devices like these too infrequently because they tend to constrain themselves. Master decision-makers don't constrain themselves unnecessarily.

SUMMARY

Finding the cause is the second step in the SCRIPTS procedure. The process begins with situation analysis. When we identify a problem, we perform root-cause analysis to identify the causal sequence responsible for the problem or threat. While performing root-cause analysis, we are constantly on the alert for the various illusions and biases that can result in errors in identifying and understanding the cause. In the process, master decision-makers recognize that they must take a systems approach, that the outcome may result from human decisions as well as physical systems, and that multiple causes may come together to create a problem.

After the basic problem or problems has been identified, we then seek to find a set of alternative solutions. We recognize that it is important to identify as many solutions as possible. The most frequent error in this phase is to truncate the solution-identification process too early. To maximize the number of possible solutions, master decision-makers apply creative rules of thumb, such as the inversion principle. As we move through the SCRIPTS process, we will eliminate most alternatives. Much of this simplification of the decision process occurs in the next stage of the SCRIPTS procedure—the evaluation of risk.

Causal Principles

1. Use-root cause analysis to identify the cause or causes of the threat or opportunity.
2. Analyze causes from a systems perspective, and recognize that failures are often overspecified.
3. Avoid causal illusions by acknowledging that neither you nor mysterious outside forces can influence events governed by chance.
4. Avoid the availability bias by knowing that the cause of an outcome may not be the most available factor that comes to mind.
5. Defensive, ego-driven attributions can lead to a failure to identify causes. Learn more by realizing (a) that the situation is not always the cause of our poor outcomes and (b) that we are not always completely responsible for our good outcomes.
6. Avoid the fundamental attribution error by recognizing that situational factors (e.g., good/bad luck or the difficulty of the task) may be a serious influence in the performance of others.
7. Avoid the hindsight bias; that is, don't exaggerate in hindsight what you could not have anticipated in foresight.
8. Don't constrain yourself. Instead, use creativity heuristics to identify as many solutions to the threat or opportunity as possible.

4

EVALUATE THE RISKS

The reader deserves an honest opinion. If he doesn't want
it, give it to him anyway.

John Ciardi

David Gordon had a terrific idea. To raise money for charity and spark interest in his favorite sport, he created the idea of a round-the-world hot-air balloon race for a million-dollar grand prize. Half of the prize money would go to the team's favorite charity; the team and its members would keep the remaining half. A world-class enthusiast himself, he quickly received support from leading balloonists, all of whom agreed to put the logos of corporate sponsors on their capsules.

When David contacted potential corporate sponsors, he approached them cautiously. He made each sign a nondisclosure agreement prior to hearing his pitch. His proposal was very detailed and contained many pages of description of the event. It even included a drawing of the trophy for the winner. In addition, he obtained the cooperation of Ted Koppel of *Nightline*, who promised to help publicize the event on his television show.

David's mistake occurred when he approached one large corporation. One of its directors was an old family friend who got David access to the CEO. Letting down his guard because of his family connections, David failed to ask for the nondisclosure agreement. After receiving an enthusiastic response from the CEO, he waited for the go-ahead on the project.

A little more than two months later, David received a call from the president of the World Ballooning Association, Jacques Sutkup. Jacques was calling to ask David about the rules of the challenge. A representative of the corporation had called him and wanted to know the details about how it worked. A shiver went up David's spine, and soon thereafter his worst fears were confirmed when the story of the challenge came out in the media. No mention was made of David Gordon in any of the news. At this point, he said, "You could have peeled me off the ceiling, I was so mad."

David went back to his original contact. The man said, "They're honorable. Let me make a call or two and I will get back to you." After a couple of days, David felt compelled to call him back, and in David's words, the conversation was "very strained." The man said that he could not help David because of his position on the company's board. He also told him a story about a woman who sued Reynolds' Aluminum claiming that the company stole her idea. She never got anywhere with her claim. The implication of the story was clear.

At this point, David consulted various members of his extended family, including a Harvard MBA and a Harvard-educated attorney. Their response was unanimous: "Don't sue; you'll only lose and they could really hurt you." David also contacted a friend who owns a National Football League team. He told David to forget it because the company's owners would be intransigent. For a year and half, David followed their advice. Meanwhile, his anger never dissipated.

Finally, David Gordon decided to sue. After checking with his boss to ensure that it would not impact his own job, he proceeded. He was turned down by a number of law firms but finally found attorneys willing to pursue his case on a contingency basis. As is pretty standard, the law firm would take one-third of anything he received. The attorneys asked him how much he wanted, and he said $1 million—the amount of the prize money. He didn't tell them, however, that if the company would come to him and apologize, he would settle for $10,000.

After the lawsuit was filed, the corporation's initial reaction was to claim that the idea was not David's but one of the balloonists who just happened to be a friend of the CEO. David's attorneys persisted, however, and explained to the firm how a jury would see this as a David and Goliath story—the big corporation ripping off an individual with a good idea. In response, the corporation offered to settle for $50,000. David said no.

As the negotiations proceeded, the company's offer continued to increase. After six weeks, they were offering $375,000. At this point, David's lawyers were pushing him to settle. They had done very little work, and their payoff from such a settlement ($125,000) would be like free cash. David told his lawyers that he wouldn't settle for anything less than $500,000.

After additional negotiations, the offer reached $400,000. David knew that going to trial would take a long time, that appeals would drag out the process, and that he might not do any better than this. Even if he won, it could take years to receive his settlement. In addition, during the process, the other side would try to make him look as bad they could. He also knew, of course, that their costs would also go up dramatically if the case went to trial. And he liked the idea of forcing the company's CEO and its top officers to come to court. (They are very busy people, and it would punish them to have to appear.) David's attorneys, however, were really pushing for him to take the settlement. They believed that they were not going to get a better offer from the corporation, and they might get nothing if they went to trial. In essence, David's negotiations had expanded: He was not only negotiating with the company; he was also being forced to negotiate with his own lawyers.

At a point earlier in the negotiations process, David had concluded that his attorneys had not done very much. As a result, he suggested that they might lower their fee. His attorneys viewed the situation quite differently, and they refused. Now they were pushing for a settlement that would give them a tidy payoff.

Here is the high-stakes question: What would you do if you were David Gordon? Would you take the settlement and receive your portion of the $400,000 ($267,000), or would you push your lawyers to continue the negotiations? The cash would really improve your own finances—especially since your children are soon going off to college. But the potential payout in this case could be much higher.

ASSESSING RISK

Humans have an approach-avoidance conflict with risk. In some cases, we actively seek and relish it; in others, we become petrified upon sensing the remotest possibility of a negative outcome. Consider the issue of treating drinking water with fluoride. Fear of its side effects has caused 3 of the 10 largest cities in the United States to elect not to add fluoride to their water supply. Yet after two generations of use, fluoride has revealed no measurable ill effects while simultaneously preventing dental cavities in 50 percent of youth under 17 years old. Clearly, the benefits of fluoride overwhelm the costs; yet in some communities, an imaginary risk dominates the decision.

Now compare the fear of fluoride to the love affair Americans have with automobiles. Americans act as though they are oblivious to the fact that auto accidents kill nearly as many people every year as did the entire Vietnam War. In this instance, the risks are very real. Yet for almost everyone, the perceived benefits overwhelm the perceived risks.

We make choices between risk and security with surprising frequency. When a business makes a decision not to launch a promising new product, it chooses short-term security and eschews risk and possibly long-term gain. Similarly, when we remain in a safe but boring job, we choose security over risk. When we choose security in our business or personal lives, we not only select safety but we also forgo the possibility of excitement and the possibility of large gains. When we seek risk, we increase the potential for harm, as well as the possibility for change, excitement, and innovation.

Many companies must make huge risk-security decisions. For example, Boeing is a company founded on risk taking. During World War II, the company prospered, making the B-17 Flying Fortress and the huge B-29 Superfortress that dropped the atomic bombs on Japan. When demand for warplanes ended in 1952, Boeing's managers gambled most of the company's net worth on building a prototype passenger jet. Boeing built the first 707 in the face of serious competition from the industry giant, Douglas Aircraft, and its prop-driven planes. The gamble paid off, Boeing prospered, and Douglas eventually filed for bankruptcy.

Boeing still bets the company when it introduces each new generation of plane. If a new line of passenger jets fails in the marketplace, the multibillion-dollar investment required to launch it can sink the company. But as one of Boeing's past CEOs noted, "You don't succeed in this business by being cautious. I don't want to lose that can-do attitude. The willingness to gamble, whether in product innovation or product introduction, is very important. The worst thing for us is to overreact and get so conservative that we try to live off our past accomplishments."

In 2000, Boeing faced just such a decision. Airbus launched a new jet (the A3XX) whose seating capacity of 650 passengers surpasses the 747's by more than 50 percent. Boeing's high-stakes decision was whether to launch its own new plane or take the more modest, safer step of extending the current 747-X to increase its capacity to 520 seats. After proposing the stretched 747, no customer orders emerged. As a result, Boeing took another route and proposed a smaller, faster jet named Delta Wing that would fly at 95 percent of the speed of sound. Costing twice as much to develop as the 747-X, Delta Wing represents a totally new and unproven concept. A true high-stakes decision, the future of Boeing rests on the success of the $6 billion investment.

We have all heard the expression "perception is reality." This axiom is particularly true when we consider the risks and benefits of a choice. Because of the ambiguity of the information available, it is impossible to precisely measure the probability and the value of the outcomes that can result from our actions, especially when we are making high-stakes decisions. For example, the decision to build a plane far larger than the 747 is contingent on future demand for such a big plane. In 2000, Boeing estimated demand for only 365 big planes. In contrast, Airbus forecast a market for more than 1,500. In a similar manner, David Gordon could not determine with certainty either how much he might possibly obtain or the likelihood of obtaining it if he continued his lawsuit. In addition, his emotional involvement probably led him to react differently to the situation and make different estimates than less-involved people, like his family advisors. In sum, the perception of risk is very often in the eye of the beholder.

Risk perception is in the eye of the beholder.

As John Ciardi declared in the opening quote to the chapter, even if the reader (i.e., your client or boss) does not want an honest opinion, give it to him anyway. David Gordon's attorneys gave him their honest opinion, but it is not clear that he wanted to hear it. What he really wanted was to punish the corporation. As a result, his view of acceptable risk diverged from his attorneys'.

With these facts in mind, how should high-stakes decision-makers go about determining the risks of action or inaction? The answer depends first on how people perceive risks.

Understanding Risk Perception

Depending on their field, academics define risk in different ways. For example, in the field of financial investing, risk is described in terms of the variance or volatility of a stock or bond. Thus technology stocks are viewed as extremely risky because their value fluctuates widely. In contrast, in the field of decision theory, risk is described in terms of the probabilities of a small set of clear outcomes. The classic examples are flipping a coin and tossing dice. In these instances, probability theory can precisely determine the risk (i.e., the expected value) of a gamble based on the known probabilities and the values of the potential outcomes.

In the arena of high-stakes decision-making, however, rarely can analysts obtain precise estimates of probabilities and outcomes. Technically, tough calls are made under conditions of uncertainty rather than risk. Even with uncertainty, it is still useful to describe the results of our actions in terms of the probability and value of the likely outcomes. Although it is impossible to precisely know the likelihood and the value of each outcome, we can make estimates. These estimates can be very helpful because they place a structure onto our high-stakes decision processes. And when we have some time to decide (i.e., we are facing a strategic decision), it is easy to show that considering both the probabilities and the values of the key outcomes is critical for making an effective decision.

Figure 4.1 is a new version of the signal detection matrix that we first presented in Chapter 2. Recall that there are two types of errors. The first is a needless blunder, that is, acting when we should not have acted. The second is the converse, a missed opportunity, that is, not act-

FIGURE 4.1   The Evidence Detection Matrix

ing when we should have acted. The needless blunder and the missed opportunity are the two basic risks in making a tough call.

This revised matrix includes three important new ideas. First, we have moved from identifying signals of problems to evaluating the evidence for action. We implemented this change so that we could apply the ideas from signal-detection analysis to the problem of assessing risk and ultimately to making the choice of whether to act.

The second change is shown at the bottom of the diagram. The horizontal line of the matrix represents the amount of evidence for action. At the far left of the line, the evidence for action is very low. The far right of the line represents strong evidence for action. As we will describe later in this chapter, the amount of evidence for action will be expressed in terms of the percentage likelihood of success if the action is taken.

The third change involves the vertical line that cuts through the middle of the matrix. We have labeled this line as the trigger. It represents the amount of evidence required to act. When placed in the center of the matrix, the trigger is neutral, which indicates a 50 percent chance of success. In this case, the cost of a missed opportunity and of a needless blunder are equal. This is indicated by an equivalent size of the rectangles that represent a missed opportunity and a needless blunder.

Figure 4.2 illustrates a hair trigger. As you can see, the vertical line is far to the left. As a result, the size of the missed opportunity is smaller and the area of the needless blunder is larger. In this case, the error of a missed opportunity is more costly than the error of a needless blunder. As a result, the decision-maker wants to minimize the chances of a missed opportunity and sets the hair trigger for action.

Figure 4.3 illustrates a sticky trigger for action. Because of the high costs of a needless blunder, the trigger is set far to the right. As a result, high confidence in the success of the action must exist prior to going to trial.

What does this analysis say about David Gordon's decision? How much evidence did he have, for instance, about the ultimate outcome of a trial? He could certainly marshal considerable evidence that the idea was his and that he was the first to present it to the company's directors. But how well could he predict a jury's ultimate decision? And even if he could, how much might they award in damages?

In addition to evaluating the likelihood of a successful or an unsuccessful trial, David also needed to consider the consequences of the two types of errors. If he chose to settle, he risked a missed opportunity. On the other hand, the settlement provided him with a sure gain of $267,000. If he chose to continue his suit, he risked a needless blunder but had the

FIGURE 4.2   Setting a Hair Trigger

FIGURE 4.3   Setting a Sticky Trigger

opportunity to score a great victory (i.e., a hit) by obtaining far more from the jury. As we ponder how he might have evaluated his risks, we next explore the factors that can influence his and other decision-makers' perceptions of the consequences of action and inaction.

Anticipating Regret: Evaluating the Negative Consequences

Six risk factors are important when we evaluate the negative consequences (i.e., the risks) of a missed opportunity or a needless blunder. Each is concerned with anticipating the regret that we would experience following the ultimate outcome. We use the acronym SMILES to identify the six factors:

The Six Risk Dimensions

Social risk: How will others view me? What will it do to my reputation?

Monetary risk: How will the outcome impact my financial and material resources?

Information risk: How much will I learn from the experience?

Life/health risk: Will the outcome threaten my life or health?

Experience risk: How much will I enjoy or hate the experience?

Sink-the-boat risk: Does a false action create the potential for a catastrophic, irretrievable loss?

To assess the consequences of a needless blunder or a missed opportunity, we try to anticipate potential regret for each of the SMILES dimensions. Table 4.1 summarizes these consequences for David Gordon's decision. Consider first the six negative consequences of the needless blunder—going to trial and losing. In addition to the obvious monetary loss of $267,000, David would also suffer a variety of social losses, such as time spent away from his family and other work opportunities. The costs of these outcomes could be quite high. Going through a trial can be highly stressful and a generally negative undertaking.

The negative consequences of a missed opportunity result from the failure to receive the gains that would accrue had he gone to trial. If he did not act when he should have, he would take a monetary loss of the $667,000 that he would receive if the jury awarded him $1 million. In addition, he would not obtain the information on whether he was able to defeat the corporation in a trial.

> **Use the SMILES acronym to identify the dimensions of risk.**

Table 4.1 SMILES: Risk-Assessment Matrix for David Gordon's Decision

Risk Dimensions	Risk of Needless Blunder (I went to trial and lost.)	Risk of Missed Opportunity (I didn't go to trial; if I had, I would have won.)
Social risk. How will the outcome and experience impact my family, friends, and those for whom I am responsible?	I missed out on a lot of time that I could have spent with my family.	I missed out on my family seeing me push a big company around.
Monetary risk. How will the outcome impact my financial and material resources?	I missed out on a sure $267,000.	I missed out on a possible $667,000.
Information risk. What will I learn from the experience?	I learned a lot about the legal system.	I missed learning whether I could beat the corporation in a trial.
Life/health risk. How will the experience and the outcome impact my health and quality of life?	The entire experience was stressful.	Does not apply.
Experience risk. Will I enjoy implementing and living with the decision?	The difficulties were pretty draining. Going after a major corporation might also hurt my career.	I missed the thrill of successfully navigating the litigation.
Sink-the-boat risk. If I go to trial and lose, will that cause irreparable harm to myself and my family?	It is unlikely that losing the trial will cause any severe long-term consequences that cannot be rectified.	Does not apply.

The Outcome of the Hot-Air Balloon Case

Most of the time, we don't structure our decisions to the extent shown in Table 4.1. In fact, however, we could add even more structure to this decision-making process. (We'll do that in Chapter 8.) But let's assume that David stopped his structuring here and was ready to move to making a decision. As it happened, when he had the $400,000 settlement offer, he was leaning toward settling because he felt that the company would not offer him much more. But he was bothered that he had to negotiate with his attorneys as well as with the company. In essence, they were telling him that as things stood, they wouldn't push hard to get him more.

At this point, David approached one of the authors of this book, Keith Murnighan, with the problem. After hearing the details of the case, Keith suggested a new strategy that would increase the incentives for the attorneys to go after more money while giving David a good outcome if they still wanted to settle at $400,000. David took his suggestions and proposed a new system for his attorneys. If they settled at $400,000, the attorneys would receive a 20 percent contingency fee. If they got a settlement of $600,000, they would get 33 percent. If they got the full $1 million, the attorneys would get half—a full $500,000. David convinced his attorneys to accept this escalating scale rather than a fixed percentage (33 percent) of his winnings. With the scale, his attorneys would be better off than they were previously—if they got him a better settlement offer. On the other hand, if they settled now, they would get less, and David would get more money.

After a couple of days and additional negotiations with the company, David's attorneys decided to settle and take a 20 percent contingency fee if David would accept the $400,000 settlement offer. This clearly made David happy. He no longer had to negotiate in an adversarial way with his own attorneys, and his payout increased to $320,000, an increase of $53,000 over his previous share of this settlement.

The actions of the attorneys suggest that their estimate of the odds and of the potential outcomes of a missed opportunity and a needless blunder diverged from David's. The costs of going to trial were very high for the attorneys. Not only could they lose the trial, but the added expense and time required to go to trial also made the consequences of a needless blunder more negative for them than for David. In addition, they had a better understanding of the capabilities of the opposing attorneys and the vagaries of juries than David. As a result, their estimate of the probability of success of a jury trial was probably substantially less than David's.

The analysis also suggests how a different set of risk factors may have affected the corporation. For them, the monetary cost of the settlement may not have been as important as the information risk. If the public learned about the lawsuit, the negative publicity would not only harm the balloon-race promotion, but it would also tarnish the company's reputation. As a result, they were willing to offer a relatively large settlement, possibly more than a jury would have awarded.

A critical problem, of course, is determining the actual value of the risks of the different choices available in high-stakes decisions. There is no true "reality" as to what the actual risks and benefits are because they are based on perceptions, not objective reality. The problem is even more difficult because several perceptual and motivational factors often bias our estimates and perceptions. The next section identifies a number of these factors.

DISTORTIONS OF PROBABILITY
ESTIMATES AND OUTCOME EVALUATIONS

As we have already noted, when we make a high-stakes decision, the level of risk that we perceive depends on both our probability estimates and our evaluations of the possible outcomes. Thus, if our evaluation of a negative outcome becomes more negative, our perceptions of risks should increase. The same thing happens if our estimates of the likelihood of a negative event increase. It is critical to recognize that two people's perceptions of the risk of the same problem can be very, very different. Thus, David Gordon's family and friends viewed the likelihood of a successful lawsuit to be much lower than David did. As a result, they felt that the risks were greater than he did. Also, both the estimation of probabilities and the evaluation of outcomes are subject to substantial distortion. The next two sections identify some of the factors that can bias and distort our probability estimates and our outcome evaluations.

Factors Distorting Probability Estimation

Four of the factors that can distort our probability estimates emerge from the illusions of causality that we discussed in the last chapter. The availability bias, the illusory correlation, the illusion of the run, and the illusion of control can all act to distort probability estimation. One additional phenomenon can also impede our ability to accurately estimate probabilities: anchoring and insufficient adjustment.

Illusions of Causality and Probability Estimation   One of the illusions of causality that often biases our probability estimates is the availability bias, which causes people to assess the probability of an event by the ease with which they can bring instances of the event to mind. Two psychologists, Amos Tversky and Daniel Kahneman, performed a classic demonstration of the availability effect. In their study, respondents looked at two lists that contained the names of equal numbers of men and women. In one of the lists, the men were famous celebrities and the women were unknown. In the other list, the women were more famous than the men. The results showed that when the list included names of famous females (and unknown males), respondents incorrectly estimated that it contained more names of females. Conversely, when the list contained the names of famous males (and unknown females), respondents incorrectly estimated that it contained more names of males than females. That the people could remember the names of the famous people much more easily than those of the unknown people provided clear evidence that the availability of the names in memory caused their different judgments.

How does the inaccurate estimation of the frequency of names lead to a misestimation of probability? The answer is that if respondents can easily recall from memory more male names, their confidence increases and they provide a high probability estimate. People act as though they consider possible answers to the problem and then give the one with the highest probability of being right.

A variety of factors may influence the ability of decision-makers to more easily recall certain events. One factor is based on egocentric biases. For example, researchers have found that the availability of our own actions in our memory leads us to attribute greater responsibility for ourselves in a joint project—particularly if the project goes well. Quite simply, our own actions are almost always more available to us than are the actions of other people. Thus, if several individuals are involved in a joint project, each person will tend to believe that he or she contributed more to the outcome than others because one's own actions are more salient and more readily recalled than the actions of others. Similarly, salespeople may take greater credit for a successful sale than a sales manager gives them because their own actions to make the sale are highly salient to them.

A second critical factor that influences our ability to easily recall certain events is the way our short-term memory works. We both encode and retrieve vivid information from memory more readily than we do pallid or obscure information. In the fall of 2000, for example, the Middle East was again in turmoil as skirmishes erupted daily between Palestinians and Israelis. As a result, many people perceived the risk of visiting Israel as quite high. The vivid news stories of the fighting caused potential tourists to substantially increase their estimation of the probability of a negative event.

Because of the importance of vividness in impacting availability, pallid information is often overlooked or ignored. In particular, base-rate information—that is, the overall, underlying average rate of an event—is often overlooked. The data actually show that almost no tourists have been harmed in Israel. In other words, the vivid news stories overwhelm the objective, historical data.

People generally fail to adequately consider base rates in their decision-making. Managers, for instance, tend to overuse focus groups in developing advertising or product strategies. Because of the small number of people employed, focus groups are not representative of all consumers. In addition, even if managers collected data from multiple focus groups, they would still have only sampled the preferences of fewer than 50 individuals. Valid conclusions about a target market require hundreds of customer interviews. The views expressed by focus-group participants, however, can be particularly vivid, leading managers to think that they are more representative than they actually are. The net effect is that managers often fail to collect sufficient data to make strong and valid conclusions about their marketing strategies.

Illusory correlations can also bias our probability estimates. In the *Challenger* disaster, NASA failed to consider all four cells of the cause-effect matrix. As we described in Chapter 3, O-ring damage was relatively rare when temperatures were low. But then again, there weren't many instances of low temperatures at all. As a result, the managers could not see the correlation between temperature and O-ring damage that they would have easily seen if they had also looked at the relationship between temperature and no O-ring damage. Their inappropriate conclusions of correlation led them to an estimate of the probability of a disaster that was too low.

The illusion of control was also a contributing factor to the space shuttle disaster. The team had successfully launched 24 straight missions. As a result, they assumed that they had mastered the technology of the launch. Instead, they failed to sufficiently consider how chance events, such as changes in air temperature, could impact their operation. In the end, they underestimated the likelihood that such conditions would affect the flight.

Anchoring and Insufficient Adjustment   Another important biasing factor is the anchoring-and-insufficient-adjustment bias. Anchoring and insufficient adjustment refers to our tendency to make estimates by starting from some initial point (an anchor) and then adjusting from that value to generate a prediction. Two neat results summarize the research in this area. First, as an anchor changes (i.e., the starting point shifts), so will the final decision. Second, even if the anchor is reasonably accurate, the adjustments from it are often insufficient.

The effects of anchoring-and-insufficient-adjustment biases can systematically influence managerial predictions. For example, as part of their job, marketing managers estimate consumer activities, interests, and opinions. In one study, marketing experts (marketing managers and marketing researchers), "regular consumers," and MBA students made predictions about the percentage of married American male and female consumers who would agree with 11 consumer-oriented questions.

The results revealed a systematic tendency for people to anchor on their own opinions. For "regular consumers," the tactic was effective because their own ratings more closely matched those of the sample than did either the MBAs or marketing professionals. Managers recognized that they would have to adjust away from their own position because they would respond differently than the average consumer. Their adjustment process significantly improved their estimates to a point that they were almost as accurate as the regular consumers. The students were least accurate because they anchored too much on their own opinions and failed to adjust sufficiently.

Another study also provides fairly startling results about the anchoring-and-insufficient-adjustment bias. Groups of real estate agents and students looked at two different houses that were for sale in Tucson, Arizona. They were given extensive information on other similar houses in the area that were for sale and had sold (i.e., comparables). Some were given high prices on the two houses ($83,900 and $149,900); others were given lower prices for the same two houses ($65,900 and $119,900). All of the other materials that the agents and the students saw were identical.

When they were asked for their opinions on the houses' actual value and their likely selling prices, both the agents and the students were greatly affected by the list prices. Those who saw the high prices thought that the houses would go for $71,000 and $133,000; those who saw the low prices thought that the houses would go for $65,200 and $109,000. In other words, they were affected to the tune of 10 percent and 15 percent by the different list prices even though their actual estimates were not near those prices. They had adjusted away from the list prices, but insufficiently. (In addition, although they did not differ much in their estimates, almost half of the students acknowledged that they had been affected by the list prices, but only 20 percent of the agents acknowledged this. Instead, the agents said that they were only affected by the true value of these houses.)

Now, think back to our hot-air balloon case. The effects of anchoring and insufficient adjustment may also have contributed to the recommendations of David Gordon's family and friends not to pursue the lawsuit; that is, they may have anchored on the fact that very few people have succeeded in previous lawsuits like this. The specifics of David's case may not have caused them to adjust their assessments of the probability of success sufficiently.

Anchoring and insufficient adjustment also explains why people have difficulty staying ahead of the power curve. Recall that the power curve describes the geometric compounding of the effects of something, such as money, a disease, or word-of-mouth communications. Consider the process of saving for retirement. When people estimate how much a stock portfolio will grow in the future, they almost always underestimate the future earnings. One reason is that they anchor on the initial investment. Most people know that it will grow faster than just adding the simple interest to the investment each year. Yet they still fail to adjust sufficiently to account for the staggering increase that occurs after the investment has had a chance to grow for 20 or 30 years. Anchors act like magnets to attract our estimates.

Anchoring-and-insufficient-adjustment processes also apply to managerial judgments concerning compound (multiple) events. With conjunctive events, two or more things must both occur for a good outcome to occur. If only one part of a complex system fails, the entire system will fail.

Researchers have found that decision-makers tend to incorrectly adjust, often overestimating the probability of success of conjunctive events. Consider, for example, the problems involved in estimating the likelihood of success for a new product. The research indicates that managers' estimates of success are too high. The reason is that when developing complex products, a number of events must be successful for the product to succeed. Even when each event is likely (e.g., has an 80 percent chance of success or higher), because of the conjunctive relationship, the overall mathematical probability of success can be surprisingly low. For example, if four milestones must be reached to launch a product and each has an 80 percent probability of success, the overall likelihood of success is only 41 percent. Because people anchor on the initial probabilities of .80, or 80 percent, they fail to adjust sufficiently and their estimate is too high.

Think back to the problem faced by Katherine Williams in Chapter 3. For her team to be successful in doing the audit of the bankrupt firm, many different actions must work. Her team needs to detect fraud, any and all problems with unpaid debts, and any and all problems with collecting accounts receivable. Let's assume that her team is 90 percent certain that it can accomplish each of these tasks. What is the probability of the success of the overall audit? The answer comes from multiplying .9 by .9 by .9, or .73. This means that there is only a 73 percent chance that the audit will go well. Put another way, there is over a one in four chance that it will fail.

Because people focus on the starting point of a 90 percent chance of success, they fail to consider the compounding effects of requiring each of the events to succeed. If 10 separate things have to go well, which is often the case with launching a new product, and each has a 90 percent chance of success, the overall likelihood of *failure* is 65 percent. Because the starting point for the estimate of the likelihood of success is often an initial probability estimate, the tendency is to adjust insufficiently from that point and arrive at a success estimate that is too optimistic. In these examples, the decision-makers suffer from the anchoring-and-insufficient-adjustment bias in addition to insufficiently recognizing the effect of compounded probabilities.

In sum, a variety of factors can inflate or deflate our probability estimates. The availability bias, the illusion of control, the illusion of the run, and anchoring-and-insufficient-adjustment effects can all cause decision-makers to make systematically biased probability estimates. In addition, the overconfidence bias discussed in Chapter 1 can also lead to inflated probability estimates. The managerial implication is that when we are estimating the probability of a needless blunder, missed opportunity, hit, or correct rejection, we need to carefully evaluate whether our perceptions are being inappropriately influenced by any of these distorting processes.

Factors Distorting Outcome Evaluations

As discussed previously, risk perceptions depend not only on our probability estimates but also on our evaluations of the value of the outcome. For example, David Gordon had to decide how much he wanted from his lawsuit. Similarly, the president of Texas A&M University, Ray Bowen, had to estimate the value of the bonfire tradition to his university when he decided not to continue it in 2000 and 2001.

Two of the biases that we discussed in the last section can also affect our evaluations. For example, the anchoring-and-insufficient-adjustment bias almost certainly impacted David Gordon's monetary-outcome decisions during the course of his negotiations. His $1 million figure probably came from the anchor of the grand prize for the first person to successfully navigate the world in a balloon. Each of his expectations during the process was likely to have been an adjustment away from that figure.

The availability bias can also influence our outcome evaluations. In fact, what is available in memory can become an anchor that we use to make our adjustments. Whenever nuclear power is mentioned, for instance, the specter of Three Mile Island may come to mind. The horrible negative consequences that could have occurred from TMI provide a reference point for estimating the possible outcomes of a nuclear accident.

Other factors, however, also can distort the interpretation of information on the value of an outcome. One of the most important is the law of decreasing marginal effect.

The Law of Decreasing Marginal Effect   How people value possible outcomes is influenced not only by their perceptions of those outcomes but also by the outcomes' importance to them. The difficult thing about importance of outcomes is that it can vary a lot, even for the same person, depending on the surrounding circumstances and conditions.

A central goal of science is to identify "universal principles" that explain behavior across a wide variety of situations and in varied fields of study, be it economics, psychology, or biology. One universal principle is the law of decreasing marginal effect. The law states that the reaction to each new unit of a stimulus declines as it is added to the previous amount. Thus, economists and psychologists have observed that each additional dollar obtained provides less value than the preceding dollar. (The principle is called "decreasing marginal utility.") For the homeless, a hundred-dollar bill means a great deal because it may be all the money that they have. For people in the middle class, a hundred dollars is nice but may not be a really big thing, especially if they have a home, a car, and a bank account. For someone who is truly wealthy, a hundred dollars provides a nice tip for a bellboy.

The law of decreasing marginal effect works for losses as well as gains. Thus each additional loss means less than the first loss. Think of a basketball team playing a 25-game season. Imagine that the team has played 20 games and won each of them. Consider how the players would feel if they lost their 21st game. After the long winning streak, that first loss would be hard to take. Now compare this experience to how the same players would feel if they had lost their first 20 games and then lost the 21st game. One more loss would have little impact. Team members do care about how many games they lose, but a 21st loss is simply not as bad as a first. This is true in many realms.

The law of decreasing marginal effect explains both conservative and risky patterns of behavior. Continuing with the basketball analogy, imagine that you are the coach of the team that has won 20 games in a row. Things are going very well, and you feel good about your work and your team. Your next game is with an extremely tough opponent, however. Will you take an unusual risk to win, perhaps by inserting an unproven but highly skilled player into the starting lineup? Most coaches will not take such a risk when they are doing so well. Like many of us, they follow the old advice, "When it ain't broke, don't fix it." The reason is that the possibility of an increase in team capability would be overmatched by the possibility of a decrease in performance. The law of decreasing marginal effect states that each additional increment of performance is less valuable than the last. It also states that in such circumstances, regressing from a high level of performance would have greater negative impact than increasing performance a similar amount would have a positive impact. As a result, people typically want to avoid taking risks and tend to stay with the status quo when they believe that they are doing well.

Conversely, people tend to take greater risks when they face a potential loss. Suppose that instead of being the coach of the team that has won 20 games in a row, you are the coach of the team that has lost 20 games in a row. You are going through a miserable season, and your next opponent is particularly tough. In this case, would you take the risk of inserting an unproven but skilled player into the starting lineup? Because each additional defeat means less than the preceding one, you may be much more willing to risk another defeat to have a chance of a victory. This suggests that our risk preferences change when we are doing badly, and as a result, we may be influenced by the situation to take greater chances.

Many experiments have demonstrated that our initial positions of doing well or doing poorly affect our risk taking. For example, in one research study, a group of managers was given the following information:

A large car manufacturer has recently been hit with a number of economic difficulties, and it appears as if three plants need to be closed and six thousand employees laid off. The vice president of production has been exploring alternative ways to avoid this crisis. She has developed two plans:

Plan A: This plan will save one of the three plants and two thousand jobs.
Plan B: This plan has a one-third probability of saving all three plants and all six thousand jobs but has a two-thirds probability of saving no plants and no jobs.

Most managers who have faced this problem have chosen plan A. They wanted to ensure that two thousand jobs would be saved. By phrasing the problem from the perspective of saving jobs, managers viewed the situation as a gain. Because people tend to be risk averse when contemplating gains, the managers avoided the more risky plan that could save all of the jobs but risked saving none.

In the same study, a second group of managers was given another set of alternatives. This time the plans were phrased in terms of losses rather than gains:

Plan C: This plan will result in the loss of two of the three plants and four thousand jobs.
Plan D: This plan has a two-thirds probability of resulting in the loss of all three plants and all six thousand jobs but has a one third probability of losing no plants and no jobs.

Most managers who were given these two choices selected option D. Of course, the A-versus-B choices and C-versus-D choices are equivalent; losing two of three plants and four thousand jobs is equivalent to saving one of three plants and two thousand jobs. By framing the choice in terms of losses rather than gains, the researchers changed the risk-security trade-off for managers and led most of them to choose A over B and D over C. Clearly, the notion of gains or losses influenced their decisions.

Gamblers at racetracks exhibit the same tendency to take increased risks when losses mount. Early in the day, the pari-mutuel odds fairly accurately reflect the likelihood that each horse might win. As the day progresses, however, a peculiarity surfaces. Long shots begin to receive more attention. More and more gamblers find themselves in a loss position near the end of the racing day. To get even, they are willing to take greater risks and bet on more long shots. For example, suppose that you had been making $10 wagers all day and found yourself $100 down going into the last race. The law of decreasing marginal effect says that the loss of the first $10 is worse than the loss of another $10 after having already lost $100. Within the context of a $100 loss, forfeiting another few dollars is not so bad, particularly given the possibility of breaking even. As a result, many people begin to bet on the long shots.

The tendency to take greater risks when we are facing potential losses is also common among day traders. Psychiatrist and trading coach Ari Kiev described the situation in the following words: "You start to lose, and you try to make it back, but you lose more. You lose the rent money and then the college money."

The greater risk taking that results when we face a potential loss explains in part why small companies tend to be more innovative than larger companies. A major difficulty for large companies is maintaining a dynamic entrepreneurial approach to business. As a company succeeds, it grows larger. To protect its gains, it becomes more bureaucratic and risk averse. In contrast, small start-ups are constantly facing potential losses. They are in debt, hungry, and driven to develop new products. As a result, smaller companies grow more quickly. They also create more jobs in the U.S. economy than do large companies. Small companies must innovate and grow or they will die. In contrast, large companies tend to develop a conservative culture that focuses on maintaining the status quo and not losing what they have already obtained.

In some cases, large companies recognize the greater entrepreneurial spirit of small companies and buy them. A number of years ago, General Motors (GM) purchased Lotus PLC—a small and innovative British firm known for making fast, stylish sports cars but which according to its chairman, "staggered from crisis to crisis." After the purchase, GM's European division head worked to maintain Lotus's independence because the engineers in the firm had a spirit and commitment that GM's lacked. He explained the reason for the entrepreneurial spirit at Lotus in the following way: "Lotus was a company that's been on the brink of failure—bankruptcy—since it started.... That mentality of just barely staying alive caused a tremendous commitment to make things work."

In her book, *Rude Awakening*, Maryann Keller described the engineers at Lotus as more productive than GM's because they were hungrier and closer to the market. According to one auto analyst, "The situation at Lotus exemplifies how adversity can bring out the best in people and organizations." When people perceive that they are in a loss position and have their backs to the wall, they become driven to avoid final disaster.

THE NEED FOR AROUSAL AND RISK TAKING

As we have just noted, risk taking often results when people are facing a potential loss. In addition, some people will also take extreme risks to raise their state of arousal to an optimum level. These folks often have a high need for stimulation, which causes them to take actions that seem crazy to many of us, like parachuting out of airplanes. They also react to risky situations in an unusual manner.

According to psychologist Marvin Zuckerman, our goal as well-functioning human beings is to maintain a comfortable level of overall physiological arousal. To maintain the proper level of arousal, we engage in activities that stimulate us to the appropriate degree. If we are underaroused, we seek activities that pump us up. People who want to heighten arousal might watch violent television shows and movies or seek risk. Engaging in risky activities, from gambling to jumping out of airplanes, is a quick way to raise your heart rate.

Chronic thrill seekers seem to have a different sense for rational decision-making than most of us. (More cautiously, we can say that they seem to have a different sense for rational decision-making than this book's two authors.) As one psychologist described it, "If you ask accident-prone skiers if they are scared when they are on a high-risk slope, they'll say they wouldn't bother to ski the slope if they weren't scared. They want a slope that terrifies them. Parachutists say the same thing. After you take the plunge there's an immense relief and sense of well-being in facing a fear that doesn't materialize."

For those who have a chronic need to maintain a high level of stimulation, it is possible to become addicted to sensation-seeking activities. Professor Zuckerman further argued that high-sensation seekers crave excitement from such questionable sources as taking drug trips to jumping into sexual adventures to engaging in criminal activities.

The rush, the jazz, and the adrenalin flow all describe the same intense feeling of conquering the fear that arises from uncertainty. People who have a high need for arousal tend to self-select themselves into occupations that require the ability to enjoy and handle the risk. Fighter pilots probably qualify. Day traders of stocks also match the profile. From a rational-choice perspective, it is curious that in mid 2000, there were roughly five thousand active day traders, but over three-quarters were losing money. One expert described day trading this way: "To make money, you need the combination of a Ph.D. in higher math, the reaction time of a fighter pilot, and the emotional stability of a hostage negotiator." Both authors of this book have experienced this phenomenon personally. One, who remains an avid golfer, enjoys making small bets to spice up a round. The other played golf in his youth but doesn't anymore. Both have tried to drum up wagers with their notoriously conservative academic colleagues, with little success. Keith Murnighan had to hear about his "hustling" of two colleagues—for the grand prize of a single soda—for years afterward. In contrast, when John Mowen plays with friends who are entrepreneurs, they often propose wagers that entail much more risk than his desire for "a little spice."

In sum, one reason people seek out and enjoy risk is to feel the rush from the excitement. To effectively make high-stakes decisions and live with them, however, it is extremely important to understand your own need for arousal and try to make rational decisions within the parameters of your desires.

ON MANAGING RISK BY USING RULES OF THUMB

One quite effective approach to managing risk involves developing rules of thumb for action. Rules of thumb, or heuristics, specify easily understood guidelines for decision-making. Heuristic devices are nothing like computerized algorithms or decision calculus models that apply mathematical formulas and data input to calculate a correct answer. Instead, they are easily followed rules that typically result in satisfactory but not always optimal decisions. Heuristics have several advantages: They are quick to implement, they tend to be simple, and they are frequently based on years of experience. In this section, we present two heuristics for managing risk, the principles of incremental change and diversification.

Employ Incremental, Not Quantum, Changes

Successful corporations frequently follow this simple heuristic: "Strive for incremental rather than quantum improvements." Incremental strategies introduce small, easily accommodated improvements continuously. They also involve only small, repeated risks rather than the large risk that could sink a company. Incremental change also allows an organization to build a culture that expects a state of constant, minor changes. In contrast, quantum change breaks the flow of work and sends shock waves through an organization.

The waves of reengineering efforts in the 1990s illustrate the negative effects of quantum change. In one company after another, consulting firms were hired to institute sweeping organizational change. Even the gurus of the reengineering movement, Michael Hammer and James Champy, admit that in as many as 50 percent of the cases, the changes did not bring the results desired.

Breaking the rule of incremental change can lead to dire consequences, as illustrated by the attempts of GM in the 1980s to halt the slide of its ever-shrinking market share. During that time, GM spent over $40 billion on modernization and new facilities. A significant proportion of this incredible sum went to state-of-the art production equipment. One industry analyst noted that GM "ended up investing in million dollar solutions for ten-cent problems." The company attempted to make quantum rather than incremental changes in their use of technology. The result was near chaos.

In contrast, Japanese automobile companies typically work on the principle of incremental improvement. For example, when Toyota built a plant in Kentucky identical to one in Japan, visitors were amazed to find a traditional factory, lacking the scores of robots that they expected to find. The goal of the firm was to minimize risk in the United States by using existing technology. Because the equipment was identical to that used in Japan, if robotics or other problems occurred, the solution could be found quickly. Once the plant was running smoothly, new technology could be gradually introduced. Although the economic performance of Japan has severely lagged behind that of the United States over the past decade, their automotive sector is still strong, due at least in part to its conservative approach of seeking continuous small changes.

The Principle of Diversification

Perhaps the most basic risk-reducing heuristic is the principle of diversification. "Don't put all of your eggs in one basket" is one of many familiar maxims that express this strategy. Nonetheless, even professional managers and investors frequently ignore this basic axiom. When they do, they often suffer serious negative consequences. For example, in 1988, Congress recognized that a $50 billion problem existed in the savings and loan (S&L) industry, due in large part to their excessive purchase of junk bonds. To solve the problem, Congress legislated that by 1995, S&Ls would have to junk their junk bonds. This created a different problem: What would the S&Ls do with the billions of dollars of junk now in their portfolios? The only answer was that they would have to sell them. But who would buy them? As a result of their forced sale and the basic laws of supply and demand, their value plummeted. Everyone wanted to sell, and no one wanted to buy. A $50 billion problem had suddenly become a $200 billion problem.

Again, the problem was one of diversification. Financial companies need to diversify across time, industries, and instruments. In the late 1970s, banks were closing because they failed to diversify across time by placing too great a percentage of their assets in long-term securities. In the early 1980s, many banks in the southwestern United States failed because they sank too great a percentage of their assets in one industry—oil. In the late 1980s, many S&Ls crumbled because they failed to diversify across instruments by relying too much on junk bonds and risky real estate deals. In the late 1990s and early 2000, the same sad pattern surfaced again: Individuals who failed to diversify their stock portfolios and focused on technology stocks (particularly the dot-com stocks) experienced devastating losses.

Many rules of thumb are industry specific. A number of years ago, we interviewed several executives in small oil firms who had survived the bust of the 1980s. We asked them if they followed any rules of thumb. Many involved controlling risk. Some examples included the following:

~ Don't bet more than two times monthly income on any one oil well.
~ Don't use your own capital on exploratory wells.
~ Costs go up geometrically when you drill beyond six thousand feet.

The men and women who followed these rules were able to weather the plunge in oil prices that forced many of their peers into bankruptcy.

Implementing the Heuristics

A first basic principle is to identify and use the rules of thumb that apply to the tough choices that you will face in your profession. A second basic principle, however, is to use careful judgment when you employ these heuristic devices. For example, should you slavishly follow the diversification principle? One of the most successful investors of this generation, Warren Buffet, built his company by following the rule of never committing more than one-fourth of the partnership's capital in a single investment. The investment that caused his company, Berkshire Hathaway, Inc., to take off, however, violated that rule. In 1963, American Express became involved in a scandal, and its stock price fell by almost 50 percent. Recognizing a once-in-a-lifetime opportunity, Buffet poured 40 percent of Berkshire Hathaway's capital into American Express. Two years later, he sold out for a $20 million profit.

Warren Buffet violated the principle of diversification because he believed that the downside risk of a needless blunder were low. He felt that the price of American Express's stock was already at rock bottom, and he reasoned that the company's problems were short term. In addition, the benefits of a hit were very high because the company had great growth potential. Thus, when he made his fateful judgment call to violate his own rule of thumb, he understood the potential consequences, both good and bad, of his decision.

> ***Because risk perceptions vary across
> people, develop rules-of-thumb to manage
> risk in your organization.***

Shifting Gears

So far, our discussion has focused on the initial decision of whether to initiate an action. For Warren Buffet, the question was whether he should break his diversification rule and invest in American Express. In Chapter 1, we asked whether Jim Bronson should take his company public. Similarly, in Chapter 3, we asked if Katherine Williams should take on a new project when she was short-handed. There is another question, however, that David Gordon's hot-air balloon story illustrates very well: When should we abandon a course of action? The decision of whether to stay or quit is the topic of the next section.

THE STAY-OR-QUIT DECISION

At midnight, on May 10, 1996, Dr. Beck Weathers, a pathologist from Dallas, emerged from his tent at high camp, 26,000 feet up the icy slope of Mount Everest. He was about to start the final leg of his attempt to climb the great mountain. He was pursuing his goal of climbing the highest peak on each continent—the great "seven summits" endeavor first accomplished in 1985 by businessman Dick Bass. Beck had successfully climbed five of the peaks. If he could reach Everest's summit, he would only have the relatively easy climb up Danali in Alaska to complete his quest.

Only 3,028 feet long, the final leg of the climb is called the Death Zone. Its successful navigation requires climbers to exert maximum physical effort for over 12 hours to scale the peak and then return before a storm, avalanche, exhaustion, and/or oxygen deprivation strands them on the mountain. The entire endeavor is tremendously time sensitive. To complete their trek prior to nightfall, climbers must start their ascent at midnight.

The combination of high altitude, extreme cold, heavy winds, and a grueling 12-hour climb makes the decision to attempt the last section a tough call. Bad weather makes the slopes incredibly dangerous.

In fact, high winds and blizzards had battered the peak of Everest for the previous week. That night, a 50-knot wind blew against Beck's tent. Should he follow the team's leader, Rob Hall, to the top? Then, good luck seemed to smile on the team, as the clouds disappeared and the winds calmed. When they began the ascent at midnight, the stars shined so brightly that Beck could see their twinkle in the mountain's blue ice.

Several hours into the climb, however, Beck realized that he was losing his eyesight. The year before, he had undergone radial keratotomy. (Spectacles really get in the way of an oxygen mask.) Now, the low barometric pressure at the high altitude changed the shape of his eye. He was climbing strongly, however, and he didn't want to bail out prematurely.

Finally, when his vision almost totally disappeared, he had to stop. Beck's medical training told him that when the morning sun came up, his pupils would contract and allow his eyes to focus again. Rob Hall told him that once the sun came up, he could wait for 30 minutes. If his vision did not clear completely, he should not go farther but should wait for Hall to come back and take him back to high camp.

At this point, Beck Weathers was faced with a stay-or-quit decision. If his vision cleared, should he continue the climb, or should he abandon his efforts and start down the mountain as soon as the sun rose?

Beck Weathers refused to quit. When the sun rose, his vision improved and he began to climb again. He would not abandon the climb this close to the summit. But within a couple of hours, his vision deteriorated badly. He was now stuck at 27,600 feet and at a very cold temperature, about 30 degrees below zero (Fahrenheit).

Beck waited for hours and actually turned down the assistance of two groups of climbers as he waited for Rob Hall to help him down the mountain. Fortunately, the last group to leave the summit risked their lives to assist him. (Rob Hall would die near the summit when he attempted to rescue another climber.)

On their way down the mountain, a full-scale blizzard hit. They made it to within 300 yards of high camp before they collapsed in the blizzard's hundred-plus-mile-per-hour winds. The climbers were lost and afraid of walking off a 10,000-foot-high cliff. It was 7:00 P.M. They had been on the mountain for 19 hours, and their oxygen was gone. The group of 10 people lay in a dog huddle attempting to keep each other warm and awake. They knew that if they fell asleep, they would never wake up.

Finally, the storm lifted enough so that the six strongest could stand and struggle back to camp. One of the six, however, risked his life to stay with the four incapacitated climbers. The others reached camp and sent a Russian guide, Anatoli Boukreev, back to find the five who had stayed behind. Boukreev went into the blizzard but could not find them. He returned to camp, received more detailed directions and on his second try found them. With the help of the one sentient climber, Boukreev was able to get the two strongest back to camp. Left lying in the snow were Beck Weathers and a Japanese woman, Yasuko Namba. Both were near death and could not move.

The next morning, conditions improved, and team members searched for the fallen pair. Yasuko Namba appeared to be dead; Beck Weathers was lying face down on the ice. One glove had come off. He was in a hypothermic coma from exposure to wind chill that had reached 150 degrees below zero. Experienced Sherpas recommended that both be left where they were. Even if they could be moved to the tents, they would surely die from frostbite. Attempting to save them now would be a desperate act of triage, because everyone in the group could perish if they tried to transport the two incapacitated climbers down the mountain.

By 4:00 P.M., Beck had been on the mountain for 40 hours and unconscious for 12 hours. No one had ever before awakened on their own from a hypothermic coma. Then, for some unexplainable reason, his eyes opened.

In his interview with us, Beck described his experience as a miracle. "I opened my eyes. I looked at my gloveless gray hand and hit it on the ice. It went thunk. I could see before me, as clearly as I see you, that if I didn't stand up, I would be there for eternity." He struggled to his feet. He knew that if he walked directly into the strong wind that continued to blow across Mount Everest, he had a chance of stumbling into camp.

A few minutes later, one of the climbers stood outside his tent in the blizzard that still engulfed high camp. Suddenly, to his complete astonishment, an apparition emerged from the storm. It was Beck Weathers, who had been left for dead. A daring rescue got him off the mountain to medical assistance. After a long series of operations, he now has a prosthesis for his right arm. He describes his left hand as looking something like a Star Trek warship. Frostbite destroyed his nose, but a resourceful plastic surgeon has helped rebuild it.

Beck Weathers has returned to Dallas, practicing medicine and giving 70 motivational speeches a year describing his experience. He says modestly, "I'm an average guy who drew from an enormous well of strength that all of us have. . . . Anyone can do this. . . . Miracles can occur. . . . The only thing that matters are the people that you hold in your heart and the people who hold you in theirs."

What would cause an intelligent man to risk his life to climb Mount Everest? What would make him continue the climb after his vision left him? The most likely answer is summit fever—the single-minded effort to achieve a goal.

Summit Fever

Summit fever occurs when people recklessly strive to achieve a goal by taking risks that they would otherwise avoid. Rather than quitting to fight another day, they risk all to achieve a goal. For Beck Weathers, it was the desire to scale the great seven summits. As he stood nearly blind at 28,000 feet, he knew that his eyes would not allow him to ever attempt another climb of Mount Everest. This was his one chance, and he risked everything to achieve his goal.

When summit fever grips you, your focus is entirely on achieving a hit—of reaching your goal. Your desire to accomplish the goal overwhelms the risk of a needless blunder. As a result, you can become entrapped in a course of action that can lead to disaster. Indeed, rather than admit defeat, decision-makers often escalate their commitment to a losing course of action. In the case of Beck Weathers, he jumped from the proverbial frying pan into the fire.

What causes entrapment? One factor is our inability to fully understand and accept the concept of sunk costs. A sunk cost is an investment that cannot be recovered if we abandon a current strategy. Thus, for Beck Weathers to abandon his climb, he had to give up the notion that he had invested considerably, both monetarily and psychologically, in his attempt to reach the summit of Mount Everest. In monetary costs alone, he had invested over $75,000.

How can we avoid the sunk-cost effect? The answer is to be rational and recognize that sunk costs are sunk. They're gone, and once they're gone, we can't recover them. Because sunk costs are gone, they should have no impact on our future decisions. The only reasons that we should use to decide to move forward with a decision strategy are our estimates of future costs and future benefits. If future benefits exceed future costs, we can proceed. If they don't, we should quit. In particular, we should not consider sunk costs in this equation because they're gone. (We realize that we have repeated this several times here. That's because we need to keep reminding ourselves to ignore sunk costs. It's much easier said than done.)

The desire to avoid taking a loss, even if it is sunk, is extremely strong and can lead to irrational thinking, especially when we are involved in making high-stakes decisions. It seems that very few people are immune from letting sunk costs influence their tough decisions. Here is an illustration.

Sunk Costs and Financial Decisions

Water projects have long been a means for senators and representatives to bring money into their states. Unfortunately, in too many cases, past losses are used as a justification for continuing a money-losing project. For example, in the early 1980s, a battle raged over whether to terminate the Tennessee-Tombigbee water project. Begun in 1972, the project consisted of building a set of locks to connect the Tennessee and the Tombigbee Rivers to open the Tennessee River directly to the Gulf of Mexico. The largest civil works project ever undertaken by the U.S. Army Corps of Engineers, the 234-mile-long waterway made the Panama Canal seem small. It had the potential to substantially increase commerce in Alabama and Tennessee by dramatically reducing the time required to move materials to the Gulf of Mexico. Before the project was completed, it had already cost over a billion dollars. However, new estimates revealed that the cost of completing the project would exceed the potential benefits. Would you decide to abandon the project or complete it? What do you think the U.S. Congress decided?

Senator Jeremiah Denton argued, "To terminate a project in which $1 1 billion dollars has been invested represents an unconscionable mishandling of taxpayers' dollars." Similarly, Senator James Sassar stated, "Completing Tennessee-Tombigbee is not a waste of taxpayers' dollars. Terminating a project at this late stage of development would, however, represent a serious waste of funds already invested." Based on their efforts (and others), the Tenn-Tom Waterway was finally completed and ranks among the world's largest navigational projects. Unfortunately, it will never pay back the costs to build it. In essence, this was a bad decision. (It may have benefited some, but it cost many others.) The moral of this story is that tough calls of whether to stay or quit should be based only on expectations of what will happen in the future.

The fact that money, time, energy, or even lives have been lost should have no impact on whether to continue a course of action.

Avoiding Entrapment

How does a decision-maker avoid entrapment? It would be easy to say, "Recognize and avoid the sunk-cost snare." This answer is absolutely correct, but it fails to go far enough because sunk costs are notoriously difficult to overcome. In addition, social pressures to continue a course of action can be intense. The time to avoid entrapment is in the initial planning stages of a project. In all projects, it pays to develop a plan describing the sequence of events that must take place and the milestones that must be reached for the project to be completed. Most important, you must specify contingencies for what happens if milestones are not reached. If the goals are not met by the date set and within the designated budget, it often helps to bring in an outside, autonomous team who can analyze the causes of the problem and make recommendations—one of which could be the termination of the project. As an old Chinese proverb states, "If you must play, decide upon three things at the start: The rules of the game, the stakes, and the quitting time."

Knowledge of when to quit is one of the hallmarks of master decision-makers. A classic example of the failure to quit occurred in 2000, when investors in high-tech stocks found their portfolios falling by 70, 80, and even 90 percent. For these individuals, the failure to sell their stocks and take a profit proved to be incredibly expensive. Benjamin Graham, regarded by many financial writers as the twentieth century's most important thinker in applied portfolio theory, developed a series of rules for buying and *selling* stocks. He had three selling rules:

1. Sell after your stock has gone up 50 percent.
2. Or sell after two years, whichever comes first.
3. Sell if the dividend is omitted.

While other investment gurus may disagree with these particular rules, the important point is that rules exist. By following the rules, you can avoid being entrapped.

In sum, two ways to avoid entrapment are to (1) follow a set of rules for identifying when to quit and (2) ignore sunk costs. There is also a third way. Think back to Beck Weathers's situation. If he abandoned his climb, he would be giving up his great desire of climbing the highest summit on each of the seven continents. The cost of this missed opportunity was extremely high for him, so high that he almost totally ignored the risk of a needless blunder. The most likely outcome of a needless blunder in his case was death. Beck Weathers's actual survival was a one in-a-many-million event. Furthermore, attempting to climb the Death Zone of Mount Everest with impaired vision made a negative outcome highly likely. The third means of avoiding entrapment, therefore, is to give equal attention to the risk of a needless blunder and to the risk of a missed opportunity.

While abandoning a course of action is frequently the rational and appropriate course of action, no one likes to be known as a quitter. It's an insult. But knowing *when* to quit is a compliment.

The Other Error: Quitting Too Soon

Which occurs more frequently—entrapment or failing to carry through a course of action? Certainly, the consequences of entrapment can be extremely dangerous. On the other hand, quitting too soon can result in the crime of lost opportunity. Although we have little evidence for this statement, we think that quitting too soon is the more prevalent malady. Look at high school dropout rates of over 50 percent in some areas of the country. At many major state universities, 40 percent of those who enter have not received a degree within a six-year time span. Research on regret also suggests that over the long run, we regret most the actions that we did not take rather than the actions that we did.

In American culture staying the course is highly valued, and quitting is viewed with disdain. Aphorisms such as "Quitters never win, and winners never quit" abound. In children's literature, we have *The Little Engine That Could*. Americans are suckers for the story of the person who stays with a course of action and wins against long odds, as exemplified by the popularity of Sylvester Stallone's *Rocky* movies. There are even programs that teach people to avoid quitting, like Ranger School in the U.S. Army. One of the purposes of Ranger School is to demonstrate to soldiers that they can endure more hardship, stress, pain, and fatigue than they realize.

Knowing whether to stay or quit is one of the toughest calls that decision-makers face. On the one hand, if you stay too long, entrapment results. On the other hand, if you quit too soon opportunities are missed, and you may be labeled a quitter. Fundamentally, however, the rules employed to solve the stay-quit dilemma are the same as they are for any high-stakes decision. We need to estimate the probabilities and then evaluate the possible outcomes, gauging the risks and benefits for each of the four cells of the outcome matrix: the hit, the needless blunder, the missed opportunity, and the correct rejection.

> ***Stay-or-quit choices provide some of the toughest high-stakes decisions.***

The principles for evaluating risks and benefits listed here are not foolproof. In the risky world of high-stakes decision-making, even master decision-makers make errors. When assessing the risks and benefits of a decision, great decision-makers analyze the goals they are trying to reach, their value and importance, and how determined they are to achieve these goals. In addition, they recognize that intuitions and emotions can have a dramatic impact on their decision. In the next chapter, we tackle the surprisingly important roles that intuition and emotion play in high-stakes decision-making.

Principles for Evaluating Risks and Benefits

1. Estimate risks by considering the consequences and the probabilities of both the needless blunder and the missed opportunity.
2. Adjust estimations of probabilities by recognizing the distorting effects of the availability bias, illusory correlation, and the anchoring-and-insufficient-adjustment bias.
3. Adjust estimations of outcomes by recognizing the effects of the law of decreasing marginal effect.
4. Recognize that people take excessive risks such as gambling in part to create thrills, increase arousal, and maintain an optimum level of stimulation.
5. Manage risk by developing rules of thumb, such as:
   a. Strive for incremental, rather than quantum, improvements.
   b. Diversify, diversify, diversify.
6. When making stay-quit decisions, recognize that losses occurring in the past are "sunk" and should have no impact on current decisions.
7. To avoid entrapment, create milestones in the initial plan of action, which, if not reached, will result in the cancellation of the project.

5

APPLY INTUITION
AND EMOTION

When I have an idea, I turn down the flame, as if it were a
little alcohol stove, as low as it will go. Then it explodes and
that is my idea.

Ernest Hemingway

E rnest Hemingway's quote reproduced here provides an analogy
for the proper role of intuition and emotion in high-stakes
decision-making. Through intuition and quiet reflection, we can
identify solutions to problems. When the best action option surfaces,
strong emotions are activated to drive the implementation of the decision. The next story, however, describes the effects of allowing emotions to hijack the decision-making process.

The entire MBA class sat stunned. As a class exercise, Keith
Murnighan had just auctioned a $20 bill. The game was played for real
money, and the two final players were in shock—literally. The "winner"
had just won the auction by bidding $2,000 for the $20 bill. As required
by the auction's rules, the second-place bidder owed $1,950, which was
his final offer before abandoning the game. When the final two bidders
talked to their professor after the exercise, both said that they could not
remember a thing that happened in the final minutes before and after the
end of the auction. The stress was so great that it had caused amnesia.

The exercise began innocuously. Keith asked the 70 graduate students if they would like to play the $20 Auction Game. The students
were all executives enrolled in a class in organizational behavior at
Northwestern's Kellogg School of Management, which is consistently
rated as one of the top-five MBA programs in the United States. All

the students in the class had significant management experience. In addition, they are very smart—scoring in the upper 10 percent on the Graduate Management Aptitude Test. Who would have thought that such experienced and intelligent people would become trapped in the exercise? The answer is that their emotions had run amuck and short-circuited their rational thought processes.

Each semester, Keith runs the dollar auction game. Here are the rules:

1. Bidding for the $20 bill starts at one dollar and proceeds in dollar increments.
2. The auction is played for real money, and there is no jump bidding.
3. Cartels, collusions, and communications among bidders are prohibited.
4. The highest bidder pays what he or she bids and receives $20.
5. The second highest bidder pays what he or she bids.

When the bidding starts, hands shoot up everywhere. Almost the entire class wants to get in on the action. Bids escalate rapidly to the $10 to $12 range. At this point, the bidding slows as many participants have set limits for themselves in this range. A few bidders will continue, however, until the $20 point is reached. Perplexed and surprised, the $19 bidder finds himself in the position of having to bid $21 for a $20 bill. (Yes, it is usually males who become trapped in the game.) Thus, even if the person wins, he loses! The forces of the situation push the person to bid $21. Now, the worm turns, and the $20 bidder is placed in the same situation. A common stopping point for the bidding is in the high $20 range. The highest bid that Keith had previously encountered was for $250 by an executive in a class taught in Hong Kong. Interestingly, Keith always runs the auction several times in each class. He is constantly amazed that even after running the auction four consecutive times with the same class, there will always be two people who bid over $20.

On the fateful day in the spring of 1998, the pace of bidding was similar to what had happened in the past. In the first round of the auction, the last two bidders were a lawyer and a director of a high-tech firm. Both of the males tried using a "tough" strategy to drive the other bidder out. At the end of the first round, the winner bid $54, and the loser had to pay $53.

Then came the second $20. The bidding quickly reached the $20 point, with two final bidders left in the auction. Based on his previous experience in Hong Kong, Keith had made the decision to move the bidding to five dollar increments if it reached $100. This would increase the speed of the game, which became boring when bids moved in only one dollar increments.

Well, the executives went into a competitive frenzy. The bidding reached $100, and Keith invoked the five-dollar rule. When it reached $400, he moved the increment to $10. At this point, the members of the class were screaming for the bidders to stop. The two competitors, however, ignored their pleas, and the bidding quickly reached $700.

Now Keith was caught up by the excitement, too. His knees were shaking when he announced that the minimum increment would now be $20. When the bidding reached $1,200, he announced that the next bids would increase by $50.

Unbelievably, the competitors continued to bid. When the bidding reached $2,000, they finally stopped. The class was in a total uproar. Everyone was stunned—including Keith. The bids went far beyond what he imagined could be possible. As he led the class through a discussion of the experience, someone asked whether this really was for "real" money. He responded, "Yes, when I run this auction, I always hope to collect from the people who bid. I don't keep the money. I collect it and give it to charity."

Immediately after the class, a member of one of the bidder's study groups, a lawyer, quickly came to the front of the room. He gently accused Keith of changing the rules of the game in the middle and suggested that he not take all of the money. Keith agreed.

Finally, the last two bidders approached, completely chagrined by the experience. Keith talked to them for 30 minutes. Each was looking for some assurance, worried about how their classmates and professors would view them, not to mention their wives. He reassured them that everything would be okay. He let the two figure out between them how much each should pay, and they agreed on $50 each.

After a lunch break, the class came back together. Everyone agreed to keep the identities of the two bidders a secret. They could tell the story but could not divulge the names of the participants. Keith gave the money that he collected that day to a charity run by one of the participants in the class. Perhaps most important, as far as anyone knows, the wives of the two competitors never learned about the proceedings.

ON THE COMPLEMENTARY ROLES
OF INTUITION, EMOTION, AND REASON

In October 2000, John Mowen observed Keith Murnighan run the dollar auction game in one of his MBA classes. It is a fascinating exercise because in the microcosm of the classroom, the roles of intuition, emotion, and reason emerge in stark clarity. Every student in the class was a successful executive. With an average age in the early 30s, these were not wet-behind-the-ears students. They were highly intelligent, mature, seasoned managers. Yet every time the exercise is run, a few get trapped. On the occasion when John observed the class, on three consecutive bidding sequences, the final two bids were in the high $20 range. As a result, even the winners of the auctions lost money.

It is particularly interesting to observe the different tactics employed by the students. Nearly all are highly competitive people. As a result, the game has an immediate appeal to them. One group, which we call the strategic planners, takes a careful, reasoned approach. They carefully analyze the game, and quickly recognize that once the bidding goes over $10, the auctioneer makes money off the deal. As a result, they tend to set a limit bid of about $9. If the bidding goes beyond that, they stop.

Another group of participants takes a different, more intuitive approach. Familiar with auctions, the intuitive planners know that it is easy to get caught in the emotions engendered by the situation. In addition, they recognize that the real kicker in the game is the rule that the second-highest bidder must pay the amount bid. Their intuition tells them that the game is risky, and they stay out of the bidding altogether.

Finally, a few participants are overtaken by their emotions. These are the extreme competitors who focus on defeating their counterparts. Rather than concentrating on maximizing their own profits, they become fixated on winning the competition. They are the ones who become trapped in the exercise.

The dollar auction game illustrates how intuition, emotion, and reason become intertwined to influence decision-making. Although the game *usually* involves low stakes, it incorporates each of the characteristics of a tough call. Because you cannot predict what other bidders will do, the information is ambiguous. In addition, values conflict as the urge to win begins to clash with the desire to make a profit. Because of the psychological conflict that it creates, the game produces strong emotions, which are pitted against the effects of reason and intuition.

The three topics of intuition, emotion, and reason provide the subject matter of this chapter. Our goal is to describe the different roles that each plays in high-stakes decision-making. We begin by describing the surprisingly necessary and important role of emotion. Indeed, we contend that without emotions, people cannot make decisions. We then turn to a discussion of what it means to make a reasoned decision. Finally, we describe the important function of intuition in high-stakes decision-making.

EMOTION AND DECISION-MAKING

Over the past 10 or so years, scientists have made a fascinating finding: If the linkage between the emotional center of the brain and the reasoning portion of the brain is severed, people are unable to make rational decisions. The story of this finding actually begins in Vermont in 1848 when a construction foreman named Phineas P. Gage was given the assignment of blasting a path through an outcropping of rock for a railroad. Intelligent and highly skilled, Gage was entrusted with the dangerous task because of his sound judgment and efficiency.

In his usual manner, Gage approached the task with thoughtfulness and precision. He hammered out a precise narrow-diameter hole, packed it about halfway with TNT, inserted the fuse, and started to pack it with sand, which must be carefully tamped down. To tamp down the sand, he used an iron bar, which he had designed himself. The bar weighed 13 pounds, was 3.5 feet in length and 1.25 inches in diameter and tapered to a point. It fit snugly into the hole into which he placed the TNT.

As he began the task of tamping the sand, someone called to him. The interruption distracted him for a split second, and as he turned, he continued to hammer the bar. His assistant, however, had not added sand, and a spark flew when the tamping bar struck rock. It ignited the still-exposed powder, resulting in an enormous explosion. The iron bar was expelled from the hole at tremendous velocity. It pierced Gage's left cheek, traveled through the front portion of his brain, and exited through the top of his head. The rod landed more than a hundred feet away, covered with blood and brains.

Gage was thrown to the ground by the explosion. One of his workers ran to find a doctor. Surprisingly, Gage never lost consciousness. As the small group of concerned workers waited for the doctor, he conversed with them and even drank some liquid. An hour later, a doctor arrived and found him sitting in a chair. The doctor took him to his office in a wagon in which Gage rode sitting up. At his office the doctor dressed and closed the gaping wound, which was fully 1.5 inches in diameter. Over the next several weeks, Gage survived the inevitable infections that resulted from the grievous wound, and in two months he was pronounced cured!

By all accounts Phineas Gage's intellectual faculties emerged intact from the accident. In addition, he had no lasting physical effects, except that the vision out of his left eye was blurred. There was one notable change, however. His personality went through a profound transformation. He metamorphosed from a polite, well-balanced, and conscientiousness person to an individual ruled by his passions. From that point on, he could not keep a job, drank excessively, and constantly used foul language.

The story of Phineas Gage would have remained a medical mystery were it not for researcher's such as Antonio Damasio. In his acclaimed book, *Descartes' Error*, Dr. Damasio describes a modern Phineas Gage—a man whom the doctor had studied for several years. Elliot (not his real name) had undergone a radical change in personality after surgery to remove a large, fast-growing tumor from his prefrontal lobe. After the surgery, Elliot appeared to have retained all of his mental faculties. Indeed, when Dr. Damasio gave him battery after battery of intelligence and personality tests, Elliot was found to have superior intelligence and a normal set of personality traits. However, Elliot could not keep a job and constantly got himself into ill-begotten schemes of one sort or another.

After spending months talking to him and giving him nearly every intelligence and psychological test available, Dr. Damasio concluded that Elliot was normal in every way—except that while he was capable of knowing, he was incapable of feeling. He could take a problem and consider It from all angles. He could even quantify his options. But as Elliot told Dr. Damasio, "And after all this, I still wouldn't know what to do!" In sum, Elliot found it impossible to make choices.

Dr. Damasio began treating many patients with damage to their prefrontal cortex—an area that lies in the very bottom-front portion of the brain. In his research, he found one test that told him much about the underlying cause of the syndrome exhibited by Elliot, Phineas Gage, and other patients with such damage. In the gambling game, the patient must make decisions as to which of four decks to select cards from. The player is given $2,000 in play money. The object of the game is to lose as little of the money as possible. Some of the cards in each deck give the player money, and some subtract money from the stake. Decks A and B contain the high-stakes cards in which gains and losses are in $100 increments. Decks C and D contain the low-stakes cards in which gains and losses are in $50 increments. In addition, the decks are arranged so the overall losses are substantially higher in decks A and B. Dr. Damasio found that "normal" adults gravitated to the decks C and D, whereas individuals with prefrontal damage gravitated to decks A and B. It was as if the brain-damaged group had myopia for the future.

In further tests, Dr. Damasio hooked the players up to a polygraph that measured their physiological arousal as they played the game. He found that the arousal level of "normal" people went up when they drew a losing card. In contrast, Elliot and other brain-damaged players showed no changes in physiological arousal. They acted as though the linkage between their emotions and their decision-making had been severed. Dr. Damasio concluded that the injuries to Elliot and to Phineas Gage had severed the connection between the prefrontal lobe and the amygdala. The amygdala is located in a primitive portion of the brain and governs emotions, such as fear. Researchers have found that mice who have had their amygdalas damaged will fearlessly approach cats.

What do the stories of Phineas Gage and Elliot have to do with high-stakes decision-making? They tell us that both intellect and emotion are required to make tough calls. Decision-makers can possess an extraordinary IQ and an incredible memory, but it takes an emotional response to move them to appropriate action. On the other hand, as we saw with Keith Murnighan's students, extremely strong emotions can be disconnected from or overwhelm reason. In these instances, the individual is driven to act with little or no conscious control, and an emotional hijacking occurs.

> **Although emotions are required for action, they can also hijack intuition and reason.**

If the stirring of emotions drives people to action, then we should find that they influence the decisions of corporate leaders. Here is an example.

A few years ago, a Japanese manufacturing company was considering potential locations for a new plant. The company makes steel wires and cords for tires, pianos, and office equipment. When it announced that it would build a plant in the United States, dozens of cities and states began pursuing the company for the jobs and tax revenues it would bring. The company began the site-selection process by identifying its decision criteria, such as the cost and availability of labor, land, and transportation. After months of negotiations with numerous suitors, the Japanese firm narrowed the choice to Tulsa and a city in Arkansas.

The Oklahoma negotiators were ecstatic when they learned that they made the final list. On almost all of the important factors that rational executives should consider, the Tulsa site was superior. While waiting for the firm's decision, the Oklahoma group traveled to Japan to woo another firm. While there, the Japanese CEO of the first company called and invited them to a resort, "to give them the good news about the plant."

When they arrived, the team was treated to an extravagant dinner and a traditional Japanese bath. Finally, the delegation was brought into a formal room. There, the CEO greeted them warmly. After the ritualistic introductions, he made his announcement—the plant would be located in ... Arkansas!

The Oklahomans were flabbergasted. How could the CEO make such a terrible decision when all the facts pointed to Tulsa as the superior site? The delegation's leader asked, "What did we do wrong?" The Japanese CEO courteously replied, "Well nothing. You did nothing wrong. Everything we found in Tulsa we liked very much." But he continued by explaining that his company was small and family owned. The site in Arkansas was located on the side of a mountain overlooking a rice field. The scene was virtually identical to their plant in Japan. By placing the facility there, his employees would feel less homesick.

In the end, the rational economic model could not explain the final choice of where to place the plant. The hot button of a strong emotional connection overwhelmed the economics of the situation. The image of the familiar comforting hillside scene stirred the emotions of the CEO. Emotions are indeed a worthy competitor of rationality.

Emotions Are Necessary for Action

Without emotion serving as an impetus to action, little would happen in this world. Why does the United States go to war? Entry into wars usually occurs after an incident creates sufficient anger to goad the president, lawmakers, and the public to action. Similarly, regulatory agencies are created after a major event causes sufficient emotion to stir Congress to action. For example, the Food and Drug Administration was established in large part because of the emotions stirred by Upton Sinclair's book *The Jungle*. His description of the horrid conditions of the meat-packing houses moved Congress to action. Here is one of the passages from the book.

> Some worked at the stamping machines, and it was very seldom that one could work long there at the pace that was set, and give out and forget himself, and have a part of his hand chopped off.... Worst of any, however, were the fertilizer men.... These people could not be shown to the visitor,—for the odor ... would scare any ordinary visitor at a hundred yards, and as for the other men, who worked in tank-rooms full of steam, and in some of which there were open vats near the level of the floor, their peculiar trouble was that they fell into the vats; and when they were fished out, there was never enough of them left to be worth exhibiting—sometimes they would be overlooked for days till all but the bones of them had gone out to the world as Durham's Pure Leaf Lard.

Other books have also activated passions sufficiently strong to get laws passed. For example, in the 1960s Rachel Carson's *Silent Spring* spurred Congressional action on the environment. Similarly, Ralph Nader's book *Unsafe at Any Speed* led to the creation of the National Highway Traffic Safety Administration.

For good or bad, the presence of emotion causes decision-makers to pull the trigger for action. Without the presence of fear, optimism, or the sheer drive to experience stimulation resulting from the need for arousal, things do not happen.

A tragic example of the failure to implement a decision occurred in NASA prior to the *Challenger* disaster in 1986. The terrible image of the explosion overwhelmed Americans, causing immense grief and anger. The emotions galvanized the country into action and led to a series of investigations, the suspension of the program, and a redesign of the booster rockets. What is important, however, is that prior to the launch of *Challenger*, decisions had already been made to change its design. The plan had simply not been implemented.

The design of the rocket booster that caused the *Challenger* to disintegrate was based on one used in the air force's *Titan III* rocket, which had shown excellent reliability. The *Titan*'s body was made of steel segments joined together and sealed by O-rings. Engineers at NASA knew that on occasion the *Titan*'s O-rings had shown some erosion due to the hot gases, so they added a second ring to the shuttle's boosters to create a safer, redundant system. Problems with the new configuration in the shuttle system became apparent as early as 1977, however, when a test revealed that upon engine ignition, the joints could rotate and decompress the rings, making it more difficult for them to seal properly. As a result of the test, NASA engineers classified the joints as Crit-1R; that is, a failure could cause a loss of life.

When the shuttle program became operational, engineers examined the O-rings after each flight for evidence of joint problems. In early flights, few problems were found. But engineers were still aware of the potential difficulty, and in 1982, a scientist proposed a new design for the O-ring that used a "capture lip," which would inhibit the rotation of the joint that caused the decompression problem. But it would take over two years to build boosters that had this design; as a result, NASA continued to use the old design while working on the new possibility.

As the shuttle program progressed, however, increasing evidence accumulated showing that something was seriously wrong with the old design. Beginning in 1983, postflight inspections after launches and test firings began to reveal a disturbing pattern of erosion of the O-rings. Because some flights transpired in cold temperatures, the company making the boosters proposed that low temperatures may enhance the probability of "blow-by." These data had also alerted NASA to the problems, and more studies were ordered. Meanwhile, the people designing a new approach had produced positive results. In fact, in July 1985, 72 new steel case segments for the booster rocket's body were ordered that possessed the "capture lip" feature. The changes were described as a "potential long-term solution," and it was projected that they would be available starting in August 1988.

The problem was that a three-year wait would stop the program and set it back scientifically, militarily, and most important, politically. Furthermore, NASA suffered from the overconfidence bias that resulted from repeated successes. As noted by an academician writing in the *Journal of Management Studies*, "It had a magical aura. NASA had not only experienced repeated successes, it had achieved the impossible. It had landed men on the moon and returned them safely to earth. Time and again, it had successfully completed missions with hardware that supposedly had very little chance of operating adequately." According to the presidential commission investigating the shuttle disaster,

"NASA's attitude historically has selected the position that 'We can do anything.'" This overconfidence and "can-do" attitude caused NASA managers to overestimate the odds of success and to fail to heed the warnings of the O-ring problems. It was playing a high-stakes game of Russian roulette, and when the *Challenger* was launched, the bullet was in the chamber. Its management did not sufficiently fear the consequences of a failure, and this lack of respect meant that it would not move to halt the program and fix the problem. Only after the *Challenger* explosion, when anger was felt, did action occur.

> **Postponing a choice is a decision, and it takes passion to overcome inertia and implement a tough call.**

The Negative Effects of Emotions

Fear makes potential negative outcomes highly salient to decision-makers. In fact, researchers have found that simply being in a bad mood causes people to retrieve from memory more negative thoughts. For example, the fear of lawsuits causes medical doctors to order unnecessary tests, even though the probability of a serious illness is low. Similarly, when the stock market metamorphoses from bull to bear, investors suddenly focus only on negative news. Each new bit of negative information causes more selling. Positive information is ignored, and the market inevitably becomes oversold. Fear drives the market too low. Those who maintain control of their emotions can make their fortune in such circumstances. Of course, the converse will also occur. During bull markets, investors become optimistic, they focus on positive news, and their estimates of the probability of good things happening is biased upward. Their misplaced hope causes them to buy, the price of stocks is driven higher, and a bubble occurs.

Anger is the obverse of fear. Whereas fear impedes action, anger encourages it. When decision-makers face the tough call of whether to act, anger biases them to action. Of course, some people are quicker to anger than others. When George Will was writing his book on baseball, *Men at Work*, managers kept telling him to be careful about what he said about Roger Clemens. Opponents know that Clemens becomes really tough when riled, and it made no sense to unnecessarily ruffle his feathers.

When angry, some individuals focus on the importance of getting even—on punishing the transgressor—and ignore the possibility of negative outcomes resulting from the action. A classic example of anger leading to a decision debacle occurred in World War II. Hitler became enraged when Yugoslavian leaders threatened to withdraw from their alliance with Germany. To punish them, Hitler kept his armies in Yugoslavia for an extra month, raising havoc with the populace. This decision delayed his invasion of Russia. Months later, the advances on Moscow and Leningrad would fail because winter intervened on the side of the Russian military. That extra month in Yugoslavia was a major factor contributing to the failure of the Russian campaign.

Emotion and the Master Decision-Maker

As Daniel Goleman described so eloquently in his book *Emotional Intelligence*, the ability to control emotions is at least as important for success as a high IQ. The evidence of researchers such as Antonio Damasio reveals that emotional and cognitive intelligence must work together if we are to successfully navigate the world of high-stakes decision-making. In addition, it is critical that the master decision-maker recognize the emotional needs of others. We believe that those who have control over their emotions can also respond appropriately to the emotional needs of others.

John Mowen has observed firsthand the importance of combining intelligence and emotion. In the spring of 2000, he worked with a bank to diagnose why it was not performing as well as expected. Each of the members of the bank, including its CEO, completed a set of personality measures as part of a new model of motivation and personality that John has created. He was particularly interested in the CEO's score on the measure of emotional stability; the score was off the scale in the direction of extreme stability. The ratings indicated an individual who appeared to be completely even tempered. As part of the consultancy, John also surveyed the bank employees' views of upper management. He found numerous complaints that the CEO failed to recognize their existence or reveal that he cared about them.

In his lengthy discussion with John, the CEO was very surprised by the employees' reactions. The CEO did care about them. However, he had focused so intently on developing new business for the bank that he forgot to consider his employees' emotional needs. Because of his flat emotional makeup, he did not recognize that others need to be supported with empathy and visible signs of caring. In sum, in addition to giving the appropriate emotional response to a situation, master decision-makers are also able to identify the emotional needs of those for whom they are responsible.

Emotions and Three-Mile Island

As we noted in Chapter 1, emotion and stress are natural components of high-stakes decision-making. One of the characteristics of the master decision-maker is the ability to take steps to create systems that minimize the factors that cause the chaos and the emotional turmoil that frequently accompany crisis situations. Indeed, one factor that contributed to the Three Mile Island nuclear-reactor incident was the incredible turmoil in the control room. When the reactor's systems began to fail, hundreds of warning lights began to flash. Loud warning buzzers inundated the room with discordant, blaring noise. Technicians and engineers swarmed into the control room. Pandemonium reigned. The decision-makers attempting to diagnose and deal with the problem were confronted with a cacophony of sound, light, and other distractions that compounded their problem. In this tumultuous atmosphere, they were forced into a micromanagement role, which distracted them from setting priorities, understanding the global picture, and identifying the underlying cause of the problem.

After the incident, Commonwealth Edison implemented regular drills to test the systems and train the operators of their nuclear reactors. As described to us by Larry Gerner, a safety engineer at one of the nuclear plants, the drills taught them that it is critical to have a separate room for decision-makers. The room is designed to provide a relatively quiet atmosphere away from the distractions of the control room to allow for increased objectivity. Most important, the calm atmosphere minimizes the chances that emotional hijackings will take place.

> *Just as Ernest Hemingway liked to turn down the flame to let his ideas percolate, a quiet atmosphere can help to control emotions and improve decision-making.*

RATIONALITY IN DECISION-MAKING

With emotion having a pervasive influence on decision-making, what does it mean to make a reasoned and rational decision? Many different views of rationality exist. For Plato, rationality was the part of the soul that stood in opposition to animal desires. Indeed, as we have shown, strong emotions can enter the process to short-circuit the search for alternatives, distort the estimation of the probabilities of outcomes, and bias the perception of the positive or negative value of the outcomes. The rational decision-maker, then, attempts to avoid having emotion influence the analysis of the problem. Only after the decision has been made does the master decision-maker allow emotions to assist in the implementation of the action.

Another approach to rationality is found in the work of decision theorists. These academicians view rationality as helping us to avoid contradictory trains of thought. According to this perspective, rationality does not necessarily lead to any particular conclusion. Rather, it is the key to avoiding logical errors of reasoning. As one authority on decision theory asserted, rationality "dictates what *cannot* be concluded, *not* what can." The problem with an approach that defines rationality in terms of avoiding logical inconsistency is that madmen, such as Hitler, can be viewed as rational. By creating myths (e.g., Jews are dangerous and the purity of the Aryan blood must be maintained), it was possible for him to deduce what seemed like logical justifications for the holocaust.

Another approach to rationality is called subjective expected utility (SEU). When applied properly, SEU focuses on the starting points of the train of thought as well as the logic of the deductive process. The base ideas of SEU are old and go back at least to Benjamin Franklin. In a letter to Joseph Priestly (the British chemist who discovered oxygen), Franklin described how to make complex choices. He suggested taking a sheet of paper and listing the pros and cons of engaging in an action. Next, the person places weights on the pros and cons to show the relative importance of each. Over a period of several days, the decision-maker crosses out the evenly weighted pros and cons and eventually selects the option having the greatest weight.

The SEU model merely extends and formalizes Benjamin Franklin's ideas. Based on this model, a rational decision involves the following five steps: (1) Identify what options are available for action, (2) identify the possible outcomes of each option, (3) estimate the likelihood of the various outcomes happening, (4) calculate the value of the various outcomes, and (5) combine the information according to appropriate rules of probability theory to estimate the SEU of each option. The option with the highest SEU is then chosen.

> ***In the rational approach, the analyst makes choices after identifying options, the values of their possible outcomes, and the probabilities of the outcomes.***

As we discuss further in Chapter 8, we advocate using a variant of the SEU approach when making strategic or tactical decisions. In circumstances in which sufficient time is available, decision-makers are urged to move through the entire SCRIPTS formula. In the process, they identify causes, evaluate risk, employ divergent perspectives, assess the effects of time, and employ rules of probability theory to solve the problem. We also propose, however, that when time is short, decision-makers short-circuit the full SCRIPTS process and move to an intuitive decision-making approach. With this idea in mind, let us move to what it means to make an intuitive decision.

INTUITION AND HIGH-STAKES DECISION-MAKING

We begin our discussion of intuitive decision by noting that the rational approach to problem solving has received criticism. One analyst argued that top executives rarely use a "rational" decision-making approach. Rather, they employ "intuition" to make decisions. Other researchers have found the same phenomena. The higher up you go in the organization the more decision-making appears to be intuitive rather than rational.

A classic example of the use of intuition occurred during John Glenn's historic first orbital flight around the earth in 1962. The risks of the flight were enormous. Glenn rode aboard an *Atlas* missile, which at the time had exploded on liftoff about 25 percent of the time. In addition, none of the control systems for the complex flight had been tested together. The public held the astronauts in awe because they correctly surmised that the men were in mortal danger every time they rode one of the rockets.

Nonetheless, the launch went smoothly, and Glenn was fired into a near-perfect earth orbit. As he headed into his second orbit, a technician noticed that one of the meters registered that the heat shield had been prematurely released. Although it was temporarily held in place by the retro-rocket pack, the heat shield would fall away from the capsule when the retro-rockets were jettisoned after taking the spacecraft out of orbit. Immediately, hearts stopped. If the latches that held the heat shield in place had been released, the capsule would burn up upon its reentry into the atmosphere. To the casual observer watching the events from the visitor's area, the control room appeared perfectly normal. As described by one participant, "We are all in a state of shock at the enormity of the situation." If the heat shield was deployed, Glenn would die.

Those in Mission Control recognized that an alternative explanation of the reading was that the instrument had erred. But there was no way to tell for sure. Then someone thought of the idea of not jettisoning the retro-rocket pack. Could it simply be left on to hold the heat shield in place as the capsule reentered the atmosphere?

Mission Control faced a classic decision dilemma. If the instrument was correct and nothing was done, the United States' first astronaut to orbit the earth would burn to death. On the other hand, if the retro-rockets were left on to hold the heat shield in place, the aerodynamics of the capsule could be upset. The result might be the same—Glenn might die. Which was the lowest risk alternative?

Time was short. Elaborate models of how air flowed over the space capsule with retro-rockets attached could not be built in the minutes remaining. No one had ever even thought of testing the flight characteristics of the *Mercury* capsule with the retro-rocket pack attached. Intuition had to be used. The person with the most experience on the aerodynamic characteristics of the *Mercury* capsule was Max Faget. The directors of Mission Control phoned him. Faget and engineers at Mission Control carefully talked through the problem. One of the participants described Faget's thinking in the following way. He had a "first order feel that leaving the retro-pack on wasn't going to be a problem." Faget understood the engineering gestalt of the situation and could intuit the nature of the pressures and forces that would buffet the capsule. Thus, a "first order feel" was the basis for a decision that controlled the fate of John Glenn. Fortunately, the intuition proved accurate, and Glenn returned safely. Tests later revealed that it was the instrument that had failed. The heat shield had not been deployed prematurely.

For baseball managers, this "first order feel" is called instinct. The well-respected manager Tony La Russa has argued that instincts are much more than mere programmed behavior. Rather, they result from "an accumulation of baseball information." For La Russa, when you trust your gut, you are using a lot of stuff that is there from the past. Indeed, in some instances, baseball players totally disdain thinking and the use of rationality. George Will in his book *Men at Work* relates a story about the 1934 World Series. The great pitcher Dizzy Dean heard that the opposing team's manager was holding a series of team meetings. In response, Dean said, "If them guys are thinking, they're as good as licked right now." In a game of split-second reflexes, thinking gets in the way. You have to react. You cannot think your way through hitting a baseball or fielding a sinking line drive. Another baseball great, Branch Rickey, put it simply, "Full head, empty bat." Bill "Spaceman" Lee, a pitcher for the Boston Red Sox, said it another way: "When cerebral processes enter into sports, you start screwing up. It's like the Constitution, which says separate church and state. You have to separate mind and body."

Academic researchers have even proposed that corporate executives should use their intuition to supplement or even replace rational analysis. Writing in *Business Horizons,* one researcher argued that "top executives have learned through painful experience that analysis by itself is both inappropriate and inadequate." Another investigator, after interviewing dozens of top executives, concluded that they seldom think in ways that one might simplistically view as rational because they seldom "systematically formulate goals, assess their worth, evaluate the probabilities of alternative ways of reaching them, and choose the path that maximizes expected return." Thus, within the context of high-stakes decision-making, it seems that executives bypass rigorous, analytical planning, especially when they face tough calls involving difficult, novel, or extremely entangled problems. According to that investigator, "when they do use analysis for a prolonged time, it is always in conjunction with intuition."

Just What Is Intuition?

In the early 1980s, Herbert Simon, the Nobel Prize–winning psychologist and economist, argued that intuition is simply the accumulated knowledge of our lifetime applied to a particular problem. For Simon, the use of intuition is comparable to thinking of a word or recognizing the face of a friend. People with a good vocabulary can immediately recognize from 50,000 to 100,000 words. Similarly, chess masters can recognize over 50,000 configurations of pieces on a chessboard and can then draw from memory the appropriate next move. This is how grand masters can simultaneously play multiple opponents while blindfolded. They recognize and categorize the configuration of the chess pieces for each opponent and link the arrangement to an existing memory label. The process then becomes no more difficult for the grand master than remembering a telephone number.

Extending these ideas to intuition, Professor Simon proposed that just as we retrieve words or chess positions from memory, we draw on our thousands of previous experiences to elicit from memory a solution to a problem. Thus no long drawn-out decision-making process occurs. Instead, the solution emerges in an instant. The memory can be stored in any of our memory systems—whether verbal memory, picture memory, or muscle memory.

> *An intuitive decision is based on stored experience and is analogous to recalling a name from memory or reacting instantaneously to a curve ball.*

More recently, the psychologist Gary Klein has described an intuitive decision-making process in a slightly different way. Dr. Klein has spent over 20 years investigating how decision-makers such as fighter pilots, fire fighters, and intensive-care nurses make decisions in high stress conditions. His consulting firm works with executives in multinational corporations, and his field of study is called naturalistic decision-making. His conclusions about how people do and should make decisions differ radically from those proposed by traditional decision theorists. Dr. Klein has found that expert decision-makers use a process, which he calls primed recognition, in which they quickly assess a situation's characteristics and then match a learned set of responses to the problem. Through their experience they are thus primed, or have a learned readiness, to respond to a particular type of problem with a preprogrammed set of actions.

The concept of primed recognition is based upon research concerning how people process, encode, and retrieve information. Dr. Klein's investigations reveal that through experience, we develop schemas for action. A schema is a set of learned expectations for what should occur and of what to do in a particular situation. The seasoned fighter pilot or firefighter constantly scans the environment for signals of problems. When they identify a signal, they match the pattern and characteristics of the signal to an appropriate schema for action. It is as though the person says, "Aha, this signal's pattern matches this particular problem, and I have learned to respond to this problem with this particular set of actions."

According to Dr. Klein, because experienced high-stakes decision-makers move through a process of primed recognition, they can respond virtually instantaneously to a problem. Contrast the primed recognition process to that proposed by traditional decision theorists. In the traditional approach, decision-makers are urged to (1) identify the problem, (2) search for information, (3) evaluate alternatives, (4) make a choice from among the alternatives, and (5) evaluate the outcomes. In contrast, in the primed-recognition process, decision-makers are urged to (1) identify the problem, (2) match the problem's characteristics to the appropriate primed response, (3) take action, and (4) go to the next-best preprogrammed response if the first action does not result in the desired outcome. Because the matching of the problem's characteristics to a learned set of responses is done virtually instantaneously, the process is very fast. Indeed, Dr. Klein has found that experienced decision-makers spend more of their time identifying and understanding the problem than deciding what to do in response to it.

> *Intuitive decision-makers spend more time identifying and understanding the problem than deciding what to do.*

Implicit in the primed-recognition approach is the concept of satisficing. The word *satisficing*, coined by Herbert Simon, represents the idea that decision-makers frequently seek to make satisfactory decisions rather than optimal decisions. Frequently, in high-stakes crisis conditions, a satisfactory decision made quickly is much better than an optimal decision made slowly. Thus, primed recognition is particularly appropriate for use in crisis conditions. The time is just too short to identify a set of alternatives and then select the best approach among the options. Instead, the decision-maker recalls from memory a schema for action that appears to match the problem, runs through a brief mental simulation to see if it will work, and then acts.

In an interview with the magazine *Fast Company*, Dr. Klein described a case that illustrates the use of primed recognition. A commander of a fire-fighting unit recalled a situation in which he and his crew were fighting a house fire. The commander led his crew and found the fire burning in the kitchen area at the rear of the house. While standing in the living room, the team shot water into the flames. The flames died back, but immediately returned, burning as fiercely as ever. Completely baffled by the fire's persistence, they sprayed the inferno a second time, only to have it return with even greater intensity.

The firefighters moved back a few steps. The series of events did not match the commander's expectations. He had matched the problem to a standard action sequence, and it was not working. Something was wrong. The commander described his subsequent action as a sixth sense. He ordered his men to exit the house as quickly as possible. Just as the crew reached the street, the living-room floor, on which they stood only seconds before, collapsed. The fire had been raging in the basement and quickly consumed the first floor. The commander described his action as resulting from extrasensory perception, and he recognized that his sixth sense had saved the lives of his crew.

In his analysis of the events, Gary Klein argued that the sixth sense described by the commander was actually the operation of intuition. When the fire did not respond as expected to the crew's actions, the commander's experience told him that something was wrong. In hindsight, it is clear that there must have been a much larger source of the flames than a mere kitchen fire. In the heat of the moment, however, it was unnecessary for the commander to reach such a conclusion. He knew that the behavior of the fire did not match his schema for action, and he took his men out of the danger. As Dr. Klein put it, "Intuition is really a matter of learning how to see— of looking for cues or patterns that ultimately show what to do ... Experienced decision-makers see a different world than novices do. Ultimately, intuition is all about perception. The formal rules of decision-making are almost incidental."

The primed-recognition approach advocated by Gary Klein is fundamentally the same process as that described by Herbert Simon. Intuition is a matter of applying past experience to recognize and label situations and then responding with learned action sequences.

In an interview with Dr. Klein, we wanted to obtain his opinion on the standard decision-making approach. We asked him if people should search for options and evaluate each prior to making a choice. Dr. Klein's position is that high-stakes decision-makers do not generate options. Furthermore, examining the options "takes them down the wrong path." Dr. Klein described decision-makers as performing a mental simulation of what would happen if a course of action is chosen. This mental simulation results in an "emotional sense of how comfortable they will be going down this pathway." This emotional sense is based on intuition in which the skilled decision-maker picks up patterns of relationships—a process that may not even be conscious. Dr. Klein suggested to us that this subconscious emotional processing is faster than if a conscious thinking process is activated. The bottom line is that the psychologist agrees with that baseball sage Dizzy Dean: Thinking can create problems when the stakes are high and fast action is required.

> **Intuitive decision-making is faster than rational decision-making.**

Evidence against the Efficacy of Intuition

While management consultants claim to teach intuitive judgment and provide anecdotes and testimonials of its incredible effects, is there hard evidence that intuition works? The answer is equivocal. The problem is that when researchers compare the intuitive judgments of people (including experts) to a standard, the intuitive decision-makers invariably do poorly.

In one classic study of intuitive decision-making reported in the *New England Journal of Medicine*, a panel of physicians examined a group of 389 boys. The doctors identified 45 percent as needing a tonsillectomy. The 214 boys judged to be *healthy* were then examined by another set of physicians, and 46 percent of these boys were diagnosed as requiring a tonsillectomy. The researchers then took the 116 boys judged to have been healthy in *this* group and had them seen by a third group of physicians. What do you think happened? Of this group, 44 percent were found to need to have their tonsils out. It seems that no matter what the state of health of the patient, the physicians diagnosed about 45 percent as needing tonsillectomies.

Over a hundred studies have compared intuitive judgments to an objective standard. Not one has found intuitive judgments to be superior. But what is the standard? In some cases, it is the answer obtained from a mathematical formula. In others, the decision is compared to actual outcomes. Finally, intuitive decisions have been compared to subjective expected utility models similar to that suggested by Benjamin Franklin over two hundred years ago. In many instances, the model has been put into a computer, and the computer mechanically ground out an answer. Today, these models are called expert systems. Of course, the idea that a computer program can outperform an expert drives medical doctors, clinical psychologists, bankers, and stock-market gurus crazy. But the data clearly support the formulaic computer over human judgment. As a past president of the American Psychological Association noted, "There is no controversy in social science which shows such a large body of qualitatively diverse studies coming out so uniformly in the same direction as this one."

As a result of the work on expert systems and of an overall goal to assist human decision-makers, the designers of aircraft, nuclear power plants, and other complex systems (e.g., medical diagnosis) have increasingly built computer-controlled expert systems into the plane or plant. As illustrated by the demise of American Airlines flight 965, however, the interface between the decision-maker and the computer-controlled system can result in fatal problems. (Recall that in flight 965, the spoilers did not automatically retract when the emergency maneuver was initiated to avoid the mountain peak.) The question thus becomes: When is it appropriate to use intuition or computerized decision support systems?

What Is the Role of Intuition?

How should we interpret the evidence against using intuition in decision-making? There are two responses. First, in some cases, the so-called experts are inaccurate in their judgments, such as the physicians who erroneously diagnosed tonsillitis. Second, it is clear that in many circumstances, expert systems can act as important aids to decision-making.

Researchers who have studied the question, however, have found that research critical of intuitive decision-making has taken place in the sterile confines of the laboratory. As described by Judith Orasanu and Terry Connolly, the laboratory requires decision-makers to make choices that do not have any meaningful context. In real life, a continuous flow of behavior occurs in which the decision-maker influences events. Real-world decision-making is very different from the gambling tasks on which much of the literature on rational decision-making is based. Furthermore, the confines of the laboratory emphasize characteristics of the decision process for which computerized expert systems are particularly adept at handling. Thus, computers are particularly good at computing probabilities and combining them with values to obtain expected values. They are not good at understanding the global situation and reacting creatively to it.

In an important article, Kathleen Mosier identified a number of myths surrounding computerized decision aids and expert decision-making. She noted that in the real world, situational factors are critical for identifying problems and for making decisions. Humans have the flexibility required to diagnose and respond to novel events. In contrast, while good at integrating the information directly relevant to a problem, expert systems cannot look at the big picture and adapt to changes in the definition of the problem. Dr. Mosier cited the example of a passenger jet landing at an airport. Automated flight systems are excellent at picking up electronic signals from the ground and landing the aircraft in heavy fog. But they are inept at recognizing that a maintenance truck has stalled on the runway or reacting appropriately if the computer has put the aircraft on a collision course with another jet.

So, just what is the role of intuition in high-stakes decision-making? We believe that intuition has three roles. First, intuition and rational decision analysis play complementary roles. When time is available, each approach should be employed in a triangulation process in which one acts as a check on the other. If the two approaches give similar answers, the decision-maker can feel confident in taking the suggested action. If the two approaches give different answers, the decision-maker needs to step back, reevaluate, and use caution.

The second role of intuition is in crisis situations. When time is short and the stakes are high, an intuitive judgment *must* be made. The problem of how to handle the heat-shield problem in John Glenn's 1962 flight exemplifies such a situation.

Third, intuition plays a role in the high-level decisions in which only the difficult choices remain. By the time a decision problem gets to the CEO's level, it has gone through a series of managers who have analyzed it from numerous perspectives. In today's corporations, filled with MBAs trained in SEU theory and quantitative methods, most options have been data-crunched to death. Clearly inferior alternatives will have been discarded long before they reach the CEO's level. Henry Kissinger has described the situation well. When asked about presidential decision-making, he stated "All decisions that get to the president are 51/49, ... and frequently they must be made quickly." In other words, decisions at the highest levels frequently require the use of intuition. A computer will not help. Experts will differ on the solution. Values will conflict. In such instances, the master decision-maker must use his or her accumulated experience to make the choice.

> *Intuition should be employed to double-check*
> *rational decisions, in crisis situations, and when*
> *a rational process cannot make a selection*
> *between two options.*

SUMMARY: INTUITION AND
EMOTION IN HIGH-STAKES DECISION-MAKING

We have argued that reason, intuition, and emotion all play an important role in high-stakes decision-making. The tough call is *when* to use reason, *when* to employ intuition, and *when* to allow your emotions to influence your actions. We recommend that when a strategic decision must be made, the decision-maker should use reason and guided intuition. The reasoning process involves moving through the seven SCRIPTS steps prior to taking action. The decision-maker then compares the conclusion derived from the SCRIPTS procedure to the solution that emerges from employing guided intuition.

Whether we are employing the full SCRIPTS procedure or using intuition, emotion can get in the way to bias how we estimate probabilities and how we value outcomes. For example, in crisis situations, the emotions of anger and fear can activate flight or fight responses that are highly dysfunctional. Taking the time to think through the situation and develop options can be critical. Once a decision has been made, however, emotions can add that extra spark to get the decision implemented and to provide the energy to perform the work quickly and efficiently.

Finally, we propose that decision-makers employ a guided-intuition process whether making crisis or strategic decisions. We define guided intuition as the instantaneous use of the SCRIPTS procedure to make experienced-based intuitive decisions. As we propose in Chapter 8, thoroughly practicing the SCRIPTS procedure on many problems allows the steps to become ingrained and reflexive. When a crisis situation occurs, the decision-maker can then automatically engage this intuitive process, in which causes are sought, risks are identified, alternative perspectives are taken, and time is considered in a matter of seconds or minutes. Thus the SCRIPTS procedure guides the use of both reason and intuition in high-stakes decision-making. Throughout this process, keep in mind Ernest Hemingway's quote that began the chapter. While using intuition or moving through the SCRIPTS procedure, turn down the flames of emotion and avoid letting anger, fear, or greed hijack you. When you identify a solution, however, allow your emotions to provide explosive force to implement the course of action with overwhelming energy and drive.

> *Guided intuition is the preprogrammed use of the SCRIPTS procedure to make fast, experienced-based intuitive decisions.*

Principles of Intuition and Emotion

1. Guided-intuition is best employed by experts when time is short and/or when a rational analysis has resulted in two or more essentially equivalent options.
2. Emotions are required to move a decision-maker to action and to implement solutions energetically.
3. When time is available, use rational decision analysis to identify alternative courses of action, the probability of success of the options, and the positive and negative outcomes that may occur.
4. Emotions exaggerate and bias perceptions of the probability of outcomes and the perceptions of positive and negative values.
5. Fear increases the belief that negative outcomes will happen and causes people to view bad outcomes more negatively.
6. Optimism increases the belief that good things will happen and increases the perceived value of positive outcomes.

6

TAKE DIFFERENT
PERSPECTIVES

Clear writers assume, with a pessimism born of experience,
that whatever isn't plainly stated the reader will invariably
misconstrue.

John R. Trimble

With a voice resonating from long experience, Janice Kline
summarized her story by stating, "Sometimes you have to
leave money on the table." Why would a hard-nosed certified public accountant and former chief financial officer, who is totally
involved in our hypercompetitive economy, conclude that money should
be left on the table? As much as anyone, we would have expected her to
scrape for every dollar possible. Our immediate question, then, was,
"What would have caused her to make this statement?" The answer says
much about how changes in our perspectives can influence the choices
we make in high-stakes decision-making. As we will show, our frame of
reference, or perspective, impacts how we make tough choices. Honed
by our professional training and by our experiences, the perspectives that
we take influence our values and ultimately how much importance we
place on key information when we make high-stakes decisions.

A few years ago, Janice Kline was the CFO for an $80 million pub-
lic company that owned 80 franchises of a major fast-food company.
The fast-food business is a highly competitive industry with narrow margins and huge cash-flow problems. Janice's firm always seemed to be
on the brink of disaster. In addition, it was a public corporation. As a
result, it had to constantly expand to meet its investor's expectations for
growth. There were days when Janice would do a cash-flow analysis

and realize that she had one week to find $500,000 to pay the franchiser who supplied their food products. To make matters worse, she had to accumulate cash each summer to compensate for the negative cash flows of $1 million to $2 million that inevitably appeared each winter.

In her role as CFO, Janice had to approach problems from a variety of perspectives. First and foremost, she had to take a financial perspective and constantly monitor the company's cash flow, along with its profit and loss position. In addition, because she was involved in negotiating contracts, she had to view the world from a legal perspective. It was in her capacity as a negotiator that she discovered some of the problems that come with taking a one-sided legal view on an issue.

Her learning opportunity occurred when serious differences of interpretation of a contract erupted between her company and its franchiser. The attorney representing her firm delved into the case aggressively and relentlessly pushed her company's side, fighting hard to obtain a settlement that would be favorable to the fast-food franchisee. One Tuesday during the negotiations, however, Janice received a call from the CFO of the franchiser. He said bluntly, "You will be here on Thursday and you will come alone or you will lose your franchise."

Janice pulled together all the materials that she could and took a flight the next day. As so often happens, Murphy's Law (whatever can go wrong will) was in effect that day, and the airline lost her luggage. She arrived at the meeting the next day in the same clothes that she had traveled in, "having that camping look," as she described it. She met with the president, the CFO, and the treasurer of the corporation. The meeting began with the corporation's president forcefully indicating how unhappy they were with the attorney that was representing her firm. After this inauspicious beginning, Janice focused on being as straightforward as possible. Her mantra was "play no games." Because of her direct and forthright approach to the problem, she negotiated a deal that pleased everyone.

In discussing the problem with us, Janice described her company's attorney as someone who tackled the case as though this one negotiation would make or break her company. Janice knew, however, that her company was in a long-term relationship with the franchiser. This is why she described the situation as one in which "you sometimes have to leave money on the table." By being willing to compromise and not go for the jugular, she was able to change the tone of the negotiation (and of future negotiations as well). Her shift to a political perspective built rather than destroyed trust and helped her to establish business and personal connections that may be able to last indefinitely.

THE DOMINANT PROFESSIONAL PERSPECTIVES IN BUSINESS

When making high-stakes decisions, master decision-makers should consider the perspective, or frame of reference, from which to approach a problem. Janice Kline's story illustrates three divergent business perspectives—the financial, competitive, and political frames of reference. By taking a competitive, confrontational perspective, Janice's attorney nearly cost her company its franchise. By taking an accounting perspective and recognizing the financial implications of the problem, she realized the danger that the attorney's confrontational attack created. Finally, by taking a political perspective, she was able to negotiate, compromise, and save her company from disaster.

The perspective that we employ provides a set of values and salient issues that influence the factors that we consider in our decision-making processes. As a result, it influences our final choice. By explicitly viewing decision problems from divergent perspectives, master decision-makers ensure that they develop a full understanding of the situation. Paraphrasing the chapter's opening quote by John R. Trimble, clear-headed decision-makers know that if they do not plainly evaluate the decision from alternative frames of reference, their decision will almost invariably be misconstrued.

> *Our professional perspectives influence the factors that we consider in our decisions and ultimately impact the choices that we make.*

Our perspectives act as lenses that focus our attention on particular decision elements and personal values. In the next section of this chapter, we discuss eight divergent perspectives that are prevalent in U.S. corporations. We describe how each perspective can have both positive and negative effects on decision-making. We then show how the perspectives have influenced decision-makers in a variety of high-stakes contexts. After discussing the critical importance of viewing decisions from an ethical perspective, we conclude the chapter with a discussion of the principle of multiframe superiority.

EIGHT PROFESSIONAL PERSPECTIVES

The eight professional perspectives we identify here are engineering/technology, sales/marketing, production, political, legal, accounting/finance, competitive, and ethical. At the risk of overloading on acronyms, note that the eight perspectives can be remembered via the phrase ESP-PLACE.

Engineering / Technology Frame

The first important frame of reference in organizations is the engineering/technology perspective. This frame is at its best when it causes executives to focus on producing innovative, high-quality products in an efficient and timely manner. On the downside, the engineering/technology frame can result in look-alike, cost-ineffective products designed for the engineer rather than the customer. At its worst, the needs and wants of consumers are ignored. This can result in the creation of products that are easy to use for the engineers. For consumers, however, the products may be so complicated as to be nearly incomprehensible and useless.

The Sales / Marketing Frame

The sales/marketing frame represents another lens that many professionals use to view the world. At its best, the sales frame causes managers to take a customer perspective in which they focus on increasing customer satisfaction and developing innovative products that fulfill the needs and wants of consumers. Unfortunately, the sales viewpoint can result in a P. T. Barnum–like focus on hype and gimmicky sales-promotion efforts. At its worst, the sales perspective results in the use of misrepresentation and deceit to foist inferior products onto unsuspecting consumers.

The Production Frame

A production focus represents a third lens that managers use to view the world. At its best, it emphasizes efficiency and productivity. The goal is to optimize output by having long production runs with a similar design and minimal changes to reduce costs. When overdone, however, a production mentality results in a loss of focus on the customer's needs and wants. If the market changes and product innovation fails to keep pace, everyone loses. A production focus can also cause managers to search out and use the latest production technology and then find themselves saddled with dramatic overcapacity. Matching production to the market can be overlooked when a production frame dominates a person's view.

The Political Frame

Another important frame of reference for decision-making is a political focus. On the positive side, a political perspective allows a manager to use a combination of relationships, compromise, power, and persuasion to bring disparate sides together to get things done. When a person views the world with a political lens, the goal also becomes one of staying in power and building alliances with and rewarding those who either contributed to the process or are likely to contribute in the future. On the negative side, a political perspective can lead to decisions that are based on ideology and favoritism rather than on a focus on getting the job done most effectively.

The Legal Frame

A legal frame is another important perspective for managers. At its best, a legal perspective causes executives to carefully consider the relationship of high-stakes decisions to appropriate laws and regulations. Because the U.S. legal system is adversarial in nature, a legal perspective can inculcate a high degree of competitiveness in decision-makers and negotiators (e.g., Janice Kline's attorney). Like the other perspectives, however, an overuse of the legal frame can cause problems. It can lead managers to focus solely on whether a particular action is legal and forget about the effects of the action on consumers and suppliers. As a result, an action can be taken that is legal but that also has extremely negative consequences for public relations. In addition, as we have already seen, the legal frame can result in an extreme competitiveness that alienates potential partners.

The Accounting/Finance Frame

When appropriately used, the accounting/finance perspective keeps costs under control and a company on solid financial footing. When improperly used, it focuses attention on achieving short-term profits and stifles innovation. For example, during the 1990s reengineering craze, U.S. corporations dramatically cut personnel. The short-term result was a dramatic increase in productivity and profitability. Unfortunately, over the longer term, the remaining employees were overworked. As a result, they could not attend to their customers or to research and development. The net effect was a decrease in consumer satisfaction and new product innovations. These effects were particularly strong in the banking industry; as the headline in the November 2000 issue of the American Banking Association's *Banking Journal* stated, "Put Away the Axe: You Can't Cut Your Way to Profitability Anymore."

The Competitive Frame

Those who employ a competitive perspective think in terms of military campaigns or sports contests. Managers frequently use military and sports terminology in the hallways of giant corporations, start-ups, and small retailers. On the military side, managers will employ phrases that come directly from the jargon of war: an advertising campaign, launching a new product blitz, battling competitors, biting the bullet, identifying the flagship brand, being under the gun. On the sports side, the phrases and metaphors are almost as numerous. We often hear managers describe themselves or others as running a two-minute drill, dropping the ball, running interference, quarterbacking the team, being a team player, punting on an issue, and scoring a touchdown.

Employing a competitive perspective in the language that we use to communicate our ideas influences how we actually perceive the situation. At its best, a competitive perspective emphasizes the values of teamwork, achievement, and winning victories. Each of these values can make a positive contribution to making high-stakes decisions. At its worst, a competitive orientation can result in a cutthroat mentality that emphasizes secrecy and winning at any cost. The results of the dollar auction game that we discussed in Chapter 5 illustrate the negative effects of a total focus on defeating an opponent. As we show later in this chapter, an excessive focus on secrecy can also be highly detrimental.

The Ethical Frame

The last of our perspectives is an ethical frame of reference. Increasingly, major corporations include a position called the ethics officer. When used appropriately, viewing the world from an ethical perspective will result in long-term benefits. By asking what the "right" thing to do is, managers can avoid talking themselves into taking actions that can lead to short-term profits but long-term disaster. When used improperly, however, the constant questioning of choices that can result from an ethics perspective can slow the decision-making process to a crawl.

> ***Use the acronym ESP-PLACE to recall the eight professional perspectives.***

ILLUSTRATIONS OF THE EFFECTS OF PERSPECTIVE ON DECISION-MAKING

In the sections that follow, we investigate how the eight perspectives impact high-stakes decisions in a variety of contexts.

The Perspectives at Ford Motor Company

Within organizations, differences in professional frames of reference among key executives can create major conflicts. For example, at Ford Motor Company in the 1960s, three distinct frames were operating. Historically, Ford was a company dominated by a production lens. The focus on manufacturing may have been best illustrated by the classic Henry Ford line, "We'll give the consumer whatever color he wants, as long as it's black." People with a manufacturing orientation want to have long product runs, few models, and maximum efficiency. By the 1960s, however, the production frame at Ford had been replaced by an ongoing battle between those with a sales/marketing frame, those with a finance frame, and those with an engineering/technology frame.

The battle over whether to produce the Mustang is a perfect example of the collision of frames at Ford. The idea for the Mustang came from Don Frey. One year Lee Iaccoca's junior, Frey was an engineer— a product man who loved cars. For Frey, a car was an end in itself. When he looked at a car, he wondered what it felt like, how it handled, how much power it had. But around Ford, Frey was viewed as a disrespectful egghead. Henry Ford II once said, "The trouble with Frey is that he's too goddamn smart for his own good. Maybe he's a genius. Maybe not. But he's certainly a pain in the ass."

Whereas Frey represented the technical, product man, Iacocca symbolized the marketing man. When Iacocca looked at a car, he wondered whether the public would buy it, how many options could be added to it, and whether he could sell it to finance. In addition, Iacocca was the consummate politician within the firm who knew that to get his way, he had to know how to use power.

Frey originated the idea of the Mustang as an inexpensive, two-seat sporty car to go up against GM's Corvette. His goal was to build a vehicle that would appeal to the expanding youth market. Ford's market researchers, however, reported back that only about 50,000 units of such a vehicle would sell. Finance looked at the numbers and nixed the project, arguing that it would diminish standard volume. Standard volume was simply last year's sales, which the finance people naively assumed could be sold the next year without anything being changed. In the minds of the finance group, maintaining standard volume guaranteed profit without risk. Unless a new product could surpass standard volume, it should not be produced because it was too risky. A new product that added to the budget without guaranteeing sales was described as "decremental." The Mustang was deemed decremental. Even after Iacocca came up with the terrific idea of putting jump seats in the back and marketing research increased sales estimates to between 100,000 and 125,000, finance still wanted to nix the project.

The Mustang case also illustrates the use of a political perspective in which players use power, persuasion, compromise, and cunning to implement their ideas. The problem faced by Iaccoca in launching the Mustang was largely political in nature. His strategy for implementing his ideas involved bringing Henry Ford II along very slowly. He avoided going through channels to reach Ford because that would make it all too clear what he wanted. Rather, he would show his ideas in informal settings. His goal was to create a situation in which Henry Ford II would grow to believe that the car was his.

Within the Ford culture, the Mustang proved to be a tough sell. Finance continued to oppose it, based on the ill-conceived standard-volume heuristic. When Iacocca finally got Henry Ford II to the design center, the CEO said, "I don't even want to talk about it."

Iacocca then took a major risk. He began informally to talk up the car inside Ford corporate headquarters. Worse, he began to leak information about it to the automotive press. Reporters and other outsiders then began to pepper upper management with questions about this hot new car and when it would be introduced. Finally, Henry Ford II went back to the design shop and said, "I'm tired of hearing about this god-damn car. Can you sell the goddamn thing?" Iacocca responded "Yes," and Ford reacted by saying, "Well you damn well better."

Iacocca's risk taking didn't stop there. Right up to the Mustang's launch, market research still estimated that demand would exist for only 100,000 or so units. Early sales, however, were hot, and Iacocca per-suaded top management to add a second plant. Eventually, three plants were built to produce Mustangs, with a total capacity of 400,000 plus units. The Mustang came out in 1964 and in the first year sold 418,812 units. In the first two years, the car made over $1.1 billion in net prof-its—in 1964 dollars. Iacocca's photo appeared on the cover of both *Newsweek* and *Time* in the same week. But Iacocca had overstepped the bounds of political power. He had become a public figure, which did not sit well with Henry Ford II. Over the next 10 years their relation-ship would deteriorate.

> *Lee Iacocca's sales and product focus conflicted with a political frame and ultimately was a key factor in his leaving Ford Motor Company.*

In the mid 1970s, Henry Ford II was touring the design studios. He encountered a young designer who excitedly showed him a clay model of a new car. The effusive young man said, "Look Mr. Ford, we've got a hot new car here. Why, it could be another Mustang." Ford looked at him and said, "Who needs that?"

The Coke-Pepsi Wars and the Competitive Perspective

The competitive frame, if implemented improperly, can derail deci-sions. The beverage industry often seems to take competitiveness to the level of outright warfare. In particular, the two major combatants, Coca-Cola and Pepsi, have a long history of military-like battles.

Because the soft-drink industry is mature, Coca-Cola and Pepsi are constantly battling for market share. They live in a zero-sum world in which the only way to achieve an increase in sales is at the expense of the other. To do this, they have a variety of choices, including advertising and marketing programs or offering a lower price than the competition. Both Coke and Pepsi executives believe that short-term volume gain will translate into a better stock price and consumer loyalty. Thus, they offer ever-increasing marketing funds to large buyers so that they can receive coveted front-page ads, low advertised retail prices, and preferred display-space positioning. These programs are aimed at producing profits and beating the competition rather than focusing on what many insiders feel has been the hallmark of Coca-Cola—great marketing and long-term consumer loyalty.

Particularly after the disaster that Coca-Cola experienced in Europe in 1998, when people got sick from drinking Coke and major retailers were clearing their shelves, Coca-Cola's senior management team in the United States felt that their focus on profits was the right path for the organization to follow. All of their actions were geared to pumping up the stock value. This position ignored the data that showed that cola sales were flat or declining. As one insider put it, "At times, we all believed that by throwing deeper discounts than our competition we could win the battle. But the only true winners were the consumers."

He went on to explain, "What we were really doing was implementing a Pavlovian response to low pricing and destroying brand loyalty." Rather than increasing profits, the deep discounting during the past several years devastated the profitability "of two of the strongest brands in the consumer goods industry." Coca-Cola's "laser-like focus on short-term gains" and "winner-takes-all position" led to losses in revenue, production efficiencies, and brand-loyalty erosion. "We may have won the battle [market share] but our company was losing the war [profitability]." One outcome of their short-term vision was a stock price that began to free fall, losing almost half of its value, and the layoff of six thousand employees, creating additional turmoil within the organization.

There were other indirect effects to this focus as well. In the late 1990s, the fastest-growing category in the business was noncarbonated beverages. Coke's insistence on pouring more resources into a category that was extremely mature led them to ignore a quickly growing, highly profitable category. Its belief that the battle was in the grocery channel—a myopic, militaristic outlook—cost bottlers millions. In the end, Pepsi rather than Coke gained a resounding victory by capturing the single-serve water market with Aquafina and then the sports-drink market with the purchase of Gatorade.

Donald Krause's book *The Art of War for Executives* delineates well these downsides of the competitive frame. According to Krause, "If an executive is unable to control his impatience and seeks to destroy his competitors by direct attacks, he will waste at least one third of his resources without accomplishing much. The impact of such a strategy is disastrous." This is exactly what has happened recently between Coke and Pepsi.

An Older Story: The "New Coke" Affair

The competitive perspective describes not only Coca-Cola's most recent history but also their actions in the 1980s. In 1985, Coca-Cola changed the taste of Coke. Responding to a long, slow decline in market share and to the Pepsi Challenge, corporate officers announced with much fanfare that a different and better soft drink had been developed in "new" Coke.

Public response was swift. Within a few days, a mass revolt was underway. Lawsuits were filed, and over 40,000 letters poured into corporate headquarters in Atlanta, Georgia. One letter stated, "I don't think I would be more upset if you were to burn the flag in the front yard."

Eventually, Coca-Cola capitulated and brought back the old flavor in the form of Coke Classic while leaving "New Coke" on the market. Even three years after the introduction of New Coke, its sales represented only 2.3 percent of the market, even though the company spent twice as much on advertising for the new product as on Coke Classic. One Pepsi executive exclaimed, "Its market share has the half-life of uranium. Every time I look, it's gotten smaller." What happened to the marketing strategy of Coca-Cola? After all, taste tests had demonstrated that people liked the "new" Coke better than the old.

Coca-Cola's decision to change the taste of Coke was made after long and careful study. Perhaps the single factor most responsible for the decision was the outcome of the Pepsi Challenge, in which person after person could be seen on television selecting Pepsi over Coke in taste tests. A rational group, the executives at Coke decided that if taste were the problem, a change in the taste of the beverage would solve the problem. They had to create a soft drink that would beat Pepsi in taste tests.

As is all too apparent, Coca-Cola executives viewed themselves as fighting a war against Pepsi-Cola. Thus, a military perspective dominated management thinking. (It still does.) The mission assigned to Coca-Cola scientists was to develop a formulation that would beat Pepsi. In addition, the testing would have to be done in total secret so as not to alert the enemy of their impending attack. To maintain secrecy, the researchers kept the tasters in the dark concerning which brands of soft drinks they were comparing. They would compare "brand A" to "brand B" and have almost no idea that they were comparing Pepsi and Coke.

The researchers, however, ignored an important psychological principle: Expectations strongly influence perception, which especially applies to taste. This principle was illustrated by an experiment sponsored by *The Wall Street Journal*. During the summer of 1987, when both Pepsi and Coca-Cola launched advertisements in which Pepsi challenged Coke Classic and "New Coke" challenged Pepsi, *The Wall Street Journal* commissioned a taste test to help clarify the muddled situation. When the identities of the brands were not revealed, the test showed that 70 percent of the 100 tasters confused the three colas. When confronted with their confusion of brands, the consumers became defensive and accused the testers of shaking the bottles. Others blamed the results on the use of plastic cups rather than glasses. Had the labels been placed on the colas, however, the results would have mirrored the tasters' prior expectations. Coke drinkers would prefer Coke, and Pepsi drinkers would prefer Pepsi. These two companies have established enormous brand loyalty.

Consider what would have happened had the Coca-Cola executives initially asked brand-loyal Coke drinkers to compare the new beverage to their old favorite, which was being discontinued. They would have immediately learned that a major problem was about to occur.

By perceiving that they were in a battle for survival, Coca-Cola executives viewed the world through a competitive military lens, which caused managers to focus on maintaining secrecy, thereby ignoring the scientific principle that expectations influence perception. By not labeling the colas, the researchers obtained an inaccurate picture of consumers' responses when they introduced the new Coke. As a result, they could not anticipate the staggering negative emotional response to the change.

> *In their battle with Pepsi, Coca-Cola executives have a history of using a one-sided competitive military perspective, which has blinded them to the importance of the sales / marketing and accounting / finance perspectives.*

The Aftermath   As time passes, our perspective on the outcomes of decisions can change dramatically. In the years immediately following the failure of New Coke, pundits—including the authors of this book—excoriated Coca-Cola's decisions. As we now look back on the New Coke affair, however, our conclusions have changed. In an interview with *Fortune* magazine in 1995, the man who introduced New Coke, Sergio Zyman, ably defended his actions. He noted that the return of Coke Classic 79 days after the launch of New Coke, produced the largest one-year rise ever recorded in the brand's sales. The incident reversed the decline in Coke's market share. In addition, Zyman argued that the affair taught the company important lessons about the emotional bond of consumers to the product. He concluded by arguing, "If I could have a New Coke situation every decade, I would. Absolutely. Judge the results. We get paid to produce results. We don't get paid to be right." Yet a mere 10 years later, it seems that the military perspective continues to hurt decision-making at Coca-Cola.

The New Coke affair is a fascinating case study. On the one hand, the strategic decision to replace old Coke with new Coke was a short-term blunder. On the other hand, in the long run, it blunted Pepsi's inroads and improved Coke's market share and profitability. Shortly after the incident, pundits criticized Zyman for replacing old Coke rather than just adding a new brand. Indeed, the question will always remain whether it was necessary to replace the brand to light the emotional fires of customers. From a psychological perspective, taking the old Coke off the market created a state called psychological reactance. Reactance occurs when a person's behavioral freedom to act is compromised. Accompanying reactance are emotions of anger and retribution. By pulling the old Coke off the market, the company unleashed these emotions, which helped fuel people's passions to get the old Coke when it returned. Thus, in a paradoxical way, the ultimate success of the New Coke venture in boosting old Coke's sales may have come primarily because by pulling old Coke from the marketplace, they deprived their longstanding customers the opportunity to purchase their favorite beverage, a drink that they may have taken for granted.

Some of our students have suggested that the actions by Coca-Cola represent a careful, deliberate plan. There is certainly no evidence that such a plan existed. In addition, we doubt that a plan of this nature would have worked. Executives at Coke were genuinely embarrassed and surprised by consumers' reactions. Their swift response to bring back Coke Classic rewarded loyal Coke customers, who responded by increasing their consumption. In addition, the incredible publicity undoubtedly created new converts. A carefully prepared plan could not have been kept secret. After it was leaked, the ensuing negative publicity would have made a bad situation even worse.

Alternative Perspectives
in the Channel of Distribution

As Janice Kline discovered in her conflict with the fast-food franchiser, competitive battles are constantly fought between companies in the channels of distribution. The company with the most clout (the channel captain) can completely dominate its smaller partners and literally jerk them around like disposable puppets. A classic example is Wal-Mart, a corporation widely known for its hardball tactics. In one case, a small company approached Wal-Mart to sell its barbecue grills. A deal was struck, and the grills sold extremely well. Wal-Mart then asked the company to increase production to supply many more units. The company agreed. After obtaining financing from a bank, it built a new facility and doubled its workforce. Things went well, and the grills sold briskly.

The next year, Wal-Mart informed the company that they would have to cut their prices on the grills or Wal-Mart would find another supplier. The president of the barbecue company was between a rock and a hard place. He had to sell grills to cover his bank loan, so he capitulated to the demand. He struggled to cut costs and increase productivity so that he could remain profitable. The next year, Wal-Mart demanded another cut in prices. Now, the CEO had nowhere to go. Threatened with bankruptcy, he was forced to sell his company to a competitor.

Wal-Mart approaches its suppliers as though they are competitors. Because it views its suppliers through this competitive lens, it wrings everything out of them until they capitulate. As the king of the retail jungle, Wal-Mart can push its suppliers with near impunity. It can take a hyper-competitive perspective and succeed—at least for the foreseeable future.

In the fast-food industry, Janice Kline's corporation had significantly more clout than the barbecue-grill company had with Wal-Mart. One of the major suppliers to her company was Coca-Cola. Like Wal-Mart, Coca-Cola often treated its customers as though it had them in a choke hold in a captive alliance. In particular, Coke executives seemed to view their relationship with Janice's fast-food chain from a military perspective, as though Coca-Cola had achieved a victory over the company and was occupying its land.

For example, to have access to Coke Classic and Diet Coke, Janice's company was required to sell flavored teas and ices. Unfortunately, neither of these products sold well in her market, which did not sit well with either Janice or her company's CEO. To make matters worse, Coke would not respond in a timely manner to her company's needs. One individual at the corporate level in particular had a chip on his shoulder. He represented the company's corporate culture at the time. Coke was pushing for dominance and behaving like a piranha. From Janice's perspective, this individual and his company, Coca-Cola, acted like jerks. The straw that broke the camel's back occurred when Coke demanded that she pull Dr. Pepper and replace it with Mr. Pibb.

Janice's reaction was to approach Pepsi with their $10 million–plus account. There, she found a very different response. They encouraged her to keep Dr. Pepper and gave her a good deal on Pepsi products. Pepsi approached the negotiations by not attaching strings to the relationship. She then called Coke and gave the jerk the news: "We are going with Pepsi." There was dead silence on the line. Then, in a sputtering voice, he said, "I will have two first-class tickets mailed to you so that we can talk in Atlanta." Janice gave the offer some thought and responded, "No thanks, I have a handshake deal with Pepsi. We are going with them." In the end, she saved her company $2 million a year by going with Pepsi—along with a lot of hassle.

The Perils of Legal Frames

In the litigious society of the United States, a legal frame has taken on increased importance. Viewing the world through a legal lens can have benefits. The law provides a formal set of rules that governs interrelations between parties. The rules in turn give the parties the confidence that they can rely on the other side to keep promises. In contrast, one of the major problems of doing business in Russia is that the laws are weak and frequently not enforced. A partner in a prestigious Denver law firm described to us the role of corporate lawyers: "Most business people have a goal in mind. They focus on what can go right to reach the goal. As an attorney, I focus on what can go wrong. My goal is to help the entrepreneur identify alternatives with the least number of negatives."

But a legalistic perspective can seriously impair progress. To avoid any possible legal problem, one solution is to do nothing. The result is a strong tendency to avoid risk taking. In addition, approaching problems from a legal frame can also discourage open communications.

In his book *Talking Straight*, Lee Iacocca discussed his approach-avoidance conflict with lawyers, describing the situation when he was CEO at Chrysler: "Altogether, Chrysler has about a hundred lawyers on the payroll—more than the number of stylists or interior designers we employ—and that doesn't include the hundreds of outside lawyers we have to hire every year." The problem, however, is that the law is often ambiguous, "and the easiest way to stay out of trouble is not to do anything. Of course, that's also a good way to go broke." To solve the problem, Iacocca hired lawyers who were also businessmen. As he explained, "I want lawyers who tell me how do something and stay within the law but who still have enough moxie to stand their ground when they have to."

Iacocca also observed that the legal perspective discourages open communications. "The sad fact is," he said, "being forthright and honest can set you up for those who aren't. Watergate gave stonewalling a bad name but whether you're guilty or innocent, the first advice you often get from a lawyer is 'clam up.'" In business, however, not communicating with customers can lead to major problems. When things go wrong, consumers want accurate information quickly.

The problems of Ford Motor Company with the infamous Pinto case illustrate the conflict between the legal frame, which focuses on limiting communications, and the marketing frame, which thrives on open communications. The exploding Pinto gas tank occurred in the early 1970s, while Iacocca was still at Ford. He noted that the Pinto "was a legal problem and a public relations problem and we chose to deal only with the legal problem." As a result, Ford was vilified by the press, which greatly increased public suspicions concerning the company. Iacocca said, "Ever since then, whenever we've had a similar choice to make at Chrysler, we've done the exact opposite. We've chosen to look past the legal consequences and go public with the whole truth."

> *A legal perspective discourages open communications with customers, which can devastate public relations and consumer confidence.*

Despite these lessons from the past, corporations in the new millennium still listen to their attorneys' admonishments to deny problems or simply say nothing. Firestone's problems with their SUV and truck tires were exacerbated because the company steadfastly denied that there were flaws in their tires. Their head-in-the-sand attitude not only harmed them in the many wrongful death trials that they face but hurt them even more in the court of public opinion.

While viewing problems from a legal frame may be paramount today, we must recognize this perspective's limitations. It can inhibit innovation and limit communications. In addition, it can lead to a hypercompetitive approach that may maximize short-term gains at the cost of developing long-term relationships.

Political and Engineering / Technology Frames

April 1961 was a terrible month for the newly elected president, John F. Kennedy, and his administration. The first blow occurred on April 12, when the Soviet Union successfully launched *Vostok 1*, which placed the first man into earth orbit. By successfully blasting Yuri Gagarin into space, the Soviets put a real scare in the American people. Congressmen called for wartime mobilization in response to the threat. Egyptian president Gamel Nasser said, "No doubt that the launching of man into space will turn upside down not only many scientific views, but also many political military trends." A newspaper in the Philippines questioned whether the launch might show the superiority of the Communist system.

The second blow to the Kennedy administration was the Bay of Pigs fiasco, which got underway just five days after the historic Gagarin flight. The ill-fated invasion by Cuban refugees trained by the United States lasted only three days before being crushed.

The same day that the news of the Bay of Pigs fiasco was being communicated to the American public, Kennedy met with Vice President Lyndon Johnson concerning the space program. Johnson had long been enamored with space and would become one of the *Apollo* program's strongest advocates. At this meeting, President Kennedy asked Johnson to get answers to a series of questions, the first of which were: "Do we have a chance of beating the Soviets by putting a laboratory in space, or by a trip around the moon, or by a rocket to land on the moon, or by a rocket to go to the moon and back with a man? Is there any other space program which promises dramatic results in which we could win?"

The meeting represented a major shift in Kennedy's attitudes; less than three weeks earlier, he had been a reluctant advocate of the space program. In fact, the day after Gagarin's successful orbital flight, Kennedy had stated in a press conference that the United States should not attempt to match the Soviets in space. Rather, we should find "other areas where we can be first and which will bring more long-range benefits to mankind." The politics of the situation, however, changed Kennedy's mind.

A month after the Soviet Union's spectacular feat, the United States finally had a space triumph. Alan Shepard successfully flew a suborbital mission that lasted just over 15 minutes. Although the success of the mission was crucial, Kennedy had still not made up his mind whether to go to the moon. To help him decide, the president frequently probed the feelings of others. Jerome Wiesner, a scientist from the Massachusetts Institute of Technology who headed the Ad Hoc Committee for Space, talked about an incident in which Kennedy felt out Tunisia's president, Habib Bourguiba, on going to the moon. Kennedy said, "You know, we're having a terrible argument in the White House about whether we should put a man on the moon. Jerry here [referring to Wiesner] is against it. If I told you that you would get an extra billion dollars a year in foreign aid if I didn't do it, what would be your advice?" Mr. Bourguiba stood silent for a few moments, then said, "I wish I could tell you to put in foreign aid, but I cannot."

As a scientist, Dr. Wiesner viewed the issue through a technology lens. Previously serving on the president's Science Advisory Committee, Dr. Wiesner and others had opposed manned exploration of space for several reasons, all logical: (1) You don't gain anything scientifically, (2) it is much more costly, (3) and when failures occur, people are killed. But as he listened to the feedback that Kennedy received from others, he realized the inevitable. As he put it, the decision to go to the moon was "a political, not a technical issue." Technology was being used to serve political ends. In Dr. Wiesner's view, Kennedy had three choices: "Quit, stay second, or do something dramatic. He didn't think we could afford to quit, politically, and it was even worse to stay second. And so he decided to do something where we had a chance of really beating the Russians."

Three weeks after the successful *Mercury* flight, President Kennedy asked Congress for funds to go to the moon. In the highly charged political atmosphere in which American prestige was on the line, Congress approved the project. As we described in Chapter 4, a momentously costly program such as going to the moon might only have been initiated within a setting in which the decision-makers viewed themselves in a loss position. The Bay of Pigs debacle and the specter of Russians in orbit created a situation in which the United States was behind. We were losing and as a result, we were willing to take the major gamble, both in terms of money and prestige, to go to the moon. But the key point is that the decision was made for political not technological reasons.

Not surprisingly, political perspectives play a large role in U.S. congressional decisions. Individuals (politicians) whose very livelihood depends on their political acumen are particularly prone to viewing issues from a political perspective. This has been fairly obvious in the way that Congress has made a host of decisions, including those dealing with the space program. Two other space-related decisions provide additional evidence of the effects of perspectives and how a decision is framed.

Framing and the Space Station   In 1992, U.S. policy makers were deciding whether to build a gigantic space station in preparation for sending a man to Mars. Several parallels exist between the *Apollo* and the space-station projects. The space station was being pushed by a vice president (Dan Quayle in this instance) who was enamored with space just as Lyndon Johnson was. And as before, many scientists viewed the project unfavorably. Dr. James A. Van Allen, who discovered the earth's radiation belts, argued, "It's advertised as the world's greatest invention, but its scientific uses are pretty dubious." Furthermore, the scientific goals could be accomplished much less expensively by using unmanned rockets.

At the time, the opponents of the space station were using its high costs as a means of swaying opinion against it. For example, one strategy was to discuss the project in terms of its overall costs. The General Accounting Office estimated that over its 30-year life span, the space station would cost $81 billion. Of course, such analyses struck a raw nerve at NASA. One official argued that despite the cost overruns and the high total price, the project was worth it. "It's like building a house. If you start to calculate what it's going to cost over a lifetime to furnish it and heat it and operate it, you'd never buy it. The lifetime cost is very high. But you say, 'I want a house.' We want a space station."

Using such a metaphor to describe the space station was a highly effective strategy. Metaphors and analogies act as "miniframes" to set people's perspectives. Concrete and vivid, metaphors effectively communicate important nuances of meaning. The use of a housing metaphor for the space station creates images of a home, of protection, of a friendly safe haven.

In his 1993 book *Judgment Calls*, one of the authors, John Mowen, made the following prediction: "What will happen to the space station and the Mars expedition? With roughly $5 billion already spent on the space station, it has taken on a momentum of its own." He noted one scientist's comment: "It's going to get built. When you've got all those employees and contractors and that big an operation at stake, a project has to be more obviously preposterous than the station in order not to happen."' John observed that once a project is "turned on" and significant sums have been spent, it is nearly impossible to "turn it off" because of the erroneous principle that money spent previously should contribute to future decisions. As he concluded, "One thing that we can be sure of, however, is that political, not technological, factors will determine whether the space station is built because Congress is inherently a political body." In fact, the space station is now manned, and its construction is partially completed.

Framing and the Space Shuttle Challenger

Political considerations overruled scientific judgment to launch the Apollo moon program, and the United States did win the race to the moon. Even over 30 years after landing a man on the moon, Americans still take great pride in this technological success story. An important factor in the success of the *Apollo* program was that, while politically inspired, the politicians stayed away from its operations. The scientists and engineers received the autonomy necessary for them to work effectively. In the development of a highly technical enterprise, politics and engineering don't usually mix very well.

The *Apollo* program's director, Jim Webb, was able to announce proudly that the program came in on time and on budget. The reason for Webb's success is that he used a two-step process. First, he had NASA engineers and accountants carefully estimate how much it would cost to place a man on the moon. Second, he applied the heuristic that all research and development projects cost twice as much as estimated. So he took NASA's figures, doubled them, and gave these to President Kennedy.

The difficulties encountered by the space shuttle program provide a contrasting example of what happens when politics are allowed to intrude into the day-to-day running of scientific endeavors. Like the *Apollo* initiative, the space shuttle was born out of a political process. Even after the program was initiated, however, political considerations constantly intruded, all too frequently overriding technical considerations. The end result was the *Challenger* calamity.

In 1970, NASA managers projected that they could build the space shuttle at a cost of $10 billion to $15 billion. At the time, the Nixon administration was heavily involved in the Vietnam War and experiencing an extremely tight budget. As a result of a series of political compromises, a temporary and inexperienced head of NASA, George Low, agreed to an $8 billion budget. Tom Paine, a previous NASA head, was appalled by the decision. Paine later argued that the downfall of the shuttle program resulted from a series of small political compromises. As he noted, "The road to hell is notoriously made small step by small step. The devil always has a very tiny bargain." The Nixon administration kept picking a hundred million here and a hundred million there from the program, until it was finally whittled down to a cost of $5.1 billion, roughly one-third of the original projected costs (*before* using Jim Webb's rule to double research and development costs).

The Nixon White House, commonly used cost-benefit analysis to save money. When applied to the shuttle project, the penny pinching created a series of trade-offs that resulted in catastrophe. First, a decision was made to use solid fueled rockets to help boost the shuttle into space. The alternative, a totally reusable system that employed liquid fueled rockets, was deemed too expensive. Old-timers such as Werner von Braun viewed such a decision as highly dangerous. Once started, solid fueled engines cannot be turned off. If a malfunction occurs, it will progress until a catastrophic failure results. The photos of the ever-enlarging flame of hot gases emerging from the side of the *Challenger* booster prior to its explosion vividly illustrate just such a problem.

The focus on reducing costs rather than emphasizing safety could also be seen in the decision not to develop an escape system. In von Braun's view, the combination of solid rockets and the absence of an escape system made the system too dangerous for manned flight. A military general who acted as a liaison between NASA and the Department of Defense described the trade-offs in the following way: "NASA didn't do it because it was stupid. They did it because they were forced to do so. We can never be perfectly safe, and it's always a human decision as just how much is enough. But in this case how much was enough was not determined by the scientists and engineers but by the politicians."

When large-scale science projects are launched via a political process, political intrusions into scientific operations must be minimized after their initiation. (This is true in the realm of manufacturing, art, and education as well.) One factor that harmed the shuttle program was the appointment of key managers chosen for ideological considerations rather than for their technical and managerial skills. Such problems became particularly acute in the Reagan administration, which zealously placed conservatives with little relevant experience in key administrative positions. Ultimately, the political intrusions into the program doomed it. The politicizing of NASA also resulted in a dismantling of the careful testing procedures developed during *Apollo*. The paper trails that could track mistakes to a single person went up in political smoke. An Air Force colonel assigned to assist Sally Ride in the investigation of the *Challenger* catastrophe described the feelings of the panel members: "It just unraveled like Watergate. We felt betrayed. It was one thing to understand the technical reasons for the solid rocket explosion. But NASA had always put its people above everything. To hear how they put off and covered up the needed repairs and to know it killed your friends is a little hard to take."

> ***Political, accounting / finance, and engineering / technology frames mix like oil, water, and benzene.***

The combination of the political and finance frames that were operative through much of the shuttle program had two major characteristics. First, the hiring of key administrators was based far more on ideological reasons than on technical expertise. Second, the finance frame tied the program to a "hold-down-the-costs" attitude. This penny-pinching approach resulted in an underfunded program that made a series of trade-offs that ultimately led to an inherently risky design.

THE ETHICAL PERSPECTIVE AND HIGH-STAKES DECISION-MAKING

Because of the high stakes involved in making tough calls, ethical issues invariably become intertwined in the decision-making process, even if they are not always recognized explicitly. In one of our interviews, we spoke with Bob McCormick, a retired CEO of a large regional bank. Bob represents that reserve of talented people who do not get headlines but are the secret resources of our nation. We talked with him about the issue of means and ends in decision-making. He explained: "Means are crucial because they affect how people feel. The appropriate process allows you to sustain effort. The reason why you see burnout at 40 in high finance is not the pace. Rather, it's the problem of compromising the means."

Research results support Bob's analysis. Managers in one experiment were given a battery of tests that assessed their ethical behavior as well as their stress. The data showed that the executives who scored highest on ethics also showed the least stress. They felt little hostility, anger, or fear. Ethical shortcuts, in contrast, extracted a tremendous psychological toll. Living on the edge of what is legal and compromising personal principles imposed serious personal costs on decisionmakers and provided more stress than did a frantic pace.

Making Ethical Choices

Children's hospitals throughout the world have the sad task of treating children who often have tremendous medical problems. Medical teams who deal with children have to pay particular attention not only to their patients' physical conditions but also to their mental and emotional states. Both are important for treatment to be effective. When nonphysical conditions make medical treatment difficult, physicians must make difficult ethical decisions that go beyond their basic medical training.

Ethical decisions are particularly poignant when they affect the treatment of sick children. The sad bottom line is that the physicians at Children's Memorial Hospital in Chicago have found that they can't treat everyone. In particular, out-of-control kids whom they might have to chase around a room to get blood or give a shot are almost impossible to treat. If a physician doesn't connect with a kid, they always send the child to another physician, hoping that the emotional connection will improve. But sometimes this doesn't provide a solution.

In essence, each medical team must make a series of medical and personal decisions for its patients. If children (and their families) are emotionally stable enough to have a mature treatment relationship, the team can treat them and they will have a chance to improve. If they are not that stable, most physicians will choose to spend their limited time and resources on people who are similarly afflicted but are stable enough to be receptive to treatment.

These kinds of decisions often seem harsh. Letting a seriously afflicted child go untreated almost borders on cruelty. But the treatments for many diseases are not simple: They can require multiple visits to the hospital over long periods of time. In addition, patients and their families have to be extremely diligent in following orders and taking prescribed medications between visits. If a child or the child's family is not willing to follow directions carefully, the patient will not do well and will end up wasting the medical team's time and efforts.

Many of these kids have a lot of anger. They naturally ask, "Why do I have to have this disease?" If they can't answer this question and it affects them so strongly that it becomes impossible to treat them, physically or emotionally, a medical team can't help them and at some point, the team decides that it doesn't pay to try. In essence, they make a conscious decision not to try to solve a problem that they can't solve.

Admittance decisions also pose ethical issues for the hospital. Recently, a Mexican child with a liver tumor traveled from Mexico directly to the emergency room (ER) at Children's Memorial. How the family knew that he would be admitted into this hospital was not clear. How they were able to pay for his transportation to Chicago was also not clear. But the hospital admitted him, and a specialist was called in to check his condition. It turned out that this child had an unusual liver disorder that required a stem cell transplant. This treatment would cost $200,000 or more. The specialist had only seen this kind of disorder two or three times before, and she wanted to keep him and treat him—both to help the child and to satisfy her own academic interests in the disease.

The final decision rested with the chief medical officer. In cases like this, he gets advice from many sources and conducts a due diligence examination (e.g., Are other, state-supported hospitals qualified to provide this care?). But in the end, he says, "I have to count on the opinion of our physicians. I also have to do the right thing for the patient."

One of the early policy decisions that the hospital and its board made was that Children's Memorial would be devoted to promoting children's health in the community. One of the big problems that the hospital must deal with, however, is the admission of children with serious problems who are not members of the community. Defining "members of the community" is difficult. Is it Chicago? Is it Illinois? The Midwest? Where do they draw the line, particularly when someone from another country shows up at the ER with a very sick child?

Children's Memorial prides itself on being the very best at every possible procedure. Another of their policy decisions is that they will constantly strive to provide the best possible care for every child. As a result, they have invested in research units in every single specialty. Other hospitals are comparable in some areas, but Children's Memorial works hard to be as good or better than everyone else in all of the specialties.

So when a South American child comes in with an unusual disease and the treatment is tremendously expensive, what should they do? If the disease can be treated at a state facility, like Cook County Hospital, then a child can be transferred and all of the costs of treatment can be more widely distributed (i.e., among the taxpayers in the state).

When alternative institutions cannot provide comparable care, however, Children's Memorial must make the decision. The chief medical officer must make some particularly difficult decisions, and he must use multiple perspectives to do that. First, he must take an accounting perspective and be responsible to the institution as a whole, particularly since the money that will pay for many of these treatments is limited. Second, he must make an informed medical decision (which we would describe as being from the technology perspective). Can they treat the child effectively? Will their attempts to help, however costly, actually help? And third, he must take an ethical perspective: If he uses unrestricted care funds, which are tremendously limited, to care for one child, will he limit the hospital's ability to treat another child in the future? And what if this next child is more obviously treatable and more clearly a resident of "the community"?

What happened with the young Mexican child? They treated him, and he is doing fine. The financial cost, however, was very high. Was it the right decision from an ethical point of view? It was if it did not interfere with treatment for future patients. But like many difficult ethical decisions, that is a big "if."

In business, we often have to face the same kinds of trade-offs that confront the chief medical officer at Children's Memorial. In 1970, Milton Friedman, the Nobel Prize–winning economist, wrote that corporate executives have a responsibility of conforming to their employers' (the shareholders') desires, "which generally will be to make as much money as possible while conforming to the basic rules of the society, both those embodied in law and those embodied in social custom." Friedman is well known for his belief in the free-market system and his espousal of capitalism. It is noteworthy, then, that he suggests that making money is paramount for a corporate executive, but only while conforming to the laws, rules, and custom of society. Clearly, ethics are part of the custom of society. The truly difficult part for all of us as decision-makers is that people can differ widely when it comes to their ethical positions, especially with respect to business issues. Thus even taking an ethical perspective in tough decision-making may mean one kind of framing for one person and another kind for another person.

How do we make the tough calls in which ethical issues arise? Within a company, it is critical to develop a culture that emphasizes ethical core values. In his book on consumer behavior, John Mowen identified four rules of thumb that managers and consumers should follow

to ensure that their decisions are ethical. By keeping these rules in mind
when making decisions, an ethical culture can be developed in a firm:

1. *The golden rule.* Act in a way that you would expect others to
   act toward you.
2. *The professional ethic.* Take only actions that would be viewed
   as proper by an objective panel of colleagues.
3. *Kant's categorical imperative.* Act in a way such that the action
   taken under the circumstances could be a universal law of
   behavior for everyone facing those same circumstances.
4. *The TV test.* Always ask, "Would I feel comfortable explaining this action on TV to the general public?"

If these rules are applied to the situation of the Mexican child, it
becomes apparent that they made the ethical decision. The golden rule,
Kant's categorical imperative, and the TV test all point to treating the
child. (Interestingly, the outcome is less clear when the professional ethic
test is employed.) If the chief medical officer had only employed a finance
lens to the situation, the outcome might have been totally different. The
ethical perspective on high-stakes decision-making is an important coun-
terbalance to a cold bottom-line approach to running an organization.

> **An ethical perspective can help balance a cold
> bottom-line accounting frame.**

THE PRINCIPLE OF
MULTIFRAME SUPERIORITY

Although we have identified eight professional frames in this section
(engineering/technology, sales, production, political, legal, accounting/
finance, competitive, and ethical), other perspectives undoubtedly exist.
Which perspective should you choose when faced with a tough decision?
You will not find a cookbook recipe that answers this question, but the
principle of multiframe superiority, one of the fundamentals of high-
stakes decision-making, can help. When faced with a tough choice, master decision-makers examine the situation from a variety of perspectives.
Indeed, one of the worst offenses that decision-makers can commit is to
view the world through a one-dimensional lens.

> ### The principle of multiframe superiority is a basic rule of high-stakes decision-making.

A problem in applying the multiframe rule is that few people have the breadth of training to accurately view the world through divergent sets of lenses. A number of years ago, Don Frey argued that one reason Japan and Germany have a competitive advantage is that far more of their CEOs have a technical background. Although his conclusion that Japan and Germany have a competitive advantage is debatable, his assertion reflects his experiences at Ford Motor Company and at Bell & Howell, where he was the CEO. He has lambasted the trend for U.S. companies to be headed by financially oriented types—the "beanies" as he calls them. As he has accurately noted, universities in the United States turn out proportionately more MBAs than engineers as compared with either Japan or Germany. Because of his frame of reference, Don Frey has a visceral distrust of finance. Although he admits that MBAs do have the best interests of the company in mind, he feels that they are trained too narrowly: "Financial control and measurement is all they know. Too often the financial types do not realize that beans must be earned before they are counted." Given this situation, how might we deal with a uniformity of outlook on the part of current CEOs? Again drawing on his own experiences, he suggested that nontechnical CEOs assemble a set of technically competent and trusted advisors.

In his analysis, however, Don Frey was also looking through his own narrowly focused lens. His solution to "financial myopia" was to use a retinue of technical advisors. Such a policy, however, may only replace one filter with another. The goal of master decision-makers should be to surround themselves with a variety of advisors, each of whom carries a divergent frame of reference.

Using a multiframe approach is exactly the opposite of our normal tendencies. Most of us recognize that we can't see all aspects of every big decision that we confront and that other sources of information and other perspectives might help us to make better decisions. But as human beings, we love to hear that our opinions are sound, that our inclinations are correct, and that the decisions we are considering are on track. In a word, we yearn for support. Thus we tend to ask our friends for their opinions when we make big decisions—and our friends tend to be like us. In many instances, they may have exactly the same perspectives that we do. So they are most likely to be convinced by our logic.

As an example of this insularity, some years ago a study showed that a person's chances of achieving partnership in one of the Big Eight accounting firms went up significantly if the person was a white male over six feet tall. Needless to say, accounting firms at the time were headed by a very homogeneous group of people. And they were perpetuating themselves—and their singular perspectives. This was natural but not particularly effective.

We are biased not to ask people who are different from us to evaluate our potential decisions but only to ask people who are similar to us. But different kinds of people are exactly the people whom we should seek out. First, they can help us see things differently and give us some foresight about our potentially disastrous blunders. Second, if they do agree with our decisions, from a totally different perspective, we can be much more confident that we are making the right decision. Thus, the idea of using multiple perspectives means that we must go against our natural tendencies and consciously seek out people with different kinds of insights that can better inform our decision-making.

> *To implement the principle of multiframe*
> *superiority, we must seek counsel from*
> *individuals with maximally different,*
> *but competently derived, perspectives.*

Recently, John Mowen was working with a midsized bank to help improve its marketing functions. The bank had only been taken public a few years previous to this, and it was struggling to make the quarterly earnings improvements demanded by investment bankers. Historically, the banking industry functioned as order takers rather than aggressive marketers of products. With changing regulations, however, a merger and acquisition binge struck the industry, and the surviving banks became much more competitive. They began to ask the question, "What do our customers want and how can we supply it?"

As John began to work with the bank, he quickly realized that it had almost totally neglected marketing. The bank had been in existence for over 50 years, yet it had hired only two senior vice presidents of marketing, and their total time working for the bank was less than two years. Although the company had the strategic goal of becoming a marketing-oriented corporation, it did not have an individual on the senior management team to represent marketing issues. The corporate treasurer and the CFO more than adequately represented the accounting/finance perspective. A highly competent individual represented the production function. A compliance officer handled the legal/regulatory side of the organization. The net effect was that their marketing effort was totally uncoordinated.

Without an individual on the senior management team to balance the information provided to the CEO, the marketing function would remain rudderless. As a result, the organization would continue to be outmaneuvered by the competition in providing financial products needed by consumers and in communicating the bank's offerings.

Leaving out any single perspective means that decisions will be biased away from the values represented by that frame of reference. Similarly, when it comes to important personal decisions, consulting people with different perspectives becomes particularly critical.

Principles of Perspective

1. Decision perspectives act as lenses that focus attention on key professional values.
2. Eight frequently used professional specialization frames are engineering/technology, sales/marketing, production, political, legal, accounting/finance, competitive, and ethical (ESP-PLACE).
3. Because each professional perspective has strengths and weaknesses, viewing the world through a singular lens will lead to poor decisions.
4. Practice the principle of multiframe superiority by including individuals in the decision-making process who can represent each of the perspectives.

7

CONSIDER THE TIME FRAME

Time waits for no one.

The Rolling Stones

Imagine that you are a management consultant. You are being interviewed by a prospective client, the CEO of a highly successful software company. One of her company's strengths is the ability to develop specialized software solutions for corporations facing unique problems. You have known the CEO as an acquaintance for a number of years.

You meet the CEO at a quiet, local restaurant. When you arrive, she is seated in a booth with a stack of corporate reports in front of her. She greets you and says, "It's great to see you. Sit down. I need your help. Let me tell you a story and get your reactions to it." Here is her story.

It seems that the previous year, an important customer came to her with a difficult problem. The CEO pulled together a team and evaluated the customer's needs. Based on their analysis, she knew that her software programmers could develop an application that would solve the problem. The difficulty, however, was that the customer wanted a solution in two months. The consensus of the team members was that there was only a 70/30 chance that the program could be developed and debugged in that time period.

At this point the CEO laughed and said to you, "Fortunately, we could charge the customer an outrageous amount of money for the program because this issue was so critical to their operations." She described how she had to choose between using the cash to add people to the project or find incentives to increase the motivation of the programmers. She added, "We all knew that if we failed in our efforts, we could lose any of his future business, and he has been one of our best customers over the previous three years."

The CEO recognized that the programming task was really a five-person job, and she assigned her most reliable and experienced programmers to the task. Although she could have added additional people, she felt that that they would just get in the way.

Because of the looming deadline and the difficulty of the task, the CEO began to consider how she might give her programmers extra incentives. After considerable thought, and acting through altruistic motives, she offered them a bonus equal to one month's pay if they were successful.

At this point, the CEO turns to you and says, "Well Mr. Consultant, tell me how my programmers reacted to the bonus." You know that you are being tested. What do you tell the CEO?

A similar situation occurred to John Mowen a few years ago. The CEO was a former MBA student, whom he had taught 15 years prior to the meeting. When the CEO asked him the question, John knew that the tables were turned, and he was now the student. Thinking quickly, but carefully, he said, "Your strategy appears sound. You are connecting a reward directly to your programmer's efforts. In addition, there is no penalty for failure. So, how did your programmers react?"

The CEO looked at John, and said in a stern voice, "John, your assessment exactly paralleled mine. In reality, however, my software programmers absolutely hated it. It took me months to win back their confidence." The CEO continued, "So, you know the outcome. Now, tell me why? Did I offer them too much, too little, what happened? When you have an answer, let me know."

We do have an answer. And it has nothing to do with how much the programmers were paid. The answer lies in their view of time, which was very different from the CEO's.

TIME AND HIGH-STAKES DECISION-MAKING

The topic of time has already appeared repeatedly throughout this book. The concept of the power curve, for instance, depends entirely on time; that is, as time elapses, the slope of the power curve becomes ever steeper. If the effects of an action take time to have an impact (i.e., outcomes lag actions), then huge problems result if you get behind the curve.

The tough choices recently faced by Xerox Corporation illustrate perfectly the effects of the power curve. The company had let its prices get out of control, and it was losing market share to Japanese competitors such as Canon. In an effort to decrease its costs, in 1999 Xerox consolidated its 36 administrative centers. The decision caused massive problems in its billing procedures, however, and fully one-quarter of its customers encountered billing or payment errors. The combination of high prices and billing errors caused orders to plummet. To counter the problem, Xerox executives initiated a program to visit large clients, such as Kinko's, in person to win back their confidence. As 2001 began, Xerox was faced with the specter of bankruptcy. Its bonds were priced at 30 cents to the dollar, and it had nearly exhausted its $7 billion line of credit. They had waited too long to act, and they got behind the power curve. It would take massive efforts to get back on top of the situation. In June of 2001, Xerox restated its financial results for 2000 and showed a loss of 44 cents a share for continuing operations. In addition, a massive debt load and investigations into its accounting practices by the Securities and Exchange Commission continued. The question that could not be answered as this book went to press was whether Xerox's response to the crisis could effectively brake its deteriorating financial situation before the company plunged into the zone of false hope.

In addition to having a major impact on power-curve decisions, time also plays a decisive role in determining whether you face a crisis or a strategic decision. Remember that the distinction between a crisis and a strategic choice is based on whether sufficient time is available to use the entire SCRIPTS process.

One of the major themes of this book is that the speed with which decisions must be made in business has increased substantially in the electronic age. Developing processes that increase the speed of our decision-making, while we maintain or even improve the quality of our decisions, is a critical task for managers. As the Rolling Stones tell it, "Time waits for no one." We can go to every time-management seminar on earth, and we will stop neither the earth from turning nor its orbit around the sun—the two factors that have the most control over our sense of time.

> ***Time impacts two high-stakes questions: Does the situation require a crisis or strategic decision, and where are you on the power curve?***

Right now, you may be saying to yourself something like, "Sure, sure, time is important, but what in the world does it have to do with how the computer programmers reacted to the bonuses offered to them by the CEO?" The answer is that people from divergent cultures can hold three different time perspectives. More specifically, the case concerns a conflict of time perspectives held by the software programmers and the firm's CEO. The following section discusses the three culturally based views of time. Next, we identify three different time traps that can harm high-stakes decisions. The chapter then investigates the relationship between time and ethics in high-stakes decision-making. We follow this discussion with an analysis of how time pressure influences crisis decision-making. We conclude with eight principles of time-based decision-making.

CULTURAL VIEWS OF TIME

What is time? This simple question has a very complex answer. Perhaps the most accurate response is that your view of time depends on your perspective. From the viewpoint of a twenty-first century physicist, time cannot be discussed without reference to distance, gravity, and the speed of light. As Stephen Hawking has noted, no absolute time exists.

Here is an example. Suppose that you have three people—one on Earth, one in a spacecraft traveling close to the speed of light, and one in orbit around a nearby black hole. Each has a clock that is perfectly calibrated, and each has the task of recording how long it takes for a laser beam to be sent from Earth to the moon. The question is: Will each person get the same answer? Prior to the development of the theory of relativity, scientists would have said yes, because time was viewed as absolute. However, when Albert Einstein developed his ideas, he turned the world upside down. Instead of time being absolute, he argued, time is relative. What is absolute is the speed of light. For a physicist, time is defined as the distance that a beam of light travels divided by the speed of light. Because the distance traveled is relative, time is relative as well.

Physicists have performed experiments showing that the person traveling on the spacecraft and the person orbiting the black hole would perceive the laser beam to take less time to travel to the moon than would the person on Earth. In addition, their perfectly functioning clocks would show that it actually took less time as well. What happens is that gravity and the speed with which a person is traveling influences the curvature of space and therefore the distance that the laser beam travels (from their perspective). In other words, the person on the rocket sees the distance from Earth to the moon as contracted, so it takes less time for the light to get there. When the person on earth starts to argue, "No, it took longer," the rocket guy responds, "Of course you think so. Your clocks are so slow." Thus, depending on where they view the phenomenon, their speed relative to the speed of light, the amount of gravitational forces operating, and their actual recording of time will vary.

To those of us on terra firma who are bound by gravity, the notion of the physical relativity of time seems absurd. It is true that the passing of 24 hours in Chicago takes exactly the same amount of time as in New York City or Tokyo. In reality, however, the relativity of time has real-world effects, such as on the global positioning system. The actual passage of time changes depending on whether the clock is in orbit or on Earth. On Earth, gravity's accelerating force causes time to slow relative to that experienced in orbit. A satellite in Earth orbit experiences no gravitational field at all: that is, it is in free fall, floating in free space, in a nonaccelerating system. Acceleration on Earth slows the clock down relative to orbiting objects.

What does this all mean? According to general relativity theory, if we bring down the satellite clock or bring up the Earth clock to compare them in the same reference frame, we find that the Earth clock has gotten behind. (Interestingly, people on Earth really do age slower as a result of the acceleration of gravity!) Because the measurement of time is critical for assessing the position on the ground, corrections for the effects of relativity must be made in the calculations. So, when we use a global positioning system in a car to figure out which turn to take in a new city, the theory of relativity is being used at that very moment.

In addition to discussing how physicists view time, we can also talk about how anthropologists view time. And here, the evidence is also unambiguous; culture has a major impact on how we understand and view time.

CULTURAL TIME RELATIVITY

Anthropologists have identified three views of time held by people living in different cultures: linear, circular, and procedural. People living on linear (or Western) time divide the world into a past, present, and future. They treat time as a resource that can be saved, wasted, spent, and bought. People in western Europe, North America, and Japan liken time to a ribbon that stretches from the past through the present and into the future. A key objective is to pay attention to the past (to avoid repeating old mistakes) and to use present time wisely (to reap rewards in the future).

> ### Three cultural views of time are linear, circular, and procedural.

People who take a linear perspective act as though they have reified time. They have taken an abstract concept, which you cannot feel, taste, or hold, and made it into a concrete thing. They even talk about types of time. Thus they talk about "real time," which occurs when what they are seeing or hearing is actually occurring at that very moment. The phrase "real time" economically communicates a whole set of ideas. Most important, perhaps, it tells you that what you are seeing or hearing is not being faked in some way. In this sense, the actions that we perceive are real.

Another of our favorites is the concept of "free time." Free time refers to the idea that there is a block of temporal space that is unscheduled. For those who charge by the billable hour, time is certainly *not* free.

Other phrases describe how people schedule their time. Thus we speak of work time, down time, and party time. "Quality time" is a phrase that we are not particularly fond of. Here, a parent allocates a specific period to be with and focus on a child. Both parent and child often know that this block of temporal space is contrived, diminishing its potential for positive effects.

People living in a linear world also talk about the things that they do to time. For example, they speak of buying time, saving time, and killing time. Of course, once you have killed it, you now have dead time!

A second cultural perspective is called circular time. Associated with agrarian societies, a circular time world focuses on the natural cycles of the seasons, sun, and moon. Every spring, for instance, the ground is tilled and crops are planted. People with a circular time perspective know that over many centuries, they will complete the same tasks every spring, every summer, every fall. Time does not stretch into the future, which offers neither joy nor fear because it will be much like the present, which is much like the past.

People living on circular time tend to act when things have to be done. In the Spanish culture the word *mañana* describes this approach to life; that is, putting off what you can but doing what has to be done.

When people on linear time do business with people on circular time, conflicts can occur. Those on Western time divide the day into segments and expect tasks to begin and end "on time." People on circular time have a more flexible view of when things should be done; they often think of people who work with linear time as uptight.

Procedural time is the third perspective. Often called "Indian time," this worldview is associated with hunter-gatherer cultures, such as those that could be found on the great plains of North America a thousand years ago. Here, the focus is on completing a task successfully rather than within a given time period. Thus when a tribe set up camp, the chief could not tell anyone how long they would stay; they would stay until the buffalo left or until the local food supply was exhausted. People who live on procedural time resist scheduling because their focus is on the task rather than on time. Phrases such as "time is money" and "wasting time" have little meaning to them.

TIME PERSPECTIVES AND WESTERN SOCIETIES

Even though people living in Western societies tend to view the world through a linear time lens, some individual's professions push them to employ either a circular or procedural time perspective. For example, universities run on circular time, moving through the seasons of fall semester, spring semester, graduation, and summer school in an iterative fashion. Any businessperson who has attempted to work with MBA classes to solve problems recognizes the potential for conflict. Working on linear time, where time is money, the businessperson wants to start the project quickly and get results in a hurry. In contrast, the professor cannot begin the project until well after the semester starts, when students have sufficient knowledge to tackle the problem. Then, the results cannot be presented until the end of the semester. Rectifying these different time perspectives makes it difficult for both parties.

Other professions in Western cultures run on procedural time. Consider the following case. A number of years ago, a woman went for a routine mammogram. The X-ray revealed a star pattern, which is an indicator of breast cancer. The woman was scheduled to have a biopsy two days later. Working on linear time, she and her husband arrived precisely as scheduled at 8:30 A.M. in the morning for the procedure. They knew the surgeon, Renee, who would perform the biopsy.

After doing the paperwork, the woman had her vital signs taken and was inserted into the awful hospital gown that patients must endure. By now it was 9:00 A.M. The woman and her husband then began to wait for Renee to appear. Thirty minutes passed, then an hour. At 10 A.M., the husband searched for a nurse to find out what was causing the delay. The nurse did not have any information, but she knew that the surgeon was around somewhere. Another hour passed. Both the woman and her husband were busy professionals, and they grew increasingly angry because they were going to miss a series of appointments.

Finally, Renee arrived at 11:30 A.M. The husband lashed out— "Where have you been!" Calmly, Renee apologized and said, "Last night, I had to operate on a very fat patient to clear an intestinal obstruction. This morning at about 8:00 A.M., he went into a coughing spasm and broke the stitches. His intestines began to fall out as the coughing became increasingly violent. I could not very well say to him, 'Whoops, sorry, I have an appointment with another client. I'll just leave your guts hanging out while I go help her.'"

Procedural time for the doctor trumped linear time for the couple. She then performed the biopsy, and fortunately, the results came back negative.

Surgeons work on procedural time. Their focus is on completing the task—no matter how long it takes. Other professionals, such as plumbers, auto mechanics, and home builders, follow the same pattern. All of us have castigated members of these professions for failing to start or complete a task on time. In each case, however, the practitioner was probably focusing on successfully completing a job rather than leaving it half-completed to move on to something else. In the procedural time world, unexpected events or problems frequently intrude to make the task take longer than expected. Just as surgeons cannot leave their patients, plumbers cannot leave commodes lying on the floor simply because they have an appointment with another client.

Creative people make up another professional group that works on procedural time. Artists, research scientists, authors, and computer programmers represent four creative professions. They make their living by hunting a highly elusive prey—ideas. They cannot predict when an idea will burst forth; sometimes new concepts don't appear for long periods. As a result, creatives often work odd hours of the day and night.

Holding them to strict schedules and making them punch a clock can result in animosity and fewer ideas.

> *Conflicts frequently occur between managers working on linear time and creatives and research and development personnel working on procedural time.*

With this background, it is easy to understand why conflicts occur between managers and creatives. Managers have schedules and must meet deadlines. They are required to run on linear time. "Just-in-time" scheduling systems make the situation even worse because any slippage wreaks havoc in the system. But scheduling is anathema to creatives.

Some managers implicitly recognize the incongruity between linear and procedural time. Alfred Zeien, the chairman of Gillette Corporation, separated the research (R) labs from the development (D) process at his company, reasoning, "If you have them (together), D drives out R because of the pressure on D to get it out the door."

BACK TO THE CEO

Let's go back to the problem faced by the CEO of the software company. What steps would you have taken to motivate the computer programmers? When we discuss the situation with MBA students in our classes, they give us the following types of answers:

~ Encourage the programmers to work as a team and compensate them as a team rather than as individuals.
~ Offer extra compensation for the added hours worked, rather than for successfully completing the task.
~ Give other kinds of compensation, such as time off or something really important to programmers—new computers or software packages.
~ Do not do anything, this is their job, and they are already being well paid.

Among these answers, the last one—do not do anything—may be the best. The other solutions all represent linear time thinking. They may not only not solve the problem: they may actually cause more problems. Another, more proactive approach is to borrow a page from today's high-tech companies and give employees a piece of the profits, for example, stock options. With the vagaries of the stock market, however, stock options may not reflect profits. As an alternative, many firms give bonuses at the end of the year based on the level of profit of the firm and on the employee's contributions. This approach helps to align the perspectives of managers and creatives. It focuses the creatives' attention on the timely completion of tasks and motivates them by linking their idea-generation efforts to the success of the firm and to their own long-term welfare. It also focuses management's attention on the difficulties of idea generation. When the firm's outcomes are salient to both managers and creatives, everyone is working toward the same goal and can more readily understand the importance of the effects of divergent time perspectives.

IS TIME A RESOURCE?

We conclude our discussion of cultural views of time with a question. Is time a resource? According to the Western perspective, time is a resource that can be bought, sold, and lost. Because many of the people who will be reading this book take a Western perspective on time, the answer may seem obvious. "Are these egghead professors crazy? Of course, time is a resource."

But let's begin our analysis by posing another, more fundamental question: What is a resource? Various dictionaries define resources in terms of assets, capital, wealth, and property. Resources can also be defined more broadly to include other people; when you have friends, they become a resource that you can turn to when you are in trouble. Information can also be a resource; knowledge becomes an asset that helps you overcome difficulties.

We propose that resources have three characteristics. First, they are valuable. As a result, even though decreasing marginal utility is real, more of a resource is still better than less. (As Sophie Tucker said, "I've been rich and I've been poor, but, honey, rich is better.") Second, resources can be transferred from one person to another. Thus, I can give you money, information, or a gift. Third, different people can have divergent amounts of a resource. Thus CEOs of major corporations make from 10 to 20 times more money than professors in business schools — a fact that may be fair (and appropriate) given the risks and the relative job security of the two professions.

Now, let us apply these three characteristics to time. First, is it really better to have more time than less time? There are a couple of ways to answer this question. We can be glib and ask: What groups of people have the most time on their hands? In the United States, the answer is prisoners and the homeless. It is difficult to argue that these individuals are wealthier than time-stressed executives. A more satisfying answer is to identify the occasions when people are experiencing the most happiness. According to the psychologist Mihaly Csikszentmihalyi, the greatest happiness occurs during the state of flow. Flow happens when a person is totally absorbed in a task in which abilities precisely match task difficulty. In a state of flow, time stops. Flow does not depend on how much time is available. Rather, it depends on how time is used. Because those who have more time are not wealthier in any sense of the word, on this criterion, time is not a resource.

The second characteristic of a resource is that it can be transferred from one person to another. Can the two of us each give you an hour of our time, so that you have 26 hours and each of us have only 23 hours in a day? Of course not. You may respond to this absurd idea, however, by saying, "Well, yes, but, you can do a task for me and thereby give me some of your time." Certainly, that is right in the sense that one person can do something for someone else. Nonetheless, the altruist is not really giving the person time. The altruist is simply performing a different task within a given time frame. Thus, the phrase "giving someone your time" is just a convenient, shorthand way of describing a choice to perform a task for someone else. Time cannot be transferred from one person to another, which also suggests that time is not a resource.

The third characteristic of a resource is that different people can have it in divergent amounts. Although it may sound flippant, each of us really does only have 24 hours in a day and 60 minutes in an hour.

Based on these ideas, it is clear that time is not a resource. Then what is time? We define it as the temporal space within which tasks are performed. What does it mean when we say that we do not have enough time? Simply that we have too many tasks to perform within a given temporal space.

> **Time is not a resource but a fixed temporal space within which tasks are accomplished.**

What are the implications of these ideas for high-stakes decision-making? The answer is surprisingly simple. Identify the length of your temporal space for making the decision. Then identify and prioritize the tasks that you must accomplish to reach your goals. If the temporal space is extremely small, you will either have to do more faster or do less. In terms of tough calls, it means that you may have to make your decisions before you really want to. The flip side, however, is that you shouldn't make high-stakes decisions until you're ready or until a decision really needs to be made.

TIME TRAPS

High-stakes decisions require us to accept trade-offs. It is a rare but wonderful occasion when we can have our cake and eat it, too. We have already discussed one trade-off that managers frequently make—that of freedom versus control. For example, Boeing executives exchanged computerized control of the 757 for giving pilots the freedom to make critical decisions in flight.

Other decisions involve trade-offs between the present and the future. For example, when we make an investment, we exchange present consumption for potential future gains. Every senior manager of a publicly traded firm recognizes the difficulty of the present-versus-future trade-off. Stock-market analysts and investment bankers want to see steady quarterly growth and no surprises. As a result, managers must carefully allocate resources so as not to endanger short-term quarterly profits. Unfortunately, the focus on the next quarter can also stifle long-term growth.

Various aphorisms illustrate the difficulties with present-future trade-offs. "Good things come to those who wait" tells us to eschew current consumption and save for the future, as does Benjamin Franklin's maxim "A penny saved is a penny earned." In contrast, the aphorism of the famous economist John Maynard Keynes has just as much validity—"In the long run, we are all dead."

The difficulty of present-future trade-offs is compounded by the fact that any single decision can have both good and bad outcomes. These outcomes can occur together or separately, in the present or in the future. This juxtaposition of positive and negative outcomes over time strongly influences both business and personal decisions. For example, when a company invests in research and development (R&D), the short-term bad is decreased profitability because tax regulations require

R&D costs to be expensed as they occur. The good outcomes come later (if at all). The combination of an immediate punishment and delayed, uncertain rewards contributes to the tendency of companies to invest insufficiently in R&D.

Present-future trade-offs can lead to at least three different kinds of time-related problems, which we call time traps. The first, decision myopia, results from our natural tendency to overweight the present and underweight the future. The second and third, time snares and time fences, result because time trade-offs involve both negative and positive outcomes. However, these outcomes don't often surface simultaneously, meaning that we may seek the positives and ignore the associated and often inevitable negatives (the time snare) or that we may so stringently avoid the negatives that we miss out on the larger positives (the time fence). The following sections delve deeper into each of these problems.

DECISION MYOPIA

One of the most fundamental elements of human behavior is that people value what happens in the present much more than what will occur in the future. In other words, people give more weight to short-term outcomes in their decision-making. In one sense, this fundamental predilection makes perfect sense. The concept of the time value of money shows why. If you have a choice between receiving a thousand dollars now or a year from now, almost all of you will take the money now. One reason is that you can invest it safely and have more than a thousand dollars a year from now. Another reason is to avoid any uncertainty—a bird in the hand is worth two in the bush. We can apply this same reasoning to other outcomes, such as feeling physically good or increasing corporate profitability five years down the road.

The myopia time trap is not just about people discounting the future. The problem lies in how deeply they discount. Researchers have found that people use exceedingly high discount rates to estimate the future value of investments than that suggested by interest rates. For example, during the 1980s, long-term interest rates in the United States consistently hovered between 7 and 12 percent. Consumers behaved, however, as though their implicit interest rates were about 30 percent. Because of this extremely high discount rate, Americans acted as though they required their investments to double in about a three-year period, or they would not make them. The net effect was a systematic bias to overweight present outcomes and underweight future outcomes.

Even though this research took place well over 10 years ago, the high-tech bubble in the stock market that occurred in 1999 and 2000 vividly shows that decision myopia is still with us. Investors knew that traditional yardsticks indicated that the dot-com stocks were overvalued. Their seemingly continuous march upward in valuation, however, overwhelmed this knowledge. The focus on attaining short-term gains (also described as greed) caused even seasoned investors to take the plunge. On July 16, 1998, the Nasdaq index stood at 2,000. On March 9, 2000, it hit 5,000. One year later, it had fallen all the way to 1,700. During that time, 428 Nasdaq stocks (more than 10 percent of those listed) had lost more than 90 percent of their value. Not only did decision myopia's bubble burst, but the ride down the bubble also pushed the Nasdaq below that original starting point.

Decision myopia strikes individuals, corporations, and governments. Two researchers at the University of Arizona observed that the desire for instant gratification frequently, and negatively, impacts medical patients. The pattern goes like this. A patient, for example a busy overweight executive, is diagnosed as having high blood pressure. He understands the dire consequences of not controlling the problem (a heart attack down the road), so he promises to wake up 30 minutes early every morning to exercise. The promise is easy, especially when the torment of the calisthenics is in the future.

When the first morning comes, the pain of waking up early and exercising is now in the present. It overwhelms the executive's (distant) goal of losing weight and reducing his chances of heart disease. As a result, it's a pretty good bet that more often than not, he will turn over and go back to sleep.

Such myopic behavior also afflicts organizations. A grim example of such short-term thinking occurred at Ford. During the 1960s and 1970s, men trained in finance and operations management dominated corporate decision-making at Ford. They were the so-called whiz kids who came to the company after World War II. Robert McNamara, the former secretary of defense, and others helped to create the financial control systems that moved Ford out of the primitive management style of Henry Ford. Unfortunately, they nearly bankrupted the company with their focus on short-term profits.

Perhaps the best illustration of their focus was the infamous E-coat affair. In 1958 researchers in Ford's manufacturing section invented a technique for improving paint jobs and resisting rust. The process involved placing the entire car frame into a vat of paint and giving it an electrical charge. The charge attracted the paint to the metal, allowing it to get into every nook and cranny. Ford Europe quickly adopted it because of their highly competitive market. General Motors paid Ford a royalty and used the process. Even Japanese companies adopted it.

The process became an instant success everywhere—except at Ford USA. By 1961, Ford installed it for its prestige Lincoln Continentals and Thunderbirds. Getting finance to approve its introduction into other plants was extremely difficult, however, because marketing could not prove that it would return the $4 million to $5 million investment.

At a 1973 styling meeting, Lee Iacocca became enraged at the poor quality of Ford cars, particularly the rust problems that were causing enormous warranty difficulties. Even though he was the president of the corporation, he was unable to change the short-term thinking of Ford's other executives. By 1975, the process was installed in only half of Ford's plants. Not until 1984 did all of their plants use the E-coat process.

High-stakes decision-makers can never quantify all of the variables that will control the outcome of their decisions. In most instances, many of the variables are simply not known. At Ford, the finance department's insistence that manufacturing *prove* that the E-coat would produce a satisfactory return was simply not possible. How can you quantify the effects of having a satisfied customer in the short term? Once the effect is quantifiable, the battle has already been lost.

A fundamental element of U.S. culture is our focus on the short term. For example, when we bury artifacts in a time capsule, for how long do we inter its contents? The answer is usually in terms of decades, or at most a few centuries. In contrast, the Japanese have a much longer time horizon. A U.S. executive on a visit to a Japanese cultural center was stunned to hear that the curators did not plan to open their time capsule for another five thousand years. Perhaps the long, long history of the Japanese people cause them to have a lengthy time horizon as well. It may also explain why their savings rate is several times higher than that found in the United States, which hovered near zero in the last few years of the twentieth century.

> ***Decision myopia describes the tendency to over-weight short-term outcomes and underweight long-term outcomes of high-stakes decisions.***

Time Snares

A time snare occurs when a decision-maker jumps to achieve short-term gains that cause harm in the long term; that is, the presence of the short-term reward snares the person into performing an action or actions that cause long-term difficulties. Addictions to tobacco and drugs illustrate time snares. The short-term positive from nicotine's high overwhelms the knowledge that smoking has a high probability of causing problems in the future.

The use of sales promotions by automakers, such as rebates and low interest rates, also represents a snare. The goal of the sales promotion device is to induce customers to purchase a car in the present. Ironically, however, the practice can also trap the auto company. In the long term, the auto industry hurts itself by relying on short-term rebates and other sales promotions to bring customers into showrooms. Peter Drucker, the management guru, described his view of sales promotions in this way: "The offers attracted few, if any new buyers; customers who already decided to buy a domestic car simply waited for the next special offer. Potential customers, however, were turned off. 'If they can sell cars only by giving them away,' was the reaction, 'they can't be much good.'"

Managers should never forget that collectively, consumers are smart. They are quite capable of learning that if they simply wait long enough, rebates and other promotions will be offered. In the short term, sales promotions may sell more products; in the long term, however, they borrow from sales in the future.

> *A time snare occurs when decision-makers let short-term positive outcomes cause an action that leads to long-term negative outcomes.*

Time snares may also occur when companies compensate sales personnel through a straight commission system that pays them a percentage of their sales. Such systems reward activities that lead to short-term gains. In the short term, the salesperson can earn more by minimizing service (which takes time) and selling to regular accounts. Straight-commission systems encourage sales personnel to discount the future rewards that come from prospecting for new clients and providing excellent service. As a result, a firm can begin to stagnate. In extreme cases, the short-term orientation can lead to unethical or illegal actions. The revelations in 1992 that some Sears automotive mechanics charged customers falsely for unneeded repairs illustrate this phenomenon. As a result, Sears changed its policy of straight commission for its mechanics.

Time Fences

A time fence occurs when an action that will lead to long-term gains is impeded because it also causes short-term losses. The short-term loss in essence acts as a fence that prevents the person or organization from taking an action that would lead to long-term benefits. The time fence is insidious because many situations require people or companies to endure short-term negatives to gain larger, long-term positives. But because the costs that occur in the present dominate future rewards, decision-makers all too often fail to take actions that would lead to overall benefits for themselves and their organizations. In other words, "no pain, no gain" does at times contain some truth.

Don Cooper, the long-time sports physician at Oklahoma State University, told us a story that perfectly illustrates the time fence. In the early 1970s, Cooper was a member of the National Collegiate Athletic Association (NCAA) executive committee and was trying to get football coaches to require their players to use protective mouthpieces. The coaches, however, were against it. They argued that if the players wore mouthpieces, they wouldn't be able to communicate clearly with each other, particularly the quarterback and defensive players who called signals.

A colorful character, Cooper knew this was nonsense. To prove his point, he had a local dentist make him a clear mouthpiece. At the NCAA's national meeting, he wore it while giving a 10-minute talk on preventing athletic injuries. At the end of the speech, he asked the coaches if they had understood him. They all said "Yeah," looking puzzled and wondering why he would even ask the question. To their utter astonishment, Cooper then triumphantly pulled the plastic device from his mouth and held it in the air. Later that day, the coaches passed the rule change unanimously.

In this case, the coaches' perception of the negative outcome of making a rule change was purely imaginary. The presence of imaginary short-term costs also influences business decisions. Today's CEOs worry that if their company's profits sag for just one quarter, its stock price will plummet and the company will be perceived as a loser. Interestingly, however, studies fail to support this contention. It turns out that investors value more highly companies that invest for the long term. Firms with some of the highest price-earnings ratios (e.g., Microsoft and General Electric) invest significantly more than average in long-term projects.

> **Time fences occur when an action that would lead to long-term gains is stopped because it also causes short-term negative outcomes.**

Some companies have taken action to avoid their natural reluctance to make short-term sacrifices for long-term gains. For example, 3M developed internal procedures to encourage investment in R&D, such as the 25 percent rule, which stated that 25 percent of a division's sales must be from products produced within the last five years. When this norm was broken, managers were penalized at bonus time. To encourage individual innovation, the company also offered $50,000 grants to employees and allowed them to use as much as 15 percent of their time to prove that an idea was workable. In essence, 3M rearranged the timing of the rewards and costs that can lead to product innovation.

One way to avoid these three time traps is to frame decisions from a future perspective. When identifying the positive and negative outcomes that may occur as a result of decision, imagine that it is three to five years in the future. From that future vantage point, it is much easier to apply an even hand when making present-versus-future time trade-offs.

> **To avoid time traps, frame decisions from a future perspective in which the possible positive and negative outcomes have already occurred.**

Time, Perspective, and Ethics

In the last chapter, we talked about the role of perspectives in high-stakes decision-making. We showed that our perspectives increase the saliency of key values, which in turn drive how we interpret information and ultimately, how we decide. Clearly, our time focus can also influence our perspective. All of the time traps that we have just discussed occur when we take a present time perspective. Taking a future

time perspective when we must make tough calls—our recommendation—can minimize the effects of the time fence and the time snare.

We also talked in the last chapter about an ethical decision perspective. Interestingly, the ethical problems faced by executives almost
always involve a time trap. Ethical decision problems occur when a person is tempted to do something that will bring a short-term gain, or
avoid a short-term loss, but ends up causing a long-term loss. The following story exemplifies this situation.

The story comes from Jeffrey Seglin, a fellow at Harvard's Center
for the Study of Values in Public Life. Writing for *Inc.* magazine, Seglin
described a situation faced by a CEO of a jet engine repair company.
It seems that right at the end of the company's annual audit, the CEO
received news that 11 planes that his company had worked on had been
grounded for potential problems with their turbines. During an audit,
the CEO must sign a letter stating that there are no outstanding circumstances that have a likelihood of producing a negative financial
effect. The CEO's problem was that if his company was producing
defective turbines, they could go out of business. There was even a
remote possibility that if a turbine failed, it could cause a crash.

The CEO faced a classic high-stakes decision. Time was short,
information was ambiguous, experts disagreed, and core values were
in conflict. As described by Seglin, "The lens through which he naturally scrutinized the situation was the one he'd used over all the years
he'd been running a business: How do I do what I need to do to keep
my company alive and thriving and, at the same time, minimize my
financial and legal exposure?" On the one hand, if he said nothing
about the problem and it turned out to be a real problem, he would
expose his company to extreme legal problems. On the other hand, if
he declared the problem, the banks that were giving him credit could
pull his loans and put his company out of business. In the end, his company could be exonerated but still be out of business.

The CEO consulted his board, as well as attorneys inside and outside his company. In the end, he fashioned a vague response stating that
"the company had a problem and that we were on top of that problem." Fortunately, the auditors never inquired about the nature of the
problem. Over the next few weeks, they learned that the company's turbines were not at fault. The problem turned out to be a false alarm.

In his article, Seglin castigated the CEO for failing to consider one
key stakeholder group in his decision process—consumers. The CEO
focused on legal and financial issues rather than considering the effects

of his decisions on passengers. Had he looked at the problem through an ethical lens, a marketing lens, or a future time perspective lens, safety issues and their potential impact on consumers might have been his primary concerns. In the end, the CEO let short-term financial and legal issues drive his decision. Fortunately for him—and for airline passengers—this time the roll of the dice went his way.

Did the CEO make the right decision in writing a vague disclosure statement to his auditors? Actually, we think that he did. The information that he had at the time was simply too ambiguous and too uncertain to cause him to write something that would put his company in immediate jeopardy. In fact, his disclosures closely matched the information that he had.

As with any big, risky decision, we hope that the CEO tried to manage the risks he was facing by temporizing, which would give him time to determine whether his company's turbines were actually posing a danger to passengers and, if so, how to alleviate those problems as quickly as possible. If he found serious problems with his companies' turbines and no quick and safe means for correcting them, *then* it would be incumbent upon him to share that information, even if it meant possibly sacrificing his company.

> ***Most ethically challenged decisions result in part because of a time trap.***

CRISIS DECISIONS AND THE EFFECTS OF TIME PRESSURE

What happens to the decision-making process when the time available is short and the stakes are high? Consider the following incident, as related to us in a recent interview.

While Dr. Jeff Vender was in a meeting, he received an emergency call from a colleague. A woman was suffering life-threatening complications following labor and the delivery of her first child. As the head of the intensive care unit, he immediately rushed to the hospital. Upon arrival, he carefully examined the woman and then searched for her husband, who was in the waiting room with his mother-in-law. Jeff walked up to the anxious pair and reluctantly gave them the news. His wife (her daughter) "was extremely ill and had a high probability of dying."

The story actually began about eight months earlier, when the young, well-educated couple had begun an exhaustive search to find the best hospital in the Chicago area to have their first child. Eventually, they settled on a hospital in Evanston, a medium-size suburb just north of Chicago. Everything had gone well through the pregnancy, as had the delivery. A C-section was performed, and the baby was doing fine. Now, however, the mother was in serious trouble. Highly toxic amniotic fluid had entered her bloodstream. This situation occurs in approximately one in every 10,000 deliveries, and the National Registry reports a mortality rate of 65 percent, most often within the first several hours.

The mother and husband looked at the doctor, horrified. Here was a complete stranger telling them that their loved one could die. As Jeff told us, "Needless to say, they wondered who I was and what the hell I was talking about."

Jeff spent the next eight hours with the woman. The amniotic fluid embolus caused her lungs to fill with fluid, making it difficult for her to breathe. He considered a number of therapies. The most aggressive was a major surgical procedure, a form of heart-lung bypass, which could relieve her from having to breathe on her own and improve her oxygenation. Jeff consulted a heart specialist, who said that the procedure could be done. But this invasive procedure had issues of its own that could seriously affect the patient. As Jeff described the situation, "She could bleed to death from the therapy. But of course, we didn't expect her to survive anyway." Meanwhile, a priest was called in to give her last rites.

One of the most commonly heard decision-making recommendations is to take action. "Do something," is a frequent war cry, particularly when a crisis is at hand. This is particularly true for physicians, who are trained to do everything they can to assist their patients. It is also true in business. In their classic book *In Search of Excellence*, Tom Peters and Robert Waterman called for managers to have a bias to action. Performing a heart-lung bypass was definitely doing something, and doing something big. But Jeff Vender decided to wait. Although her condition was critical, he wanted to know more about her condition before he acted. So he rapidly searched the Internet for additional information. He also called a colleague for advice.

After his search, Jeff decided on two courses of action, both of which were reversible. First, he and seven other people carefully turned the woman over so that she was on her stomach. "By flipping her, we transferred the fluids in her lungs from her back to her front, which gave her a better opportunity to make use of the oxygen she was getting." This procedure had been noted in the literature but was not commonly employed at the time. It was based on his intuitive analysis of the situation, previous experience, and recent medical findings.

The second action he took was to increase the pressure of the oxygen that they were pumping into her lungs, to a pressure higher than he had ever done before. It was a calculated attempt to provide enough oxygen to her bloodstream to keep her alive. An incredulous resident asked why he was doing this. Jeff responded that although it was risky, it was less aggressive than the heart-lung machine. Because he was at the patient's side the whole time, he could react quickly if something began to go wrong. With a bypass, there was no turning back. Amazingly, the monitors and lab tests revealed that the woman was doing better. She survived the night.

Over the next two weeks, Jeff gradually turned down the pressure on the ventilator. But the woman was still in a drug-induced coma. Over a four-month time period, her condition slowly improved. As it became apparent that she would survive, everyone's worries shifted from "Will she survive?" to "What will her condition be should she survive?" Many people who suffer an amniotic fluid embolus emerge with neurological damage.

After 13 weeks, the sedatives were gradually removed so that she could wake up. Over time, they discovered that she had movement in all her limbs and she could talk. She was going to be all right!

Jeff told us that as he reflected back on the event, the biggest decision he made was not to do the heart-lung bypass. "We had a crashing patient, not a crashing airplane," he said. Both the heart-lung bypass and the increased ventilator pressure were time consuming. But hours were important here, not minutes. In our interview, he explained that, "The key was vigilance. By staying with her continuously, I had the ability to respond immediately to an adverse response and rapidly alter therapies." He continued, "We also had no nursing mistakes, no line infections; nothing major went wrong. It was like the wind stopping when we needed it to. Everything went right."

Jeff Vender handled this crisis with tremendous skill and great good fortune. His analytical approach to the problem, coolness under pressure, and diligent and prolonged efforts represent three requirements for successfully navigating a crisis situation.

Research on Time-Pressured Decision-Making

One of the central features of a crisis is the lack of time available to make the tough call. Over the past 20 years, academic researchers have begun to investigate how people handle time pressure. Perhaps the single most consistent finding in the literature is that the accuracy and quality of decisions decrease under time pressure. An important issue, then, is to determine the factors that lead to these decreases in decision accuracy. Current research suggests that five factors are critical in harming the quality of decisions. Time pressure leads decision-makers to:

1. Increase their information processing speed but decrease the amount of information that they consider.
2. Increase the weight that they place on negative information.
3. Increase their use of simpler rather than more complex decision models.
4. Lock in on and defend their first chosen strategy.
5. Be more influenced by their emotions, which can interfere with guided intuition and rational analysis.

Master decision-makers are able to minimize these negative effects of time pressure, as illustrated by the actions of Jeff Vender. He kept his emotions in check and was able to employ a reasoned approach to the problem. He identified multiple options and collected additional information that helped him to make better decisions. He avoided the trap of locking in on the first option (the heart-lung bypass). He also maintained optimism and focus on the positive actions that he could take to deal with the situation.

One additional factor emerges from the analysis of Jeff Vender's handling of the crisis. He focused on taking actions that kept his options open and extending the amount of time he could take to make his high-stakes decisions. Had he immediately gone to a heart-lung bypass, he would have eliminated all of his other options. Analysts who have investigated crisis decision-making propose that the one characteristic of individuals who can deftly handle emergency situations is the ability to determine how much time is available to make the decision. Even in a crisis, acting prematurely can be catastrophic. By taking his time, even within the confines of a crisis situation, Jeff Vender was able to identify options that minimized the downside risk should they fail.

Life-or-death decisions, of course, can also occur in business. One work domain in which a crisis can literally explode into a life-threatening situation is the offshore oil and gas industry. In July 1988, for instance, an oil platform far out in the North Sea exploded, causing the death of 167 workers. The situation began with an initial explosion of natural gas vapors. Over the course of a few hours, the crisis escalated as a chain reaction of explosions followed, culminating in the structural collapse of the platform. Subsequently, a detailed review analyzed how the manager of the platform performed. The reports suggested that the manager became paralyzed by the situation and was unable to give orders during the turmoil of the crisis. With the breakdown of the command structure, no effective action was taken to combat the crisis.

A number of recommendations emerged from the analysis of this catastrophe. One finding concerned the critical importance of rehearsing how to respond to crises. Preplanning responses to emergency situations provides decision-makers with learned sequences of actions that minimize the detrimental effects of strong emotions. This preplanning requires the development of a crisis-management plan.

The analysis of the oil-platform disaster also suggested that rehearsals that most closely approximate actual crises are most effective. One survivor of the catastrophe described how the noise caused by high-pressure gas escaping made communication nearly impossible. In such circumstances, rehearsal drills must incorporate extreme noise to provide the realism required. Even football coaches recognize this principle. In the days before their teams leave to play an opponent in a noisy stadium, many coaches will make their teams practice with loudspeakers blaring the same raucous cheering that they will soon face.

> **Both preplanning and "live-fire" rehearsals help to minimize the negative effects of time pressure on crisis decisions.**

We need to add one more consideration to this brief discussion of the management and preparation for crisis decisions: AVOID them. Through careful preplanning, master decision-makers can minimize the likelihood that crises will occur. Some well-known management consultants have proposed that managers should keep their organizations in a constant state of chaos. We totally disagree with this recommendation.

Because most of our environments are in constant states of flux, organizations are always experiencing change. Effective organizations build change into their cultures. Although some professions are built around dealing with crises (e.g., hospital ER personnel), in most organizations, steps should be taken to avoid crises.

By their nature, crises cause managers and employees to deal with short-term, time-pressured, high-stakes problems. As a result, they must overlook ongoing tasks, such as building customer relations and product development. Of course, circumstances beyond a manager's control will inevitably cause crises to occur. The goal, however, is to minimize the likelihood of facing a crisis by continually scanning the environment to stay ahead of the power curve.

Principles of Time Framing

1. Recognize that conflicts may occur as a result of individuals working on different types of time—linear, procedural, or circular.
2. Time is not an expandable resource; rather, it is a temporal space that provides the opportunity for task accomplishment.
3. Time fences result from overweighting short-term costs and underweighting long-term gains.
4. Time snares result from overweighting short-term gains and underweighting long-term costs.
5. Avoid time traps by approaching decisions from a long-term perspective.
6. Ethical decisions represent one type of time trap.
7. The time pressure that occurs in crises inevitably harms decision-making quality.
8. Preplan and practice how your organization should respond to crises.

8

SOLVE THE PROBLEM

Art, like drawing a line, consists of drawing the line somewhere.

Gilbert K. Chesterton

The last step in the SCRIPTS process is to solve the problem. Gilbert K. Chesterton's wry quote reproduced here well depicts the issue. Solving a problem involves making a choice by drawing a line somewhere and then stepping across it to take action.

Another way to approach solving the problem is to view it from the perspective of the great philosopher and baseball player Yogi Berra, in what may be his most famous quote: "When you come to a fork in the road, take it." He was wrong, of course, when he implied that you only have two choices when you reach a choice point. You can take either of the two branches of the fork, but you can also turn around and go back. Or you can leave the beaten path and take a new route. Finally, you may decide that you've come as far as you need to and that the status quo isn't too bad. A first principle in solving the problem, then, especially when it involves high-stakes decisions, is to be creative and recognize that there may be many possible alternatives for action.

A second principle in solving the problem is to add some structure into your decision process. Structure will not only help you make a better decision; it will also help you save time. (You won't have to agonize so much over high-stakes decisions as you may have in the past.)

The goal of the SCRIPTS procedure is to provide a structure to assist you in making high-stakes decisions. As we noted in Chapter 2, when you have identified a signal for action, you must determine whether you face a crisis or a strategic decision. If it's a crisis, you immediately move into guided-intuition decision-making. If you have sufficient time to gather information, you are facing a strategic decision. Then you can move systematically to find the cause, evaluate the risk, apply intuition and emotion, take different perspectives, consider the time frame, and finally, solve the problem.

This chapter provides a three-step process for solving the problem, which is based on the signal-detection approach that we presented in Chapter 2, "Search for Signals of Threats and Opportunities." If you are not facing a crisis, the first step is to set your decision trigger by calculating what we call a risk ratio. This involves performing some simple calculations of your maximum downside risk (the numerator of the ratio) and the range of possible outcomes that might follow action (the denominator of the ratio). Prior to finalizing the ratio, we recommend that you adjust your calculations by moving through the first six steps of the SCRIPTS process again, if you have the time.

The second stage in structuring a strategic decision is to carefully analyze the probability that choosing to act will be successful. As with the risk ratio, we recommend structuring your analysis by considering a series of factors to ensure that your estimate is not unduly biased. This determination will reflect your confidence that action is the right choice.

The final step in the three-step process is to compare the trigger setting (your risk ratio) with your estimate of the probability that acting will lead to success (your confidence). If your probability estimate exceeds your risk ratio, then it's on to action and implementation. If not, the status quo should look very good.

As we have already noted, before you can do any of this, you have to first decide whether you are facing a crisis. How many high-stakes decisions are crises? We think that true crisis decisions rarely happen. These situations, such as the incident at Three Mile Island or the firefighter who removed his team seconds before the floor collapsed into an inferno, are unusual. Even cases such as the near disaster of *Apollo 13*, in which an explosion occurred on the spacecraft, leave decision-makers with sufficient time to move through the SCRIPTS process.

In the unusual circumstance when you face a true crisis, the key to survival and success comes from the knowledge that you have gained from past experience and training. Even in a crisis, however, the structuring that comes with SCRIPTS still plays a role, an implicit one. The repeated use of the SCRIPTS process during strategic decision-making will help train you to make high-stakes decisions quickly and at the extreme, automatically. If all has proceeded accordingly to plan, the SCRIPTS process becomes a central part of your guided-intuition process. Thus, even when you face a crisis decision, experience should allow you to use SCRIPTS, however instantaneous your decisions.

In this chapter, we continue our focus on improving decision-making by presenting a case study of a tough call that occurred in 1998. The situation involved a decision of whether to invest funds in a new company that was producing an innovative product. We use the story as a foil for reviewing the SCRIPTS process and for discussing the seventh and most crucial step—solve the problem.

THE CASE OF ZEPHYR TECHNOLOGY

Calvin Johnson was attending a conference in February 1998 in Tampa, Florida. Although he would not admit it publicly, he enjoyed the conference more for the sun and the chance to renew old acquaintances than for the often-boring research presentations. At the opening-night cocktail party, he literally bumped into a colleague whom he had not seen for almost 10 years. Well known in his field, Calvin had been asked on several occasions to write letters of reference for the colleague, an extroverted psychologist who now taught courses in marketing management and consumer behavior. Most recently, Glenn Knight had spent a couple of years teaching in Australia. Now he was back in the United States with his new wife. After exchanging pleasantries, Glenn asked Calvin if he had dinner plans for the next night. When Calvin indicated that he was available, Glenn responded, "Wonderful, I have a new project that I want to tell you about."

The next night Calvin, Glenn, and a couple of other colleagues were eating fresh seafood at a quiet restaurant overlooking Tampa Bay. Curious, Calvin asked Glenn about the project. Immediately, Glenn's mood transformed, and he launched into a discussion of his new company—Zephyr Technology.

While he was teaching at the Australian university, Glenn had required teams of MBA students to create new product ideas. One of the teams developed an idea for a new type of shoe. The product concept was to create a cushioning system that would take outside air and force it up and through the sole of the shoe to the foot. It would accomplish two things. First, it would help cool the foot, which was particularly useful in warm climates. Second, the circulating air would lower the incidence of fungus, another serious problem in warm climates. The team had performed a market-potential analysis, and the results were astounding. Foot fungus is a major problem in many parts of the world, including the United States. Conservative estimates placed the market potential for the shoe in the hundreds of millions of dollars.

Glenn became enamored with the idea and began working with one of the students to develop a prototype. They had been working on the project for about a year and were now in the process of raising money. They had formed a company, Zephyr Technology, and had filed an application for a patent on their innovation. They had worked with a company in Australia to create prototypes. Adidas was evaluating one, and initial results were encouraging. The prototype worked as promised and was showing excellent durability.

After Glenn gave the initial overview, one of the colleagues at the table indicated that she and her husband had bought a piece of Zephyr Technology. With this revelation, Calvin became more interested and began to carefully probe the structure of the deal. Glenn told him that for $10,000, Calvin would receive 0.183 percent membership interest in Zephyr Technology. Glen indicated that his goal was to raise $300,000, which he felt would handle the costs to develop the next prototype, pay the salaries of the three principle officers in the firm for a year, and handle the legal fees required to complete getting the patents.

At this point, Calvin was fascinated. He trusted Glenn and the colleague who had already invested $10,000 in the company. He asked Glenn to send him the market-potential analysis and the prospectus for the company. The rest of the evening was spent drinking Chardonnay and discussing the vagaries of academia.

When Calvin returned home, he talked with his wife about this new investment opportunity. A cautious person by nature, his wife reminded him that most new products fail. A couple days later, the materials that Glenn had promised arrived in the mail. Calvin was impressed by their professionalism. The market-potential analysis indicated an extremely large market for the product. The competitive analysis revealed that no other products on the market could match the Zephyr technology. A letter accompanying the prospectus indicated that a meeting had been held with Adidas. A two-stage development process was proposed in which Adidas would give a cash infusion of $30,000 and provide their product facilities to assist in creating the next prototype. The letter indicated that Calvin had to act fairly quickly. Adidas's management committee was evaluating the prototype and would make a decision shortly thereafter. Once the development money was received and the contract signed, the price to buy into the company would go up dramatically.

Based on conservative estimates, Calvin and his wife estimated that if the technology could be sold, a $10,000 investment would be worth $40,000 in a year. In addition, the Adidas contact sounded very promising. The potential risk of the investment, however, was not lost on Calvin and his wife. Indeed, the prospectus that Zephyr provided clearly stated that the entire investment could be lost. Looking closely at their finances, Calvin and his wife felt that they could risk $20,000, that they could afford to lose all the money if that should occur. Their retirement was under control, and they already had secure investments that would pay for their children's college educations. On the other hand, there were many other things they could do with the $20,000, such as go on a terrific European vacation, take a sabbatical, or invest in the stock market. They faced a classic tough call. Should they plunk down $20,000 to own 0.366 percent of Zephyr Technology? What would you do if you were in their situation?

ZEPHYR AND THE SCRIPTS PROCESS

In this section, we employ the first six components of the SCRIPTS process to analyze the Zephyr case. Our goal is review these parameters of high-stakes decision-making (i.e., S through T in SCRIPTS) and to reveal their critical importance in moving toward the final step of solving the problem.

Parameter 1: Search for Signals of Threats and Opportunities

Although searching for signals of threats and opportunities is an ongoing process, in some cases, a tough call just falls into your lap. Such was the situation with Zephyr Technology when Calvin Johnson's colleague approached him with the opportunity.

Once you have identified a tough call, it is critical to determine if it is a crisis or a strategic decision. In the Zephyr case, it was clear that this was not a crisis. As a result, there was sufficient time to systematically move through the remaining six steps of the SCRIPTS process.

Parameter 2: Find the Causes

At this early stage of the SCRIPTS process, we must ask what caused this problem or opportunity to occur. More specifically, what was the root cause of Glenn Knight proposing the investment to Calvin? If Calvin had asked this question, he would have realized that it was less expensive for Glenn to give investors a piece of the company than to go to venture capitalists or to banks for loans. Calvin might also have been suspicious of this new venture. He could have asked whether Glenn had a genuine deep-seated belief in his product or if he was doing it for the short-term benefit of making money from his investors. Calvin trusted Glenn, so he believed that Glenn did have a deep and sincere belief in the product. Trust increased Calvin's confidence in the accuracy and validity of the information Glenn provided.

Parameter 3: Evaluate the Risks

As described in Chapter 4, we must consider two broad classes of factors when we evaluate risk. First, we must estimate the costs of a needless blunder and of a missed opportunity. The six risk dimensions SMILES: (social, monetary, information, life, experience, and sink-the-boat risks) can help us determine these costs. Then we must estimate the probability that our actions will succeed.

Estimating the Costs   While we must estimate the value of a needless blunder and a missed opportunity on each of the six SMILES dimensions, we typically start the process with an assessment of monetary risk. A needless blunder is the amount of money that you would lose if you acted and the result was negative. In contrast, a missed opportunity is the cost of not acting. It is the amount that you would lose if you decided *not* to act and the result would have been positive. In the Zephyr case, the cost of a missed opportunity (assuming complete success) was $80,000 and the cost of a needless blunder (a complete loss) was $20,000.

When we assess the value of a needless blunder and a missed opportunity, however, the other dimensions may lead us to adjust these potential costs. To assist in this process, it helps to construct a table that contains all of the dimensions of the analysis, as we have done in Table 8.1.

We usually insert the monetary values of the missed opportunity (i.e., $80,000) and the needless blunder (i.e., $20,000) into the table first.

Table 8.1   Risk Analysis for Investing in Zephyr

Risk Dimensions	Costs of a Needless Blunder	Costs of a Missed Opportunity
Social risk	Spouse is very unhappy.	Colleague is disappointed.
Monetary risk	$20,000	$80,000
Information risk	No loss of information.	Lost learning opportunity.
Life/health risk	Possibly experience stress from the loss.	No life risk, just disappointment.
Experience risk	May hate the whole process.	Would not have the interesting experience of participating in the creation of a new company.
Sink-the-boat risk	Is this a single-play decision that if lost will cause extreme harm? No.	Is this a once-in-a-lifetime opportunity that you will forever punish yourself for if you say "no?" No.

Next, we evaluate the social risks that may result. In this case, passing up the deal (i.e., a missed opportunity) could cause a rift in the friendship with the colleague. At the same time, a needless blunder could cause problems in Calvin's relationship with his wife. It could also negatively impact Calvin's reputation as a sagacious investor.

Our next step is to consider information risks. If Calvin passes up the investment, he would miss an opportunity for an interesting learning experience. This might be more serious than it would be for most people because as an academic, Calvin's identity is all about learning. In addition, he would miss the opportunity to tell his future students what he had learned.

The next step is to consider life/health risks. There is a remote possibility that having the project go wrong could cause stress and harm his health. There is no life risk in this case, however, if the deal is a missed opportunity. On the dimension of experience risk, Calvin should have asked how much he would enjoy the experience of being involved in the development of a new product as a passive owner. This possibility intrigued him at the time, so this would increase the costs of a missed opportunity. The experience of a needless blunder, however, could be extremely negative: Watching an investment gradually (or even quickly) disappear could be quite disconcerting.

Finally, we must consider sink-the-boat risk. If this investment is a needless blunder, will the loss of $20,000 cause irreparable harm to Calvin and his spouse? Is this sum of money integral to their retirement, the education of their children, or the paying off of critical debts? On the other hand, is this a once-in-a-lifetime opportunity? If he said "no" to the deal, would he forever second-guess himself and regret the decision? Recent research has consistently shown that when we look back on our lives, we regret most the actions that we have not taken rather than the actions that we did, meaning that we regret missed opportunities more than needless blunders.

If a needless blunder would cause irreparable harm, the decision is a true single-play tough call. This would change the entire analysis, and action would only be warranted when confidence for the positive outcome is extremely high. On the other hand, if you are facing a once-in-a-lifetime opportunity, then experiencing a missed opportunity would be extremely negative. In either of these cases, your decision becomes a strategic, single-play tough call rather than a tactical choice. These kinds of high-stakes decisions call for extreme caution, a point that will be extremely important in the final phase of the decision-making process—solving the problem.

Estimating the Probability of Success   In addition to evaluating the risk, we must also estimate the probability of success if we act. In our example, Calvin had to identify the milestones that Zephyr needed to achieve to succeed. Each milestone represents a conjunctive event; that is, each element of the process, on its own, could lead to failure. As we noted in Chapter 4, to estimate the overall likelihood of success, we must identify the likelihood of the success of each conjunctive event and then multiply these probabilities. The result provides an estimate of the probability that the entire project will succeed.

As Calvin analyzed this new venture, he felt that Zephyr needed to achieve at least four milestones. First, the prototypes needed to pass

Adidas's tests. Second, Adidas (or another shoe company) still had to decide on a licensing agreement. Third, the company would have to commit to producing the product and adequately market it. Finally, it would have to succeed in the marketplace. If we assign a highly optimistic likelihood of .5 (50 percent) for each of the four conjunctive events, the probability of success of the entire project is 0.5^4 (.5 × .5 × .5 × .5), or .0625. Thus, optimistically, there is only a 6 percent chance that the project will succeed. In reality, the probability of success may actually be lower. Because new products have only a 20 percent chance of succeeding in the marketplace, Calvin should have reduced his estimate of the fourth of these probabilities to .20, in turn reducing the overall probability of success to 2.5 percent (.5 × .5 × .5 × .2).

The estimation process does not end, however, with our analysis of the conjunctive model. As we move through the remainder of the SCRIPTS steps, we will adjust our probability estimates up or down depending on our assessment of the implications of intuition, perspective, and time.

Parameter 4: Apply Intuition and Emotion

As we noted earlier, if you face a true crisis situation, you must immediately shift to a guided-intuition decision-making process. Even when making strategic decisions, however, we should employ guided intuition as well as the rational application of the full SCRIPTS process. Guided intuition provides a second source of information for making tough calls. When properly employed, it can guard against situations in which the numbers aren't accurate or don't seem to add up (i.e., warning signs are going off in your brain, heart, or stomach, even if you can't really explain them).

How would Calvin have used guided intuition as a check against the quantitative analysis? First, he needed to gather all of the information that he can within the time available and make a tentative decision based on what his experience tells him to do. Then, he should have performed a mental simulation that plays out a scenario of the chain of events that will result from his decision. If the sequence of events leads to a positive outcome and appears likely, his decision is confirmed. But if the sequence of events feels implausible, he needs to consider another option and repeat the process. If the scenario plays out as expected, he can finalize his decision and act. As naturalistic decision researchers have found, this guided-intuition process is often both fast and effective—*if* it is employed by individuals who are highly experienced and well trained.

It is critical that we use guided intuition without excess emotion. When strong feelings of fear or optimism enter our intuitive processes, they can bias our analysis. For Calvin and his wife, the possibility of quadrupling their investment within a year might lead to greed. The hope of quick riches is one of the most basic of human motivations and can easily short-circuit a clear, effective analytic process, as well as an intuitive process. In particular, it can bias our estimates of the probabilities of success. Thus, when he initially estimated the likelihood that Zephyr shoes would succeed, Calvin needed to take care to ensure that the possibility of large gains did not inappropriately increase his estimates of the likelihood of each milestone.

The-grapes-must-be-sweet bias is the name we have given to the phenomenon that occurs when we want something badly and are so excited by its value that we think that its likelihood is greater than rational analysis would suggest. The sweet-grapes bias is the flipside of the sour-grapes phenomenon. Sour grapes refer to a situation in which people know that they cannot have something and as a result, state that they never really wanted it and that it is undesirable anyway. In contrast, sweet grapes refer to the case in which people really, really want something and persuade themselves that it is actually achievable. A good illustration of sweet grapes is the situation in which people buy thousands of dollars worth of lottery tickets when the jackpot reaches hundreds of millions of dollars. The emotions accompanying greed and avarice cause a dramatic inflation of their perception of the odds of success.

> **The sweet-grapes bias describes how the desire to obtain a highly valued object erroneously increases estimates of the probability of success.**

For Calvin and his wife, the sweet-grapes bias had the potential to inflate their estimates of the likelihood of success of each of the conjunctive events. Thus it is likely that the 6 percent chance of success that they estimated with the conjunctive model was inflated.

Parameter 5: Take Different Perspectives

As noted in Chapter 6, master decision-makers view tough calls through the lenses of many perspectives, each of which identifies a different set of values and issues. The effect is like moving to the high ground to get a global view of the problem. It allows us to identify the full range of factors that might influence our chances for success if we act. Using the ESP-PLACE acronym developed in Chapter 6, we find that six of the eight perspectives identified apply in the Zephyr case. (The two perspectives that do not are the political and ethical viewpoints.)

First, viewing the problem from an engineering/technology perspective, Calvin would have had to assess the likelihood that the Zephyr staff could engineer a durable and cost-effective product. The engineers would have to develop a fairly complex air-intake and exhaust system in the shoe. Could a group of amateurs oversee such an effort? These considerations should have made Calvin lower his estimate of the probability of success.

The next factor, the sales/marketing perspective, should have pushed Calvin to ask how difficult it would be to successfully promote a new shoe with a $150 price tag. In addition, he should have asked how consumers would react to shoes that are marketed for their two distinctive qualities: cooling your feet and protecting you from fungus infections. Traditionally, shoes are sold on fashion, not practicality. At the same time, people with foot fungus problems may be willing to pay extra for shoes that offer the possibility of eliminating a very uncomfortable problem. Working through the marketing perspective results in a balance between the positive and negative effects. But is it an equal balance? On the face of it, it's hard to know. Thus, at least for the moment, we will make no adjustments in estimating costs or probabilities based on the sales/marketing perspective.

What issues arise from a production perspective—the first P in ESP-PLACE? When we use this perspective, we must ask whether manufacturing the shoe can be scaled up from the prototype to actual production. Can hundreds of thousands of different-sized shoes be made while maintaining quality and efficiency standards? The process of moving from the prototype to the production stage of the product-development cycle is notoriously difficult. These considerations should have led Calvin to reduce his probability estimate.

Although political issues (the fourth perspective) are not relevant in this case, the legal perspective has clear implications. The legal frame of reference suggests that Calvin should have asked whether one of the major shoe companies could steal or otherwise discover Glenn's idea. Large corporations are known for turning down the ideas of inventors and then later introducing a product based on an eerily similar concept. In addition, large corporations are notoriously reluctant to adopt the ideas of outsiders. These considerations should have also led Calvin to lower his probability estimate.

What are the implications of the accounting/finance perspective? From an accounting vantage point, Calvin must estimate the likelihood of a profit. Will the costs of designing, producing, and marketing the shoe be low enough so that a profit can be made based on sales to a limited market of nonfashion-conscious consumers who live in warm climates? These considerations suggest that Calvin should have reduced his estimate of the probability of success even further.

Using the competitive perspective, Calvin should have asked how competitors would respond to the introduction of this new shoe. Although there is currently little or no competition for this new product, if Zephyr shoes are successful, competitors will almost certainly enter the market with their own designs. As a result, the window of opportunity for this cool new shoe could be short-lived. As a result of the low level of current competition, this analysis should have increased their estimates of the probability of success.

Finally, Calvin needed to investigate the tough call from an ethical perspective. Fortunately, the Zephyr opportunity did not pose any ethical dilemmas.

Consideration of all of these perspectives should have led Calvin to adjust his estimate of the likelihood of achieving the hoped-for successful outcome. Table 8.2 summarizes the entire analysis. Four of the eight ESP-PLACE dimensions indicate that Calvin and his wife should have reduced their estimates of the probability of success. Only one suggests that they should have increased it. Clearly, Calvin should have lowered his estimate of the likelihood that Zephyr shoes would be successful.

Parameter 6: Consider the Time Frame

Because Calvin faced a strategic rather than a crisis decision, he had considerable time to decide. When considering time issues, we must also evaluate which cultural view of time is most appropriate: Does the tough call involve linear, circular, or procedural time? In addition, are

Table 8.2   Using Multiple Perspectives to Adjust
Probability of Success Estimate

ESP-PLACE Dimensions	Probability of Success Adjustment from the 6% Initial Estimate
Engineering	Adjust down for engineering difficulty.
Sales/marketing	No change.
Production	Adjust down for production difficulty.
Political	Not relevant.
Legal	Adjust down for defending patents
Accounting/finance	Adjust down for high costs.
Competitive	Adjust up because of low competition.
Ethical	Not relevant.

there conflicts between people who employ divergent time perspectives? The Zephyr case illustrates a classic linear-time situation in which an investment in the present generates hopes of achieving larger gains in the future. Both Glenn and Calvin were operating on the same linear time frame, and as a result, time conflicts were unlikely.

But what about time traps? It is possible that decision myopia could have caused Calvin to undervalue future outcomes and over-value initial investment costs. This combination of valuations could create a time fence in which giving up the $20,000 initial cost would act as a barrier to making the investment required to earn a far larger amount in the future. In this case, however, Calvin had an extra $20,000 to invest. In addition, he was focusing on the prospect of quick future gains. As a result, he was not suffering from decision myopia (although he may have been affected by the sweet-grapes phe-nomenon).

Another time-based factor, however, did influence Calvin's decision. Glenn skillfully and artfully created a sense of time pressure by giving Calvin and his wife the impression that a decision by Adidas was immi-nent. They not only felt time pressure, but they also experienced reac-tance; that is, they believed that their freedom to act (to get in on the deal) was endangered. Reactance feelings elevate our valuations of whatever may be lost. Just as we tend to increase our perceptions of the value of goods that are becoming more and more scarce, the perceived value of the Zephyr investment increased. Thus, while they estimated the future monetary value of the investment at $80,000, Calvin and his wife's state of reactance led their psychological valuations to be much higher.

> **Reactance describes how a perceived threat that blocks a valued outcome causes people to desire the outcome even more.**

In sum, Glenn's expert salesmanship overcame the effects of decision myopia to create a state of psychological reactance. Calvin felt that unless he and his wife made a decision quickly, they would lose out on the deal. As noted in the last chapter, when people feel time pressure, they place greater weight on negative outcomes. For Calvin, the possibility of losing the chance to get a deal represented a negative outcome that he wanted to avoid. The net effect of these forces was to increase his perception that if he didn't act, he would miss a big opportunity. Thus a key issue for Calvin was to avoid allowing reactance to cause him to erroneously increase his fears that he might lose out and miss a golden opportunity.

SOLVE THE PROBLEM

As we proceed through the Zephyr example, we are now ready to move on to the seventh SCRIPTS element, solving the problem. When we are making a strategic decision and time is available, we should delay making a choice until we have moved through the SCRIPTS process. It is important not to rush to a conclusion and to try to remain unbiased throughout the decision process. Keeping an open mind as we proceed through the six parameters is critical. By delaying the decision, we can consider the effects of each parameter without having a particular end in mind. After assessing their effects, we can be in position to make a choice that will stand the test of time.

A Three-Step Process for Solving the Problem

Our approach to solving the problem is to take our philosophy of structured analysis to its logical conclusion. We do this in three steps. The first step is to set our trigger, that is, determine how sticky or how quick it should be. Second, we assess how the evidence that we have been able to accumulate contributes to the probability of success if we act. Finally, we compare our evidence to our trigger setting. If our estimate of the probability of success surpasses the trigger setting, we act; if not, we remain in a status quo position. Through this three-step process, we provide a simple, but powerful, means for making high-stakes decisions. In the sections below, we discuss each step in the solve-the-problem process.

Step 1: Set the Trigger   As we noted in Chapter 2, the trigger identifies the amount of evidence that we will require for action. We discussed what it means to set a sticky, a neutral, or a hair trigger, settings based on which type of error is more costly. Thus, we set a sticky trigger when the risk of a needless blunder is substantially higher than the risk of a missed opportunity. An example is the criterion for guilt employed in the criminal justice system in the United States. The instruction that the defendant must be found guilty "beyond a reasonable doubt" means that we have set a sticky trigger because we believe that it is worse to convict an innocent person (a needless blunder) than to let a guilty person go free (a missed opportunity). In contrast, the instructions in civil trials represent a neutral trigger; the jury (the set of decision-makers) is told that a verdict for the plaintiff can be based on a "preponderance of the evidence," which implicitly indicates that the risk of a needless blunder is no greater than the risk of a missed opportunity.

We should set a hair trigger when the costs of a missed opportunity are higher than the costs of a needless blunder. An example is the decision by President Bush in 2001 to push hard for a large tax cut to spur an economy that was moving rapidly toward a recession. Thus the negative consequences of not acting when actions were needed were higher than the risks of committing a needless blunder (acting when you should not).

Another way to view the trigger is to think back to Gilbert K. Chesterton's quote at the beginning of the chapter: "Art, like drawing a line, consists of drawing the line somewhere." In the context of high-stakes decision-making, the trigger setting tells you where to draw the line.

Thus far, we have described the trigger setting in terms of a process of balancing the risk of a missed opportunity versus the risk of a needless blunder. There is a simple way to quantify this balancing process. We recommend the creation of a risk ratio. We produce a risk ratio by dividing the value of the needless blunder by the sum of the values of the missed opportunity and the needless blunder. The risk ratio will range from zero to one because the value of the denominator (the sum of the value of the needless blunder and the value of the missed opportunity) will always be larger than the value of the numerator (the value of the needless blunder). The denominator represents the range of possible outcomes, from the worst to the best. The numerator represents the downside risk if you take the action and are wrong:

$$\text{Risk Ratio} = \frac{\text{the value of a needless blunder}}{\text{the value of a needless blunder} + \text{the value of a missed opportunity}}$$

The calculation of the risk ratio begins by considering monetary risk. Using the Zephyr example, we divide the financial cost of the needless blunder (i.e., \$20,000) by the sum of the costs of a missed opportunity and a needless blunder (\$80,000 + \$20,000 = \$100,000). This sum gives a proportion of .20 (\$20,000 / \$100,000), or a proportion of 20 percent. The proportion represents the criterion value for how much evidence we must require to take action. The closer the proportion is to 0, the less risks we face and the less evidence we should need before we act (i.e., set a hair trigger). A risk ratio of .50 indicates that we have set a neutral trigger. Finally, a risk ratio above .75 indicates that we should set a sticky trigger and require confident predictions of success before we act. Thus the higher the value of the risk ratio, the greater the risk if an action is taken.

> **The risk ratio provides a quantitative means for setting the trigger.**

Remember, however, that this initial risk ratio depends solely on monetary risk. It is also important to consider nonmonetary factors when setting a trigger. As a result, we recommend that you adjust the risk ratio after analyzing the remaining five risk dimensions. Our monetary risk ratio provides an anchor point; other considerations can push us away from this anchor.

Table 8.3 is based on a SMILES risk analysis of the Zephyr situation. We have used the monetary risks of a needless blunder and missed opportunity to develop the risk ratio of .20. We then considered each of the other SMILES dimensions to determine whether the trigger should be adjusted up (indicating that the decision is riskier than it initially seemed and requires more evidence) or down (requiring less evidence). As the table indicates, our analysis suggests that we increase the trigger setting for two dimensions (social and life risks) and reduce it for three (information, experience, and sink-the-boat risks).

To adjust the risk ratio, we recommend balancing the weight of the nonmonetary risks that would result from a needless blunder or a missed opportunity. Think of placing the weight of the missed-opportunity risks in your left hand and the weight of the needless-blunder risks in your right hand. Whichever is greater will cause you to move the trigger in that direction. Thus, if your needless blunder weight is greater, you increase the stiffness of the trigger and require more evidence before acting. In this case, it would mean moving the trigger setting from the anchor point of .20 to .25 or more (depending on how important you felt the nonmonetary risks of a needless blunder were). On the other hand, if the weight of a missed opportunity is greater, you would loosen the trigger and require less evidence before acting, perhaps moving the risk ratio from .20 to .15 or even .10.

When we apply this procedure to the Zephyr case, it's pretty clear that the weight of a missed opportunity is only slightly greater than the weight of a needless blunder. That is, the three risk dimensions that suggest loosening the trigger (i.e., information, experience, and sink-the-boat risks) slightly outweigh the two dimensions that suggest stiffening the trigger (i.e., social and life risks). The net effect is to decrease the risk ratio from .20 to something slightly lower—say, to .18.

This ratio represents a criterion for how much confidence we must have before we act. To simplify our analysis, we convert the risk ratio from a fraction to a percentage. Thus, in this case, Calvin would need an estimate of more than an 18 percent chance of success before making this investment.

Step 2: Assess the Evidence for Acting   After setting the trigger, Calvin needed to assess the strength of the evidence that he had that the project would succeed. As his estimates of success increased,

Table 8.3 Calculating the Criterion Value for Trigger Setting

Risk Dimensions	Value of a Needless Blunder	Value of a Missed Opportunity	Risk Ratio and How Adjusted
Social risk	Spouse is very unhappy.	Colleague is disappointed.	Increase, because spouse's reaction is more important.
Monetary risk	$20,000	$80,000	Risk ratio = .20. Requires a probability estimate of success greater than 20%.
Information risk	No loss of information.	Lost learning opportunity.	Decrease because of information value.
Life/health risk	Possibly experience stress from the loss.	No life risk, just disappointment.	Increase slightly because of higher weight of needless blunder.
Experience risk	May hate the whole process.	Would not have the interesting experience of participating in creation of new company.	Decrease slightly because missing the experience is more serious.
Sink-the-boat risk	Is this a single-play decision that if lost will cause extreme harm? No.	Is this a once-in-a-lifetime opportunity that you will forever punish yourself if you say "no." No.	Decrease slightly because this could be a rare opportunity.

so would his confidence in acting. If his estimate of the probability of success exceeded the criterion that he set for his trigger (his risk ratio), he should act.

As noted previously, to estimate this probability, we begin by identifying the milestones that must be achieved for the endeavor to be successful. Then, we multiply the probabilities of each milestone together. In the Zephyr case, we used this procedure and obtained a 6 percent estimate of likely success.

Just as we adjusted the risk ratio when we set the trigger, we must also adjust this probability estimate of success. To do so, we list all of the reasons why action should work and all of the reasons why it may not. As we noted earlier, this approach borrows ideas that go back at least to Benjamin Franklin when he described how to make complex choices. He suggested beginning the process by taking a sheet of paper and listing the pros and cons of engaging in an action. He next advocated, after contemplation and thought, striking out comparable pros and cons until the process simplified itself and an obvious choice emerged. Our process for solving the problem builds on Franklin's intuitive approach.

The Zephyr case presented four reasons for success: The market potential analysis was favorable, Adidas showed strong interest in the product, a patent for the technology was in the works, and there was little competition in this segment of the shoe market. On the other hand, there were also four problem areas in its development and marketing: The technology was unproven, the management team was unproven, large companies rarely license technology from small firms, and most new products fail.

When we assess the probability that success will follow action, we must also consider the factors that could bias our estimate. For example, Glenn Knight's skillful sales pitch was immediately available in Calvin's memory. As noted in Chapter 4, the fact that this information was so readily available could have easily biased Calvin's probability estimates. If Calvin did not systematically consider all of the things that could go wrong, the positive response of the Adidas vice president and the compelling results of the market research might inflate his estimates of a likely success.

This suggests that we must also consider whether we have been affected by decision-making biases when we make our initial estimates of success, and adjust accordingly. In the Zephyr case, if Calvin put the cons in one hand and the pros in the other, he should have perceived that the cons weighed more than the pros. As a result, he should have reduced his 6 percent estimate of the likelihood of success—perhaps to something closer to 4 percent.

Step 3: Compare the Likelihood of Success to the Risk Ratio   With the calculations of the risk ratio and the probability of success, we are now in position to make a high-stakes decision. This straightforward step simply entails comparing the two figures. If the likelihood of success is greater than the risk ratio, the evidence points toward action. In contrast, if the likelihood of success is less than the risk ratio, there is a strong indication to not act.

> ***If the probability of success is greater than the risk ratio, action is indicated.***

In the Zephyr case, step one resulted in the final risk ratio being set at 18 percent. Step two resulted in an estimated likelihood of success of 4 percent. Because the risk ratio exceeds the likelihood of success, Calvin should have come to the conclusion that he and his wife should *not* invest in Zephyr shoes. Even though they set a hair trigger for acting, our assessment of the likelihood of success is so low that they should have concluded that it would not be smart to make this investment.

The Story's Conclusion

Well, you may wonder what actually happened to Calvin Johnson and his wife's decision. Yes, they opted to make the $20,000 investment. Soon afterward, the people at Adidas decided that they did not want to license the product. In the letter to Glenn Knight, Adidas's product development manager indicated that the company would be focusing on the fashion-shoe market rather than the functional-shoe market. With that blow, Zephyr's principals began to scramble to contact other shoe companies, including Nike and Brooks, that might be interested. A small shoe company finally signed a contract to work with Zephyr to develop and market the product. Unfortunately, no funds changed hands.

When this book went to press, more than three years had passed since Calvin and his wife made their $20,000 investment. Increasingly, it looks like the only benefit that will result are information gains and the chance to write a case on the topic.

SOLVING NONMONETARY
HIGH-STAKES PROBLEMS

The Zephyr Technology case illustrates a high-stakes decision in which monetary outcomes dominated the decision process. Although they considered a variety of nonmonetary risks (e.g., social and experiential costs), the fundamental question was whether Calvin and his wife would make money on the deal. As a result, the analysis began with the development of a risk ratio based on the relative monetary costs of a missed opportunity and a needless blunder. The final determination of evidentiary requirements (i.e., setting the trigger for action) depended on adjustments that they should have made to their original calculations of their monetary-based risk ratio.

It is clearly appropriate for decision-makers who are facing tough calls that have important financial components to construct their risk ratios on the basis of the monetary outcomes of a missed opportunity and needless blunder. These calculations then act as an anchor that they can adjust after they evaluate the other risk criteria in SMILES. The final risk ratio is a clear indicator of the decision-maker's criteria for action. Only if their confidence in success (as based on their final probability estimates) exceeds this ratio should they act.

Many high-stakes decisions, however, revolve around nonmonetary criteria. For example, Jeff Vender's choices in treating his patient had nothing to do with monetary criteria. Similarly, Beck Weathers's decision to continue his climb to Mount Everest's summit after he realized that he was losing his vision also illustrates the key role of nonmonetary factors in high-stakes decision-making. How then can we use the three-step approach to make nonmonetary-based tough calls?

Rather than using monetary outcomes to construct an initial risk ratio anchor, we begin with a risk ratio of .50, which sets a criterion of a 50 percent likelihood of success for taking the action. We then use the risk dimensions of SMILES to adjust the risk ratio up or down. After estimating the likelihood of success, we compare it to the risk ratio. If the likelihood of success is greater than the risk ratio, action is indicated. To illustrate these ideas, we present the story of Melisa Dedovic's high-stakes decision.

> *When a tough call does not involve monetary*
> *outcomes, we initially set the risk ratio at .50*
> *and adjust this neutral trigger up or down based*
> *on the relative costs of a missed opportunity or*
> *needless blunder.*

Leaving Sarajevo?

Melisa Dedovic was born in 1972 in Sarajevo, Bosnia. Highly preco-
cious, she began doing stories for local television at the tender age of
14. By the time she turned 22, she was anchoring the news for Sarajevo's major television station. This was during the height of the shelling
of the city during the ethnic conflict there. One day in 1995, an artillery
shell exploded in the building where she did her broadcasts. The shell
had a delayed fuse, so the bomb was able to penetrate deep into the
building prior to exploding near her studio—some 50 feet underground.
Christiana Amanpour of CNN was in the same building at the time,
and together they fled the inferno caused by the bomb. Finding her
camera crew, Melisa went from hospital to hospital to report on the status of her colleagues. At the end of the day she collapsed from exhaustion. Only then did she realize that the blood on her blouse was from
a wound that she received when the shell exploded.

Later in 1995, Melisa was with her camera crew reporting on the
housing situation of refugees. This was during a truce, and the markets were full of people buying food. Out of nowhere, an artillery
shell exploded, killing 76 people. Initially, she and her crew ran for
cover. Then, composing themselves, they returned. Her cameraman
grabbed her by the neck and told her that pictures were all that was
needed. They recorded the massacre and transmitted their images for
the world to see. Melisa told us, "Nothing had to be said—the pictures described it all."

We asked Melisa if she liked the fame of being the premier journalist in Sarajevo. "Certainly, yes, it was phenomenal," she said. She
continued by explaining, "I was responsible for keeping three million
people informed." Her goal was to keep her people up to date on what
was happening.

One of her toughest calls was the decision to leave Bosnia to come
to the United States. At the urging of a colleague, she applied for a
scholarship to study in the United States. Almost a year after her

application, she received news that she was one of two people in Bosnia to receive the scholarship. The question was, should she stay in Bosnia or go to the United States to earn a degree in communications? At the time, it was five days before her wedding. She would have to leave her home, her family, a new husband, and a new job as the public-relations director for the Open Broadcast Network, a television station that was run by Western sources. Her job continued to be reporting the personal stories of the victims.

Melisa Dedovic faced a classic tough call. The stakes were high, people who advised her provided different recommendations, the information was ambiguous, and there was conflict among her loyalties and values.

SCRIPTing the Decision

What does the SCRIPTS analysis say about Melisa's decision? Systematically moving through each of the steps, let's start with the calculation of a risk ratio, preset at .50.

Search for Signals   The near-continuous warfare in Serbia represented a signal for action that was impossible to miss. As Melisa noted, however, it was a conversation with a friend that initially moved her to apply for the scholarship. This older man told her to think about herself and her future rather than approaching the problem from the point of view of her community. The culture of Serbia asks its people to place their family and friends first. Her mentor suggested that now was the time to think of herself and her future. When the news arrived that she had received the scholarship, she was forced to make a single-play, high-stakes decision. Because she had time to make the decision, it represented a strategic choice. She may, however, have been facing a power-curve situation. If she decided to stay, it was always possible that events could rapidly accelerate in Sarajevo to prevent her from taking the scholarship later.

Find the Cause   Melisa well understood the cause of her situation. Ethnic strife had coursed through her homeland for centuries. In Serbia, the problems are so deep and so varied that warfare could resume at any moment. Her nation seemed to be constantly at a breaking point (or tipping point, in Malcolm Gladwell's terms) from which the slightest event could cause it to move from a state of peace to a state of all-out terror. On the other hand, however, she could play a causal role in ameliorating the situation because, as a journalist, she had a voice that could help to reduce tensions and decrease the probability of an outbreak of violence.

Evaluate Risk   The SMILES analysis of the risk of a needless blunder and a missed opportunity provide important information here. On the social dimension, a needless blunder would mean the certain loss of contact with her family and friends in Sarajevo for at least two years, maybe forever. In contrast, a missed opportunity would mean that she would not expand her expertise and make new contacts in the United States. On balance, the risk of a needless blunder seemed greater to her than the risk of a missed opportunity on the social dimension. Quantifying the monetary dimension is extremely difficult. There is, however, some likelihood that missing the opportunity to go to the United States could lower her earnings potential in the future. In fact, the range of her professional opportunities might increase dramatically with a master's degree in communications. Thus, for money, the weight of the missed opportunity was greater than the weight of a needless blunder.

On the risk dimension of information, missing the opportunity to go to the United States would result in a loss of knowledge and information gained from pursuing a master's degree. Staying in Sarajevo would mean more experience of the same sort that she already had, in other words, a smaller increase in her information base. Thus the weight of a missed opportunity was greater here.

Thinking through life risks was perhaps the easiest analysis of all. Melisa had already survived several artillery shells and one execution attempt. Missing the opportunity to go to the United States could literally cost her life. Thus this was a very heavy factor for her.

Perhaps the most difficult of the risk dimensions for her to analyze was the experience risk. On the one hand, foregoing the opportunity to enter the master's program would prevent Melisa from going through a challenging and rewarding program. On the other hand, her current job was extremely exciting. As she explained to us, "There was a new danger every day. Because I was blacklisted, just going from home to work placed my life at risk." As a person who enjoyed arousal, she liked the taste of danger. Although most of us would probably want to avoid life-threatening risks, on the experience risk dimension for Melisa the scales were fairly balanced between the cost of a missed opportunity and the cost of a needless blunder.

Finally, she needed to consider sink-the-boat risk. The opportunity to go to the United States for a master's program was a once-in-a-lifetime opportunity. Afterward, she could always go back to Serbia. Thus, on this dimension, the risk of a missed opportunity was far greater than that of a needless blunder.

In sum, the risk analysis suggested that, on four of the six SMILES dimensions (monetary, information, life, and sink-the-boat), the risks for Melisa Dedovic of a missed opportunity were clearly higher than the risks of a needless blunder. On one (the social dimension), the risk of a needless blunder was higher. On the other (experience risk), they were the same. Thus, the risks of a missed opportunity were clearly higher than the risks of a needless blunder, leading to a much lower risk ratio than .50; we set it at about .30.

Step two in this kind of analysis is an initial calculation of the likelihood of success. Then we can adjust our estimate on the basis of considerations of emotion, perspective, and time. To do this, we first identify the milestones that we would have to achieve for the action to succeed. In Melisa's case, she would have to have the endurance and the smarts to succeed in a difficult academic program. In addition, she would have to have the social skills to make friends and adapt to a new culture. Finally, she would have to be able to find a good job when she finished the program. Melisa had good reason to be confident on all of these dimensions. She knew that she was smart (probability of success on this dimension probably equals .95). She knew that she would make friends (another estimated probability of success of .95). She also knew that she would put in the effort. As she described to us, "I am a driven person. I can always find something to do; I can read; I can put puzzles together in different ways." So her probability of success here was also .95. Finally, she was highly confident that she could find a good job when she finished. Her ultimate goal was to return to Serbia to teach journalism at a university. Again, she was highly confident (probability of success of .90). When we multiply these probabilities together (using the conjunctive model), the result is a probability estimate of 77 percent for success if she acts.

Apply Intuition and Emotion   As we discussed in Chapter 5, we should use guided intuition in times of crisis or when we have considerable experience. Melisa did not face a crisis. In addition, she had been in the United States once, and then only briefly. Thus she had little experience and training and was not well positioned to make an intuitive decision. As a result, intuition would not be a good basis for reaching her decision.

Emotional factors, however, played a major role in her decision. When Melisa learned that she had won the scholarship, she was only days away from being married. She learned that, after a three-month delay, she could bring her new husband to the United States to be with her. But as she said to us, "Unfortunately, everything went wrong in the marriage." She and her new husband divorced prior to her leaving. With this event, her emotions pushed her toward taking the scholarship.

After emotions and intuition, it is critical to determine whether other factors may also have influenced her probability estimates. Thus, before proceeding to a decision, it was important for her to make further adjustments on the basis of any potential biases. We consider each in turn.

Take Different Perspectives   The eight perspectives identified in the ESP-PLACE acronym apply more to business decisions than to the career and life decision that Melisa faced. Frames of reference such as engineering, selling, production, and accounting had absolutely nothing to do with her decision. Although political, legal, and ethical considerations were certainly appropriate, they would have little impact on estimating the likelihood of her success if she took the scholarship.

Consider the Time Frame   A number of time-related factors, however, could have impacted Melisa's decision. A time snare was certainly operating; she would not be able to bring her husband to the United States for three months. The short-term negative feelings that would result from the separation mitigated against leaving her homeland. In the end, divergent cultural views of time may have been partially responsible for her divorce. Instead of working on Western time, her new husband may have been operating on circular, traditional time. He may have expected his marriage to follow the same course as his father's and his grandfather's. Clearly, Melisa employed a Western time perspective in which you invest in yourself to prepare for a better future. Her Western time perspective increased the likelihood that she would succeed in the graduate program but may have clashed with a traditional definition of a marriage.

Solve the Problem   The final step in the SCRIPTS process is to solve the problem. In the three-step process, Melisa began by calculating a risk ratio. Based on the weights of the missed opportunity and needless blunder on the six risk dimensions, adjustments from the starting point of .50 were clearly required. Our analysis of her risk dimensions suggested that the risk of a missed opportunity was higher than the risk of a needless blunder, by a substantial margin. As a result, we reduced her risk ratio to .30. (This means that we have determined that the costs of missing the opportunity to go to the United States were substantially higher than the costs of going to the United States and having things turn out poorly, by a ratio of almost three to one.)

In step two, Melisa assessed the probability that action would be successful. Our analysis led to an initial estimate of 77 percent. We adjusted this result following a consideration of the effects of emotion, perspective, and time. The divorce from her husband clearly led her to increase both her drive and her chances for success. The other perspectives had little to say about this issue. Finally, her Western time perspective also acted to increase her estimate of success. In sum, we could easily place the likelihood of her success at 80 percent or more.

In the final phase of solving the problem, we compare our two calculations, the risk ratio and our estimate of the likelihood of success following action. Melisa's success estimate of 80 percent far surpasses her risk ratio of .30 (30 percent). Thus, in the end, her high-stakes strategic decision was easy to make.

SOLVING PROBLEMS
WITH MULTIPLE OPTIONS

The problems that we have considered so far had only two options. The decision-makers could either do nothing or take one course of action. Thus, Calvin could either make or not make the investment in Zephyr Technology. Similarly, Melisa Dedovic could either take the scholarship or stay in her current job in. As we noted in Chapter 3, however, it is critical to identify as many options for solving the problem as possible. What does our approach say about multiple-option high-stakes decisions?

Fortunately, the solution to these more complex decisions is straightforward. Although it entails more work, to be truly systematic about our high-stakes decisions, we should go through this same analysis process for each viable decision option. In other words, we should calculate a risk ratio and an estimated probability of success for reach of the possible actions. Luckily, doing this for two alternatives is not twice as much work as doing it for one; as we evaluate the risk ratios and the probabilities of success of each alternative action, we naturally get better at the process. For each option, we determine whether the likelihood of success is greater than the risk ratio. If the likelihood is higher than the risk ratio for only one option, we choose that option. If the likelihood is greater than the risk ratio for both options, we choose the option that has the greatest difference between the likelihood estimate and the risk ratio. We call this difference between the likelihood and the risk ratio the *confidence margin*. Thus the alternative with the greatest confidence margin should be the alternative that we select.

> ***When choosing among multiple options for action, we should select the option that has the greatest confidence margin.***

For example, suppose that Melisa Dedovic had a second option of going to work as a journalist for a television station in Italy. She could go through a full SCRIPTS process to assess this action versus staying in her current job in Sarajevo. She would compare the confidence margin for this option to the confidence margin of going to school in the United States. Imagine that for the Italy option her risk ratio was .32 and that her estimate of her success was 80 percent. Her confidence margin for going to the United States is .50 (.80 −.30). Her confidence margin for going to Italy is .48 (.80 −.32). By the smallest of margins, she should go to the United States. Needless to say, however, because the difference in her confidence margins is so small, she should pause before she proceeds to action. This is clearly a decision that she should sleep on if she can—and delay until she really needs to make a final choice.

We conclude this chapter with a strong suggestion, an admonition, to always identify as many options as possible. As we noted in Chapter 3, one of the most frequent mistakes of high-stakes decision-makers is to focus quickly on a single solution and then act to justify its selection. Once we identify the possible causes of a problem, we should identify as many solutions as possible. By the time we have moved through the SCRIPTS process and have reached the stage of solving the problem, we will quickly eliminate most options.

As master decision-makers, we should strive to employ the three-step process on several alternatives, not just two. In this way, we can be more confident that we haven't eliminated any better solutions.

Principles for Solving the Problem

1. Move through a three-step sequence to calculate a risk ratio, estimate the probability of success if you act, and choose action if your probability-of-success estimate exceeds your risk ratio.
2. When faced with multiple options for action, select the option that has the largest confidence margin.
3. When monetary considerations dominate, use them first in calculating your risk ratio. Then adjust on the basis of the other SMILES risk dimensions.
4. When nonmonetary considerations dominate, start with a risk ratio of .50. Then use the six SMILES dimensions to adjust it.
5. Calculate the likelihood of success by (1) estimating the probability of achieving each milestone necessary for an action to succeed and by multiplying the prob abilities together and (2) adjusting your result by considering the effects of intuition, emotions, perspective, and time.

PART III

Putting It All Together

9

THE MASTER DECISION-MAKER

It's none of their business that you have to learn how to
write. Let them think you were born that way.

Ernest Hemingway

As suggested by the Ernest Hemingway quote that opens this
chapter, no one writes well without training. A similar learning
process is required to consistently make successful high-stakes
decisions. What are the characteristics of a master decision-maker?
How would you know a master decision-maker if you met one? One
approach would be to find people who have been highly successful over
a considerable time span. For example, consider William E. Simon. He
was the 63rd secretary of the Treasury, under President Gerald Ford.
Previously, he was the deputy secretary of the treasury, where he super-
vised efforts to restructure and improve U.S. financial institutions. He
founded three successful companies and served on the boards of over
30 corporations, many of them *Fortune* 100 companies.

Another option is to look to universities. For example, consider
Scott C. Lederman, who was the treasurer of the University of Pennsylvania for 12 years. He created the first cash-management program
and was the director of investments for this world-class university.

We may also find master decision-makers among highly successful
investors, such as John Templeton. Born in rural Tennessee, he earned
a scholarship to Yale, became a Rhodes scholar, an Oxford graduate,
and a member of Phi Beta Kappa. In 1937, he opened an investment
firm and, as described by Louis Rukeyser on *Wall Street Week*, became

one of America's authentic investment heroes. His Templeton Growth Fund and Templeton World Fund became two of the largest and most successful mutual funds. In 1972, he created the Templeton Prize, which is a cash award larger than the Nobel Prize. The Templeton Prize rewards those who have advanced the world's understanding of spirituality. In 1987, he was knighted Sir John by Queen Elizabeth II.

In addition to high levels of success, what do William E. Simon, Scott Lederman, and John Templeton have in common? These well-educated, highly successful individuals all participated in the New Era Foundation in the mid 1990s. Founded in 1989, the charitable fund was run by John G. Bennett Jr., who promised to double the money of nonprofit organizations that donated funds to his organization. Bennett claimed to represent anonymous donors who would match the money of these nonprofit organizations. Under the terms of the agreement, charities donated their funds to New Era; after six months, they would receive twice their initial donation. Bennett indicated that the six-month wait was a requirement of the benefactors.

The fund grew through word-of-mouth contacts and through the testimonials of people like William E. Simon and John Templeton. An affable and apparently sincere individual, Bennett charmed the directors of the charitable and nonprofit organizations that he targeted. Although the promises made seemed unbelievable, in the early days, the results were astounding. The initial investors received the promised return on their donation. Many of these organizations then placed additional funds with New Era. The positive word-of-mouth communications from these satisfied customers lured more and more moths to the flame. In 1994, contributions to the charitable organization had reached $100 million. In the first four months of 1995, the fund received an estimated $135 million in additional money.

Unfortunately, the New Era Fund was a scam. The scheme's bubble was burst by a persistent accountant named Albert J. Meyer. Working part-time in the business office of tiny Spring Arbor College in Michigan, Mr. Meyer discovered a $294,000 bank transfer that was made to New Era in 1993. Highly suspicious, he thought that it may have been sent to the discredited television evangelist Jim Baker. When he learned that it was connected to New Era, he tried to find information on the organization. Finding nothing in the library, he made numerous telephone calls. Finally, he concluded it was a Ponzi scheme. Administrators at the college, however, ignored his warnings and plunked down another $1.5 million. Described as a pit bull by his wife,

Mr. Meyer intensified his efforts to expose New Era. He first went to the Internal Revenue Service and the American Institute of Certified Public Accountants. Although expressing agreement with his suspicions, they did nothing.

Finally, a letter to the Securities and Exchange Commission prompted an investigation. In May 1995, the Ponzi scheme unraveled. The final estimate placed losses at $54 million. The scheme touched over a thousand individuals and charities, including 180 evangelical groups, colleges, and seminaries. Bennett pleaded no contest to an 82-count indictment and was convicted and found guilty of the biggest charity fraud in U.S. history. He was sentenced to 12 years in prison, and the judgment was upheld by the U.S. Supreme Court in 1999.

THE CHARACTERISTICS OF A MASTER DECISION-MAKER

While luminaries such as William G. Simon, Scott Lederman, and John Templeton were ensnared by the New Era Fund, a lesser-known man, Robert Montgomery Scott, escaped. As president of Philadelphia's Museum of Art, Mr. Scott was approached by Bennett—the mastermind of the Ponzi scheme. While other nonprofit organizations in Philadelphia were dumping money into New Era, Mr. Scott played devil's advocate. He told a *Wall Street Journal* reporter that he kept saying, "Show me the prospectus. Show me where the money would go." He explained, "I've been involved in raising money enough that I know there isn't a wide pool of anonymous donors. I had a skepticism that those people existed." Because of these suspicions, Mr. Scott made the tough call of turning down the offer to invest in New Era. Meanwhile, numerous nonprofit organizations in Philadelphia (e.g., the Academy of Natural Sciences with $2.7 million and the Free Library with $1.45 million) took the plunge. Until the final demise of New Era, his fellow fund-raisers rolled their eyes at his skepticism.

One analyst who was involved as a creditor in the sordid affair noted, "It proves that experienced people are as foolish as anyone else. ... A lot of it is done on the cumulative weight of people who had had a good experience. People make their decision based on talking to other people." Summarizing the debacle, columnist Roger Lowenstein concluded, "This is the dirty secret of experts. Outsiders view them with awe, particularly when their field is an abstruse one such as investing. But in truth, experts are courageous or impressionable, independent or conventional, in the same degrees as other two-legged beasts. And all of an expert's brains and training will not count for much if, at the crucial moment, he relies on somebody else's brains instead of his own."

So, are Albert Meyer and Robert Scott master decision-makers while William Simon, Scott Lederman, and John Templeton are mere mortals? Although it is true that those who became embroiled in New Era showed poor judgment, it is also true that one bad decision does not preclude someone from being, or becoming, a master decision-maker. One of the characteristics of master decision-makers is that they are willing to make high-stakes decisions. While they will consistently make sound choices, errors in judgment do happen. That is the nature of tough calls.

As we noted in Chapter 1, tough calls are chancy by their very nature. Because luck plays a role, even the best decisions can have bad outcomes. To identify master decision-makers, we must look not only at decision outcomes but also at the decision process. Master decision-makers focus on ensuring that the process is structured and thorough.

When Simon, Lederman, and Templeton failed to employ a systematic process and instead depended on others' recommendations, they violated a cardinal rule: Do your own research. But as we all know, it's understandable if we make a mistake once. We become personally responsible when we make the same mistake twice. People who make successful high-stakes decisions over an extended time period are rare. These exceptional individuals understand the nature of tough choices and the trade-offs they produce. They have deeply ingrained structured processes for making tough calls. Our SCRIPTS approach can help you achieve the same thing.

Why is developing a deep understanding of SCRIPTS so important? Consider the training that the flight engineers in the *Apollo* space program endured—days and days of practice in which one problem after another was thrown at them at twice the normally expected pace. At one point, they nearly rebelled. Their reaction was that this stuff would never occur in their flights. Chris Kraft, who ran flight operations, had a sage response. By practicing problems over and over, you learn the systems and you develop a way of thinking. When a real crisis arises, even if you have never trained specifically for it, you have the knowledge of the system that allows you to respond coolly and creatively. To maximize the chances of successfully navigating tough calls and high-stakes decisions, master decision-makers take their practice time—their decision-making on lower-stake decisions—seriously. They learn from the process. By carefully analyzing our decision processes, we can all improve our decision-making abilities.

As you practice the SCRIPTS process on simulated (or real) problems, implementation of the process can become second nature, an almost reflexive response. As we noted in Chapter 5, decision-making then becomes intuitive, and we almost automatically control our emotions. This is the highest level of skill for a master decision-maker. At this level of expertise, when a tough call surfaces and the pressure is on, your decision processes are clear, and you can respond appropriately within the required time frame. You will find that because of your expertise, your decision-making processes will evolve from deep thought to guided intuition.

The New Era Fund illustrates two of the characteristics of the master decision-maker. First, master decision-makers follow a tested process when they make tough calls, exemplified in Robert Montgomery Scott's decision not to invest. Second, they do their own research. Albert Meyer is the prototype here. If it is impossible to do your own research, it is critical to employ trusted advisors to do it for you. And even then, it is important to be honestly skeptical when their results don't add up.

In addition to having a deep understanding of the SCRIPTS process and doing their own research, master decision-makers have four additional characteristics: (1) They gain and then learn from experience, (2) they have fun and experiment, (3) they know when to ask for help, and (4) they implement decisions with precision and forcefulness. With these characteristics, they look forward to the opportunity to make high-stakes decisions. The following sections dig deeper into these ideas.

Gain and Then Learn from Experience

We are convinced that a major cause of the great dot-com bubble of 2000 was the inexperience of a substantial proportion of its investors. The steady gains in stock prices in the 1990s drew millions of new investors into the stock market. Most analysts and professional funds managers had entered the field during the 1980s and 1990s, having not experienced the last substantial bear market that occurred in the 1970s, when stock prices traded between 700 and 1000 on the Dow for over ten years. Possibly due to this lack of experience, investors divined all sorts of explanations to justify the enormous valuations given to stocks like Priceline and Amazon, whose price-earnings ratios were infinite because they never made a profit. Even the prices of stalwart technology stocks such as Intel and Lucent were priced at over a hundred times earnings. Inexperienced investors may have fallen for the "sweet-grapes" phenomenon discussed in the last chapter and let the lure of huge gains influence their estimate of the likelihood that that their choice of companies would succeed spectacularly.

Writing in *The Wall Street Journal*, E. S. Browning and Greg Ip identified six myths that drove the inflated perceptions of corporate performance and the consequent boom in stock prices. First, overoptimism caused investors in tech companies to believe that they could generate breathtaking gains in earnings, sales, and productivity for years to come. Second, they believed that tech companies were not subject to ordinary economic forces, such as a slower economy or higher interest rates. Third, they believed that some tech companies had natural monopolies that would create unbeatable advantages. Fourth, they felt that exponential Internet growth had just begun and if anything, would accelerate. Fifth, they considered prospects to be more important than immediate earnings. Finally, they fooled themselves into believing that this time things were different, that the new technologies had created a new age of investing in which old rules no longer held.

The experience of a bear market or a careful look at the historical record might have led many people to see the dangers that lurked in our new industrial age. For example, in years long gone by, the invention of the radio led to dramatic growth in the stocks of many companies. One of the hottest was Radio Corporation of America (RCA). This growth did not last forever, however, as RCA's stock price crashed in the 1930s (along with many other companies'), losing 98 percent of its value.

The boom-bust pattern of the dot-com stocks also looked like a replay of the oil boom of the 1970s. A few years ago, we interviewed several executives in independent oil firms that had made it through the great oil bust of the 1980s. This was a group of mature men who averaged well over 20 years experience in the oil business. They had seen the good times and the bad. They knew that booms followed busts and vice versa. They had learned that the worst thing that an "oil man" could do was to highly leverage his company. Those who lost it all when the boom ended were most frequently the less experienced, who had not been around to see the entire boom-bust cycle. Instead, they had seen only the good times, the exploding oil prices of the 1970s. They took on massive debt loads to expand with the times, and when the plunge hit, they crashed and burned.

Among the group who did not weather the storm, we found an amazing number of 40- to 50-year-old men who no longer owned the huge house, several expensive cars, and all of the toys that they had accumulated during the boom years. After the bust, many divorced (often for a second time) and struggled to make it back into the oil business. All of them were older and wiser after having lost their shirts. Just as experienced decision-makers survived the oil crash of the 1980s, the older, more seasoned have avoided and survived the dot-com frenzy.

In 2000 and 2001, however, another boom occurred—this time in natural gas. For years the U.S. government had encouraged power companies to build plants using this cheap, environmentally friendly fuel. At the same time, formal policies discouraged exploration. Suddenly, late 2000 produced a shortage, causing prices to skyrocket. The experienced management at one small company, Chesapeake Oil and Gas, recognized the coming problem in the late 1990s. While the price of natural gas was at all-time lows, they purchased as many producing wells as possible. Their stock prices languished at under a dollar. When the shortage occurred, their stock increased over 20-fold. These seasoned speculators actually followed the old adage of "buy low and sell high." Some sources suggest that T. Boone Pickens, the grizzled veteran of the corporate raids of the 1980s, made several hundred million dollars investing in natural gas futures in 2000.

The importance of experience also holds in manufacturing. In her book *Rude Awakening*, Maryann Keller noted the dominant but limited perspectives of General Motors' finance-oriented managers. They had no direct experience on production lines. They'd never sold a car, conducted market research, or attempted to integrate production and engineering. Because they received a company car as an executive perk, they didn't even have the normal experience of purchasing and maintaining a car; chauffeurs drove the top managers to work. How could they have empathy for their customers if they had no experience buying and driving a car? Ross Perot was right on target when he declared, "If I have a car that gets worked on by mechanics every day so that I never see, feel, or taste reality, and I am driven back and forth to work, what do I know about the product? I should have to buy a car from a dealer. I should have to negotiate for it. It should be picked at random and I should drive it. And when that sucker breaks down, I ought to have to take it to the dealer and get punched around. That's reality."

But experience is useless unless we reflect on it and learn from it. For example, the baseball great Pete Rose was particularly meticulous about examining his bat after each at bat. His goal was to identify precisely where the ball struck the bat so that he could make small adjustments at his next at bat. He even went so far as to rub down his bats before each game with alcohol so that he could find the small marks left by the ball on the bat. This relentless search for feedback was one reason for his success. In contrast, in his personal life he failed to learn from his experiences. Although his friends warned him of the possible outcomes of his gambling, he refused to listen and learn. As a result, he may never enter baseball's hall of fame.

It is difficult to become a superb decision-maker without that well-worn coat of experience. Whether in business, medicine, sports, or law, the bumps and bruises from making decisions and seeing their outcomes, both good and bad, are a critical proving ground for master decision-makers. It is equally important, however, to learn from other people's experiences.

Have Fun and Experiment

Research shows that when people are in good moods, they work harder, buy more, and are nicer to each other. Not a bad trio of outcomes!

Southwest Airlines has learned this lesson well. The company has made having fun a part of its corporate culture. Its CEO, Herb Kelleher, actually bases his hiring decisions in part on an individual's sense of humor. He argues that by hiring employees who like to have fun, he has obtained the most productive workforce in the industry. Their productivity results from a combination of low attrition, low absenteeism, high creativity, and innovation.

We first see evidence of the "lighten-up" attitude of Southwest's employees in their uniforms—khakis and polo shirts. Even during the deadly dull safety announcements prior to takeoff, flight attendants can have fun. During one monologue, an attendant said: "Speaking of smoking, there's never any smoking aboard our flights. You know what happens if we catch you smoking here at Southwest, don't you? You'll be asked to step out onto the wing to enjoy our feature movie presentation, *Gone with the Wind*." The corporate strategy of encouraging employees to have fun is in part responsible for Southwest showing a profit every year since 1973. No other airline comes close to this record.

An organization's workforce can play hard and work hard simultaneously. The ability to have fun reduces stress and increases flexible thinking. In addition, by lightening up, people are free to experiment.

In a wonderful little book called *The Max Strategy*, Dale Dauten tells the fictitious story of how a chance encounter in an airport changed his life. The main protagonist is an old, energetic, and wildly successful businessman who has become a prophet for the virtue of experimentation. The book's fundamental idea is that great discoveries and great businesses are not planned. Rather, they are accidents that happen because a person was willing to experiment and had the optimism, drive, and creativity to take advantage of good fortune when it occurred. Examples of unplanned inventions are numerous, from the development of Levi's jeans to the creation of Coca-Cola.

Know When to Ask for Help

On July 29, 1999, a seriously disturbed day trader named Mark Barton bludgeoned to death his wife and two sons. He then proceeded to downtown Atlanta, and at 2:45 P.M. he entered Momentum Securities, an office set up for day traders. Carrying two handguns with him, he shot and killed three people. When he entered the day-trading room, he first greeted people. Then he began firing. As he fired bullets into helpless people, he said over and over, "I hope I'm not upsetting your trading day."

From Momentum Securities, he moved across Piedmont Road to All-Tech Investment Group, another day-trading firm, where he had lost $80,000. When he entered All-Tech's offices, no one knew what had happened across the street. Interestingly, he had been popular among the traders and office staff at All-Tech because he was a risk taker. Sweating profusely, he said that he wanted to talk to the two officers and training person. Once in the room, he closed the blinds and said, "This is going to be very quick and visual." He then pulled out his weapons and began shooting. From there he went out into the main trading room going up and down the rows of computers, shooting the day traders at point-blank range. Four people died, and many were grievously injured. When surrounded by police, he committed suicide.

Coincidentally, the building that housed Momentum Securities also contained another firm, Crisis Management International. The president of the firm is Bruce Blythe, who in 2001 was involved in the rescue of hostages in Ecuador held by South American drug lords. The day after the tragedy, Mr. Blythe was asked if he could assist All-Tech. He told the manager that he needed to get everyone at the scene of the crime back to the building within 72 hours. At that point, he would do a group stress debriefing session with them. Based on his long experience, he knew that it was important to move quickly to get the company's clients talking about the incident and releasing their emotions. Only after going through the debriefing at the scene of the crime would they be willing to come back to the building to trade stocks. The manager hired Mr. Blythe to do the counseling. The same offer was made to Momentum Securities. Their manager, however, declined the offer. He felt that the Red Cross could handle the situation and would not charge a fee.

Three days later, after the rooms were cleaned and equipment replaced, Bruce Blythe was back at All-Tech doing group counseling for the new employees (brought in from out of town), day traders (those who were not injured at the scene), and their families. He sat down in the middle of the floor, and as he probed their feelings and reactions to the incident, tears flowed and emotions were high. The participants told stories and talked about their reactions. Mr. Blythe described the post-traumatic stress that the participants were facing as like the flu. He told them that for a time period, the stress would be in control. But like flu, their bodies would fight the effects, and over time they would heal. As the session progressed, the gloom began to lift. He knew that things were going well when about an hour into the session, one of the clients turned on a computer and began trading.

In our interview with Bruce Blythe, he told us, "It was beautiful to see the healing process beginning so quickly, but this is not to say that these people were healed. They had a lot of grieving and emotional stress to still sort through." Within a few weeks, trading activity returned to normal levels at All-Tech. It was a different story at Momentum, however. It took the manager six weeks to reopen his branch. A year-and-a-half later, his office was out of business.

Even master decision-makers do not have all of the answers. The old maxim to know one's strengths and weaknesses is particularly appropriate for high-stakes decision-making. If you do not have the skills to do a task, it is critical to seek the expertise of people who do. Master decision-makers are willing to ask for help.

IMPLEMENTING HIGH-STAKES DECISIONS

The last of our major characteristics of master decision-makers is that they implement decisions with force and precision. Because of the extreme importance of implementation, we have reserved a major section of the book to discuss its features.

As we begin this section, let's step back for a minute to discuss a larger issue. From a general perspective, what are the factors that influence the outcomes of high-stakes decisions? Three factors are critical: (1) the quality of the decision-making process, (2) the precision with which the decision is implemented, and (3) the effects of chance. We believe that employing the SCRIPTS process and executing the decision with precision will minimize the likelihood that bad luck will harm the outcome and maximize your ability to take advantage of good luck. As M. C. Alexander put it, "The harder you work, the luckier you get." In sum, by practicing and using the SCRIPTS process, you are preparing yourself to seize opportunities.

> **By practicing and using the SCRIPTS process,
> you are preparing yourself to seize opportunities.**

We identify in this section six factors that are critical for executing decisions with precision and force: (1) communicate a vision, (2) understand human limitations and needs, (3) use Ockham's razor, (4) monitor your progress, (5) attend to the details, and (6) create a crisis-management plan.

Communicate a Vision

It is absolutely necessary to have a clear vision of where you are going. Without it, it is impossible to exert leadership. As the old saying goes, "You cannot push a string—you must pull it." Clearly articulating your vision will allow you to pull people to success.

Having a vision does not require that you go through elaborate goal-setting and planning exercises. Herb Kelleher, the highly successful chairman at Southwest Airlines, has a clear philosophy about formal strategic plans: "The meticulous nit-picking that goes on in most strategic planning processes creates a mental straitjacket that becomes disabling when things change radically from one day to the next."

In place of formal strategic planning, Kelleher advocates scenario planning. In this process, a company's executive committee asks "what if" questions. For example, they might ask, "What will we do if the price of aviation fuel increases by 50 percent?" Or, "What if the competition launches a low-price airline that competes for one of our major routes?" By generating scenarios, the company can prepare itself for a variety of alternative futures. As Peter Schwartz eloquently says in his wonderful book *The Art of the Long View,* "Ability to act with a knowledgeable sense of risk and reward separates both the business executive and the wise individual from a bureaucrat or a gambler." Scenario planning creates a sense of flexibility that allows an organization to respond rapidly to change, even if change was not anticipated. Scenario planning also sharpens an organization's ability to identify signals for action.

In the early 1980s, Mr. Schwartz worked for Shell Oil. At the time, the company was planning to build a huge oil platform in the North Sea that would cost billions of dollars. His planning group began developing alternative scenarios for the price of oil and gas. One scenario anticipated a continuation of the status quo of high oil prices and a strong OPEC group. A second posited that communism would collapse and Russia would be forced to sell oil and gas to the world market. At the same time, the Organization of Petroleum Exporting Countries (OPEC) cartel could disintegrate. The net result would be a dramatic decline in the price of oil and natural gas, which would seriously harm the profitability of the platform.

When Shell presented the second scenario to experts around the world, they paid little attention. Based on this scenario, however, the corporation made significant changes in their strategy. Executives began to pay more attention to political developments in the Soviet Union. They also held down expenses and avoided paying high prices for new oil fields. As a result, when oil prices plummeted in the 1980s, the company emerged in a significantly stronger financial position than most of its competitors.

What does scenario planning mean for articulating a vision? Developing a clear vision statement becomes even more important when an organization takes a scenario-planning approach. Southwest Airlines has a clearly articulated vision—to make a profit, achieve job security for every employee, and make flying affordable by providing the best service and lowest fares to the short haul, frequent-flying, point-to-point traveler. Scenario planning helps an organization develop strategies to accomplish its vision. Without a guiding vision, organizations and individuals can find themselves bouncing like pinballs from one course of action to another.

Providing a vision has one additional critical effect. Because a vision tells a story, it is motivational and can be remembered. What famous American said, "The Declaration of Independence is a promissory note?" When we present this question to executive groups, less than one in a hundred know the answer. When we ask who said, "I have a dream," everyone knows that these are Dr. Martin Luther King Jr.'s words. In fact, both quotes came from the same speech. We remember the four words because they expressed Dr. King's vision for African Americans. Although the eight-word quote created a wonderful metaphor that spoke to the financial elite of the United States, it simply did not have the motivational impact of his vision statement.

Creating an effective vision for your organization, and for yourself, is one of the key attributes of the master decision-maker.

Understand Human Limitations and Needs

As humans, we have certain basic limitations and needs. Two of these limitations are particularly important for implementing our decisions. First, there are restrictions in our ability to remember and to retrieve information. Because our world is exploding with so much data, these limitations can easily result in information overload. With information overload comes anger and poor performance. Second, humans have a strong need to be treated with respect and dignity. Because other people often implement the decisions that result from our tough calls or they are directly affected by them, we must be ever cognizant of their effects on motivation. Leaders who fail to recognize either information-processing limitations or the need to be respected will find it impossible to effectively implement solutions to tough calls.

Information-Processing Limitations   Here is a brief example that illustrates our information-processing limitations. Below are two lists of numbers. Look at list A. First, read the numbers out loud. Then close your eyes and repeat them back out loud.

List A.   5   9   2   6   7   1   3

Were you able to recall the numbers and repeat them in their correct order?

Now, do the same thing with list B. Read the numbers out loud, close your eyes, and repeat them back out loud.

List B: 8   5   7   9   3   1   8   4   2   6

Unless you are a very rare individual, with an extremely long cognitive span, you were not able to repeat back the numbers in the second list. As you have probably noticed, list A contained seven digits—the length of a telephone number. In contrast list B contained 10 digits. According to a scientific principle called Miller's Law, people are able to process and remember seven plus or minus two bits of information at a time. This occurs because of the limitations of our short-term memory, which acts like the random-access memory of a computer. If the amount of information to be processed exceeds the upper limit of nine bits, most of us experience information overload and our performance drops seriously. In fact, many times when people try to remember the list of 10 numbers, they actually remember less than 7. Thus, when more information causes overload, we often don't achieve as much as we did before the extra information was added. In essence, excess information gets in the way of our normal level of ability.

The implications of Miller's Law are huge. It influences how fast we can train employees. It influences how quickly we can learn to use a new technological device. It also influences how much information advertisers can transmit in their messages to customers. The master decision-maker recognizes that the engineers who develop a product and the sales force that sells it have had months or years to learn the intricacies of how to make it work. Too often, we forget that a novice to the product cannot handle the information flow. The result is an unhappy customer who will look elsewhere to find someone who understands his or her needs. Master decision-makers understand these facts and design their products, their persuasive messages, and their instructions for product use to make them more "user friendly."

A failure to consider people's information-processing limitations nearly doomed Xerox when its managers decided to launch a new office copier in the late 1970s. The 8200 was packed with computer intelligence, the most advanced available. It was also reliable and worked efficiently, at least in the lab. In the "real world," however, the market rejected the product. It was the first product failure in Xerox history, and at first, no one could figure out why.

After a lengthy investigation, managers discovered that their engineers had failed to look at the human factor. The technicians who developed the product had spent thousands of working hours on the machine and knew it inside and out. Users, however, had to walk up to it and quickly figure out how it worked. As the manager who led the redesign effort explained, "The only problem was that no one paid attention to the user. People had to wade through buttons and visual noise and manuals just to copy a page or two." As a result, customers left Xerox and purchased simpler models from its competitors. Redesigning the 8200 took two years. But the result was a machine that was adapted to the needs and limitations of users, helping Xerox to recapture its lost market share.

The Need for Respect   One of the more-devastating corporate disasters in the past few years has been the decline of Motorola. The once-high-flying company failed to anticipate and respond to the movement to digital and away from analog wireless phones. In addition, it bet and lost billions on Iridium—a project to use satellites to provide wireless telephone communications. Its stock price fell from over $60 to less than $10 in 2001. While stock analysts and other pundits focused on Iridium and its wireless-phone business, some of the company's senior employees suggested that there were other causes. In particular, they identified Motorola's antagonistic culture as an important component of its poor overall performance.

In one of our interviews, a senior manager at Motorola told us how the various divisions described themselves as participating in "horizontal violence." In other words, the divisions competed against each other in the same markets. During the analog era, the cellular-phone division was the big winner. At one business meeting, an executive asked all of the cellular managers (there were about a hundred of them present) to stand up. He then asked all of the other managers to seek them out because "they are carrying you on their backs. They are responsible for your yearly bonuses." The executive whom we interviewed summarized the situation by saying in a sarcastic tone, "Needless to say, this was not a cooperative environment."

One of the reasons the president of the wireless-phone division missed the movement of cellular phones from analog to digital is that he failed to listen to people. According to a Motorola executive, this individual had "no compunction about abusing anyone anytime, whether it was a colleague, a customer, or a supplier. He engaged in frequent abuse even as the corporation's CEO was pushing a program of individual dignity with the firm." Because of his mistreatment of subordinates and customers, no one could push him to develop a new digital cellular phone. As our contact in the organization said, "We gave the second generation (of cellular phones) to Nokia."

A continuous pattern of mistreatment of employees and customers always comes back to haunt an organization. Consider the implications of the following statement from a customer of a major health insurance company: "Aetna acts like we're a bunch of liars." These bitter words emerged from a surgeon as he described how he and other physicians were treated by Aetna, the largest health insurer in the United States. In an effort to get costs under control, Aetna implemented a series of policies, including making physicians get permission before running tests on patients. As one doctor noted, you can wait on hold for an answer "longer than it takes to do a colonoscopy." You can imagine how customers who were forced to wait reacted to these policies, too.

Among other practices that infuriated physicians, the insurer took its time paying them. Hospitals and physicians grew impatient with the new policies and began to leave. These losses had an immediate impact on Aetna's bottom line. After they had implemented these draconian procedures, their earnings and stock performance steadily slipped in 1999 and 2000. As a result, a new CEO was brought in to correct the problem. As the chairman of the board described the situation, "There's no business model in the world that succeeds by making customers angry."

According to a study by the Hudson Institute and Walker Information, 56 percent of employees say that their employers fail to show concern for them. One of the worst examples of such treatment is the boss who forced his subordinate to fly to a monthly budget meeting in a distant city. The employee's wife was pregnant and already three days overdue. When he got the call that she was to have an emergency Caesarean section, it was too late to catch a plane home. As a result, he quit the company and is now the president of his own firm.

When physicians, executives, or clerks—anyone—is treated as if they are incompetent, liars, or slackers, they will rebel. Even the simple act of taking forever to respond to a telephone call indicates a lack of respect. Following the Golden Rule and treating employees as you would like to be treated is a basic principle that master decision-makers always try to follow.

Use Ockham's Razor, Not KISS

What fast-food product has the highest profitability? The answer: french fries. They can have margins as high as 80 cents on the dollar. Of course, the king of fries is McDonald's. To compete more effectively in the tough fast-food industry, Burger King in the mid 1990s made a concerted effort to create a better tasting fry. After several years of product development and a $70 million advertising budget, on January 2, 1998, Burger King launched its new french fries, which had a coating of batter on each piece of potato. With Mr. Potato Head as its spokesperson, the campaign began by giving away 15 million orders across the United States.

The early returns on the new product were good. Independent tests confirmed that people preferred Burger King's fries over McDonald's by a 57 percent to 35 percent margin. Over the first six months, sales of Burger King fries increased by more than 150 million orders. Their new approach of covering the potato in batter appeared to be working. The batter gave the fries a crispy crunch, which marketing research discovered was what consumers wanted. Burger King's goal was to create a fry whose crunch could be experienced through seven or more chews.

After the initial surge in customer interest, however, sales began to fall. Franchisees complained that the fries clumped, cooled too fast, and often seemed undersalted. Customers began to rebel when the taste of the fries began to change for the worse. Ever mindful of the need for the fries to crunch, the franchises added more batter, which took away the potato taste. When franchisees complained to Burger King, management suggested that they check their cooking procedures. Meanwhile, sales of burgers and soft drinks also began to decline. The poor quality of the fries was creating a ripple effect. Finally, 30 months after the initial launch, the CEO agreed to create a new fry. Most important, the 19 pages of french fry specifications would be replaced by a far simpler approach to producing a fry that was much like McDonald's.

Burger King's response to the french fry problem illustrates three of the SCRIPTS parameters. First, because management did not adequately search for signals of problems, it took them too long to discover that the new product was not performing satisfactorily. This caused them to fall behind the power curve. As a result, sales of soft drinks and burgers also began to fall. Once management recognized the problem, they initially failed to identify the cause and blamed the difficulty on the franchises (i.e., management made the fundamental attribution error).

In addition, managers failed to look at the problem from different perspectives. Marketing drove the process of creating a fry that consumers would prefer over McDonald's. In the process, however, they ignored the needs of production. In particular, they were unable to achieve absolute consistency, a necessary element for success in the fast-food industry. The additional fact that they consciously hire a low-pay, high-turnover, low-education, and low-commitment workforce also means that they must keep procedures extremely simple. With 19 pages of specifications and a multistep process to batter and fry the potatoes, consistency became their Achilles' heel.

The needs of marketing and of production are often in conflict. Most master decision-makers take this into account upfront and often overcome such difficulties.

At a superficial level, Burger King's experience with its batter-coated fries appears to illustrate the acronym KISS, or "keep it simple stupid." That is, the extreme complexity of making the batter-coated fry made it impossible to maintain the consistency of taste that fast-food restaurants require. Management had to find a level of complexity that its workforce was capable of implementing.

We suggest, however, that KISS is an oversimplification. The world is filled with pundits who provide simple answers to tough issues. In many cases, however, the easy answers are wrong. There was and is no simple answer to the problem of creating french fries that taste better than McDonald's. Burger King's problem was that it created an overly complicated solution. The key is to find the minimum level of complexity necessary to solve the problem.

Instead of KISS, we recommend using Ockham's razor. William of Ockham, who lived in the early fourteenth century, entered the Franciscan order and taught at Oxford. Translated from Latin, Ockham's razor states: "Entities are not to be multiplied without necessity." Applied to implementing solutions to tough calls, Ockham's razor means: "Employ the minimum level of complexity necessary to implement a solution." Even after seven centuries, this is wise advice.

> **Employ the minimum level of complexity necessary to implement a solution.**

Often confused with KISS, Ocham's razor is usually applied by scientists who are choosing between two competing theories that make the same prediction. In such situations, the principle states that one should select the theory with the simpler explanation. The key, however, is that the explanation must account for the phenomenon under study. Simplicity is only good when it solves the problem.

A classic example of the use of the minimum level of complexity necessary to solve a problem was the use of the Warthog in the Persian Gulf War. Hotshot U.S. Air Force fighter pilots wanted to send this slow and ugly plane to the scrap heap for years. The advantage of the A-10 Warthog is that it possesses sufficient armor to absorb punishment while flying slowly, destroying enemy tanks. In the Gulf War, it stole the show from the advanced Stealth fighters, the Tomahawk cruise missiles, and the Patriot antimissile missiles.

The Warthog possesses far less technology than the sleek, fast jets that U.S. Air Force jockeys love. But it exemplifies the idea of applying the right level of technology for the job. The mere sight of the plane, credited with destroying 1,000 Iraqi tanks and 1,200 artillery pieces, brought panic to Iraqi troops. The slow speed of the plane was absolutely essential for it to fulfill its mission. As described by its designer, the plane's secret was its ability to fly 30 feet off the ground at a slow speed so that it could pinpoint its target. It could then fire its missiles with deadly accuracy.

Those who fought to keep the Warthog flying demonstrated an important characteristic of the master decision-maker. They recognized that complexity and high technology have their place but that getting the job done efficiently is the most important criterion for success.

Closely related to Ockham's razor is another maxim, "Complex is easy, simple is hard," which we heard from Glenn Shafer, a statistician-philosopher. This idea is particularly applicable to the burgeoning field of information technology (IT). When we entered the KISS phrase into an Internet search engine, we found dozens of articles warning IT specialists to be wary of too much complexity. For example, in a column in the trade magazine *Network Computing*, Richard Hoffman admonished, "In the cross-platform, multi-language, Internet-enabled, n-tier, distributed datasource, componentized-code world, simplicity can be as elusive as it is crucial." In English, he said, "the longer and more complex the chain, the greater the chance of a critical meltdown somewhere along the way. The most robust and stable solutions don't necessarily use the newest, cutting-edge products, tools, and technologies."

These ideas fit precisely with our method for calculating the likelihood of success presented in Chapter 4. For example, suppose that preparing french fries is a one-step process of cooking the fries at a precise temperature for a precise time period. If there is a .9 probability of successfully completing each task, the likelihood of having a failure is 10 percent. If a total of six complicated steps are required and each has a .9 chance of succeeding, the overall likelihood of failure is now 47 percent.

Whether dealing with technology, new-product development, or motivating people, the underlying issues in implementing a tough call are extremely complex. Two types of errors can interfere with our attempts to find solutions. The first is to match a complex solution with a simple problem. The second is to employ an overly simple solution to a complex problem. The goal is to use Ockham's razor and apply the minimum level of complexity to solve the problem. Solutions that are either overly simplistic or overly complex are likely to fail. As Glenn Shafer's quote suggests, finding the right level of complexity is hard. It is also the goal of the master decision-maker.

Monitor Your Progress

The process of learning from experience begins with a simple adage to monitor your progress. The case of Palm, Inc., and the threats posed by Microsoft are a perfect example. Not only must Palm constantly keep its finger on the pulse of its own sales; it must also constantly be on the lookout for Big Competition (capitalized for emphasis). Any false step on their part and they could be behind the power curve unless they take almost-immediate corrective action.

As you work through the arduous process of implementing a decision, it is critical to monitor your progress to avoid falling behind the power curve. By monitoring your progress, you gain the feedback that is necessary for learning. In addition, the feedback may provide the signals you need to be warned in time to avoid crashing.

Attend to the Details

"God is in the details." The world-renowned twentieth-century architect Mies van der Rohe wrote these words. Van der Rohe created the International style of architecture, which is noted for its rectilinear forms and elegantly crafted simplicity. He was also a member of an association of artists and craftspeople (the Deutscher Werkbund) who advocated a marriage between art and technology. The goal of the group was to give form and meaning to machine-made things. Another of his dictums, "less is more," illustrates the concept of the Ockham's razor, which we discussed previously in this section.

Van der Rohe used the phrase "God is in the details" to describe his belief that beauty is found in simplicity and in the refinement of the exposed structural elements of buildings. Thus if an architect attends to creating beauty in the smallest details of a structure, it is unnecessary to add superfluous ruffles and flourishes to create meaning and to please the eye. These concepts represent the basis for the steel-and-glass-walled structures that marked the twentieth-century International style of architecture.

We can use these ideas when we implement high-stakes decisions. Not only should the steps we take to implement our decisions follow the principle of Ockham's razor, but we also need to implement the steps with precision and accuracy. If you work to ensure that every i is dotted and every t is crossed, the execution of your fine decision can take on real beauty. Think of the performance of top-notch athletes. Their actions are economical and flowing. They're beautifully simple.

We can't overemphasize the importance of focusing on the details when implementing high-stakes decisions. Poor execution can doom the best decisions. Conversely, great execution can salvage mediocre decisions. To turn to sports again, a great example of these ideas is the simplistic offense run by the Green Bay Packers football team under the master coach Vince Lombardi. One of the team's basic plays was the sweep. The two guards would lead the way around the end. The fullback would enter the hole first to clear out a linebacker. The half-back (most frequently, Paul Horning) would then carry the ball through the hole. Every team would prepare for the famous Green Bay sweep; they knew that the Packers would run it over and over again. Yet the Packers had practiced it for so long and had refined the details to such a point that it would work even when the other team knew that it was coming. Many would argue that deception is a key element of the offensive strategy in American football. Yet attending to the smallest detail of execution was one of the reasons the Green Bay Packers were football's best team for quite some time.

> ***Poor execution can doom the best decisions;***
> ***great execution can salvage mediocre decisions.***

Attention to detail is one of the basic components of the total quality management (TQM) movement that has revolutionized organizations around the world. Too often, however, executives fail to apply the same standards to themselves as to their employees. Thus, while employees are expected to meet high-quality standards when making products and serving customers, executives often fail to perform adequate research prior to making decisions (e.g., investors in the New Era Fund), fail to ensure that the organization is following its strategic plan, and/or fail to communicate necessary information to middle managers. The master decision-maker recognizes that God is in the details.

Create a Crisis-Management Plan

Because of their inherent risk, high-stakes decisions can go wrong. As a result, it is imperative that, in addition to identifying an initial course of action, the master decision-maker also creates a backup plan. The question, "what do you do if things go wrong?" must always be in the back of your mind. In addition, even when you aren't confronting any major tough calls right now, you still need to have a crisis-management plan in place. Things will go wrong. Having a carefully thought out plan will be invaluable when they do.

The importance of a back-up plan is illustrated in a situation that began when a lightning bolt set fire to a semiconductor plant in Albuquerque, New Mexico, in March 2000. The fire created a crisis for Nokia Corporation of Finland and Ericsson Corporation of Sweden when it shut down the factory's production of computer chips. The radio frequency chips were crucial components of their mobile phones, which the companies sell around the world. Worldwide sales of mobile phones were booming at the time, and neither company could afford to have a glitch in production. As described by Almar LaTour, the responses of the two companies could not have been more different.

Because of an outstanding information system, middle managers at Nokia identified a problem in the flow of computer chips into its distribution system prior to receiving notification of the problem from Philips Electronics, which owned the factory. Because Nokia encourages the quick dissemination of bad news, the CEO of the company quickly learned of the problem. Within two weeks of the fire, Nokia had deployed a team of 30 people to search the world to find a new supply of chips. The product most threatened by the chip shortage was handsets, which were in extremely high demand at the time. Nokia's chief troubleshooter, Pertti Korhonen, worked to have chips redesigned "on the fly" and pressured suppliers—particularly Philips—to increase production. He declared, "A crisis is the moment when you improvise."

In contrast, Ericsson moved more slowly. Violating the rule of diversification, they did not employ multiple suppliers of chips. Because of a slow start and a lack of suppliers, their production of mobile phones diminished to a trickle, and the company lost $400 million in potential sales. As described by Ericsson's marketing director, "We did not have a Plan B." As a result, Ericsson got behind the power curve. In fact, it ultimately left the handset-production business.

By using multiple suppliers, Nokia could overcome the potentially critical disruption in its supply of computer chips. The lesson is clear: Every organization needs to have a crisis-management plan in place that describes the immediate steps that they must take should calamity occur.

Another classic example of the benefits of such a plan occurred when an airplane crashed on Saturday, January 27, 2001, killing 10 people associated with the basketball program at Oklahoma State University. The president of the university, James Halligan, learned of the crash on Saturday evening. The university has in place a number of plans for how to handle bombings, kidnapings, shootings, and the like. Central to each plan is a list of people to call in a prespecified order. While the team's coach, Eddie Sutton, had the painful task of calling the families of the deceased, Dr. Halligan and his close associates were pulling together a team to handle the crisis. As a result, a plan was in place by Monday morning. Because of the plan, the university had effectively mobilized so that they could hold a memorial service on Wednesday of that week. Over 10,000 people attended. Even more complex arrangements were also in place to assist the grieving families, basketball players, coaching staff, and dignitaries who arrived from all over the United States. Counselors were assigned to each family and to each player.

Also responding quickly and professionally was the Federal Aviation Administration, which has its own crisis-management plan honed to the finest detail. It took care of handling and transporting the bodies of the deceased and making arrangements for memorial services. Their expertise went as far as taking the victims' personal effects, such as clothing and watches, to Louisiana to be cleaned of jet fuel and dirt prior to being given back to their families.

Because of the preplanning and quick implementation of the crisis-management plan, President Halligan and his associates handled the catastrophe with consummate skill. The 270 family members who attended the memorial service received individual attention, including transportation from airports and counseling assistance. Coaches and dignitaries from all over the United States flew in for the memorial service. While the effects of the tragedy will be felt for many years, the professional and careful handling of the crisis began the healing process.

DENOUEMENT

We began this book by describing high-stakes decision-making as an art. The completion of a task becomes an art when it meets four conditions: (1) Chance strongly impacts the outcome, (2) different sets of values apply to the problem, (3) information is ambiguous or incomplete, and (4) experts disagree as to the solution. When high stakes are added to the equation, we describe the situation as a "tough call."

Because tough calls are made in a risky world, even the best decision-makers make mistakes. To improve the odds of making successful tough choices, master decision-makers follow a process, such as SCRIPTS, to make the call. By following a tested process, they increase their ability to make confident decisions. In turn, as confidence increases, they enhance their ability to implement the decision with enthusiasm. The combination of making a sound decision and then implementing it skillfully and forcefully maximizes the likelihood of success. With implementation comes experience and learning. With learning comes a continual improvement in judgment. The final outcome is the ability to make tough decisions that will stand the test of time.

Perhaps one of the most important outcomes of practicing and using the SCRIPTS process is that you will develop the confidence to make and implement high-stakes decisions. Too frequently, organizations and individuals can experience paralysis of analysis. In these situations, decisions are continually delayed until more data are obtained or until a better product or plan is created.

In one of our interviews, we talked with the CEO of a public software company who described one of her recent tough calls. Shortly after she was named CEO, it became evident that there were problems with a particular employee. A brilliant programmer, he was more skilled than any of her other employees. His singular problem, however, was that he could never reach closure on a project. As a result, nothing emerged from his work. Her tough call was whether to fire this employee.

When you follow the SCRIPTS process, determining when to take action is straightforward. You assess where you are on the power curve and then weigh the costs of the two errors of not taking action when you should and of taking action when you should not. In this case, the CEO of the software company had to decide whether retaining her employee would help or hurt her company. In the end, she made the tough call of firing the employee. The costs of keeping him were simply too high.

> **Using the SCRIPTS procedure helps
> decision-makers avoid paralysis of analysis.**

When making tough choices, remember to use the SCRIPTS process. Develop the systems to identify signals of problems. Finding problems early is critical if you are to avoid falling behind the power curve, especially in our fast-paced, speed-driven world. At this stage, determine whether the problem represents a crisis or a strategic deci sion. When a problem is found, immediately find the cause. Next, use the SMILES acronym to identify the risks of a missed opportunity or a needless blunder. After evaluating risk, apply intuition and emotion. If the problem is a crisis decision, it's time to bring all of your collected experience into play and use your intuition to make the choice. Even if the problem is a strategic decision, intuition can play an important role in the decision-making process. You can then move on to taking different perspectives and considering the time frame to adjust your estimates of the risk of making a needless blunder or missing an opportunity and of determining the likelihood of success if you decide to act. Once you have all of the information that you have gathered from the first six steps, you can move into the last stage of the SCRIPTS process—solve the problem.

After we have made our high-stakes decisions, it is critical that we implement them with force and precision. In the implementation phase, we need to communicate a vision, use Ockham's razor, remember human limitations, monitor our progress, learn from experience, attend to details, and have a crisis-management plan in place.

Our long-term goal is that we all become master decision-makers. These rare individuals have a number of characteristics. They follow a tested process (such as SCRIPTS) for making decisions, they do much of their own research (or have trusted advisors help them with it), they first gain and then learn from experience, they have fun and experiment, and they implement their decisions with force and precision. When making tough choices, master decision-makers recognize that even the best decisions can turn out poorly. As a result, they focus on the process rather than the outcome. They recognize that whether the outcome turns out well or badly, they must learn from it and then put it behind them. With a top-notch process, the odds are increased that the outcome of the next tough call will be successful.

Many of the world's best decision-makers are humble and recognize that they cannot delegate high-stakes decisions. A classic example of the humble master decision-maker was Sam Walton. From a home base in Arkansas, he created the world's largest and most profitable retailer—Wal-Mart. Even after reaching the height of financial success, he still drove a beat-up station wagon to work, and to check on the performance of his stores, he flew his own airplane so that he could personally inspect them.

> ### *Master decision-makers are not born;*
> ### *they are prepared.*

As we did the research for this book, we discovered that master decision-makers are found all over, in the small towns and back roads of America and throughout the world. It is important to remember, however, that the ability to make high-stakes decisions can be taught. The facility to make tough calls is not a predetermined genetic trait. Master decision-makers are not born. Instead, they are prepared. Through their experience, the use of a structured process, and guided intuition, they practice the art of high-stakes decision-making.

Principles of the Master Decision-Maker

Master decision-makers:

1. Follow a structured process, such as SCRIPTS, to make tough calls.
2. Do their own research or rely on trusted advisors.
3. Gain and then learn from experience.
4. Have fun and experiment.
5. Know when to ask for help.
6. Implement decisions with force and precision.
7. Communicate a vision.
8. Understand human limitations and needs.
9. Use Ockham's razor.
10. Monitor their progress.
11. Attend to details.
12. Develop crisis-management plans.
13. Are often humble.

APPENDIX

Principles of High-Stakes Decision-Making

CHAPTER 2: THE SIGNAL-DETECTION PRINCIPLES

1. Employ situation analysis to identify signals of threats and opportunities.
2. Avoid the zone of false hope by identifying problem signals early.
3. Set your trigger so that a mistake will lead to the least-negative outcome.
4. Strive for accuracy in detecting signals by creating outstanding systems for gathering and interpreting data.
5. Recognize that the overconfidence bias can decrease accuracy and influence trigger setting.
6. If you are facing a short-fuse situation, truncate the SCRIPTS process by going directly to guided intuition.
7. Be realistic when making a decision, and be confident when implementing it.

CHAPTER 3: CAUSAL PRINCIPLES

1. Use root-cause analysis to identify the cause or causes of the threat or opportunity.
2. Analyze causes from a systems perspective, and recognize that failures are often overspecified.

3. Avoid causal illusions by acknowledging that neither you nor mysterious outside forces can influence events governed by chance.
4. Avoid the availability bias by knowing that the cause of an outcome may not be the most available factor that comes to mind.
5. Defensive, ego-driven attributions can lead to a failure to identify causes. Learn more by realizing (a) that the situation is not always the cause of our poor outcomes and (b) that we are not always completely responsible for our good outcomes.
6. Avoid the fundamental attribution error by recognizing that situational factors (e.g., good/bad luck or the difficulty of the task) may be a serious influence in the performance of others.
7. Avoid the hindsight bias; that is, don't exaggerate in hindsight what you could not have anticipated in foresight.
8. Use creativity heuristics to identify as many solutions to the threat or opportunity as possible.

CHAPTER 4: PRINCIPLES FOR
EVALUATING RISKS AND BENEFITS

1. Estimate risks by considering the consequences and the probabilities of both the needless blunder and the missed opportunity.
2. Adjust estimations of probabilities by recognizing the distorting effects of the availability bias, illusory correlation, and the anchoring-and-adjustment-insufficient-bias.
3. Adjust estimations of outcomes by recognizing the effects of the law of decreasing marginal effect.
4. Recognize that people take excessive risks such as gambling in part to create thrills, increase arousal, and maintain an optimum level of stimulation.
5. Manage risk by developing rules of thumb, such as:
    a. Strive for incremental, rather than quantum improvements.
    b. Diversify, diversify, diversify.
6. When making stay-quit decisions, recognize that losses occurring in the past are "sunk" and should have no impact on current decisions.
7. To avoid entrapment, create milestones in the initial plan of action, which, if not reached, will result in the cancellation of the project.

CHAPTER 5: PRINCIPLES OF INTUITION AND EMOTION

1. Guided intuition is best employed by experts when time is short or when a rational analysis has resulted in two or more essentially equivalent options.
2. Emotions are required to move a decision-maker to action and to implement solutions energetically.
3. When time is available, use rational decision analysis to identify alternative courses of action, the probability of success of the options, and the positive and negative outcomes that may occur.
4. Emotions exaggerate and bias perceptions of the probability of outcomes and the perceptions of positive or negative values.
5. Fear increases the belief that negative outcomes will happen and causes people to view bad outcomes more negatively.
6. Optimism increases the belief that good things will happen and increases the perceived value of positive outcomes.

CHAPTER 6: PRINCIPLES OF PERSPECTIVE

1. Decision perspectives act as lenses that focus attention on key professional values.
2. Eight frequently used professional specialization frames are: engineering/technology, sales/marketing, production, political, legal, accounting/finance, competitive, and ethical (ESP-PLACE).
3. Because each professional perspective has strengths and weaknesses, viewing the world through a singular lens will lead to poor decisions.
4. Practice the principle of multiframe superiority by including individuals in the decision-making process who can represent each of the perspectives.

CHAPTER 7: PRINCIPLES OF TIME FRAMING

1. Recognize that conflicts may occur as a result of individuals working on different types of time—linear, procedural, or circular.
2. Time is not an expandable resource; rather, it is a temporal space that provides the opportunity for task accomplishment.
3. Time fences result from overweighting short-term costs and underweighting long-term gains.

4. Time snares result from overweighting short-term gains and underweighting long-term costs.
5. Avoid time traps by approaching decisions from a long-term perspective.
6. Ethical decisions represent one type of time trap.
7. The time pressure that occurs in crises inevitably harms decision-making quality.
8. Preplan and practice how your organization should respond to crises.

CHAPTER 8: PRINCIPLES FOR SOLVING THE PROBLEM

1. Move through a three-step sequence to calculate a risk ratio, estimate the probability of success if you act, and choose action if your probability-of-success estimate exceeds your risk ratio.
2. When faced with multiple options for action, select the option that has the largest confidence margin.
3. When monetary considerations dominate, use them first in calculating your risk ratio. Then adjust on the basis of the other SMILES risk dimensions.
4. When nonmonetary considerations dominate, start with a risk ratio of .50. Then use the six SMILES dimensions to adjust it.
5. Calculate the likelihood of success by (1) estimating the probability of achieving each milestone necessary for an action to succeed and by multiplying the probabilities together and (2) adjusting your result by considering the effects of intuition, emotions, perspective, and time.

CHAPTER 9: PRINCIPLES OF THE MASTER DECISION-MAKER

Master decision-makers:
1. Follow a structured process, such as SCRIPTS, to make tough calls.
2. Do their own research or rely on trusted advisors.
3. Gain and then learn from experience.
4. Have fun and experiment.
5. Know when to ask for help.
6. Implement decisions with force and precision.
7. Communicate a vision.

8. Understand human limitations and needs.
9. Use Ockham's razor.
10. Monitor their progress.
11. Attend to details.
12. Develop crisis-management plans.
13. Are often humble.

NOTES

CHAPTER 1 Tough Calls in a Speed-Driven World

3   The quotation from W. Somerset Maugham comes from "The Public Speakers Treasure Chest" (New York: Harper & Row, 1977), 467.

3   In the story of the growing brew pub company, the names of the individuals and the companies have been changed at their request. The details of the story, however, are true and were obtained from interviews with one of the partners in the company.

4   The American flight 965 discussion is based on an article by William Carley, "Could a Minor Change in Design Have Saved American Flight 965?" *Wall Street Journal,* January 8, 1996, pp. A1, A8.

6   "Decision-Making in the Digital Age: Challenges and Responses," Research Monograph 2, December 2000, <www.kepner-tregoe.com>, (June, 12, 2001).

9   Dennis Kleiman, "How Fast Are You," *Fast Company,* May 2000, pp. 137–154.

10 The General Motors information comes from Gregory L. White, "As GM Courts the Net, Struggling Saturn Line Exposes Rusty Spots," *Wall Street Journal,* July 11, 2000, pp. A1, A10.

10 "Decision-Making in the Digital Age: Challenges and Responses," Research Monograph 2, December 2000, <www.kepner-tregoe.com>, (June, 12, 2001).

13 Daniel M. Wegner and John A. Bargh, "Control and Automaticity in Social Life," in *The Handbook of Social Psychology,* 4th ed., edited by D. T. Gilbert, S. T. Fiske, and G. Lindzey, pp. 446–496 (New York: McGraw-Hill, 1998).

13 Polling exiting voters is not perfect, however. Recall that in the November 2000 presidential election, projections from the state of Florida first went to

Al Gore, were then retracted, then went to George W. Bush, and then were retracted again. The reason was that the statistical margin of error in the polling numbers was greater than the actual difference in the margin between the two candidates.

15 The statistics concerning seat belts comes from Larry Landan, *The Book of Risks* (New York: Wiley, 1994).

15 The information on the home-and-auto store emerged from interviews with two individuals who worked for the company.

CHAPTER 2 Search for Signals of Threats and Opportunities

25 The quotation from Marshall McLuhan comes from H. V. Prochnow and H. V. Prochnow Jr., eds., <www.elibron.com/english/sayings>.

27 The Pearl Harbor discussion is based on Abraham Ben-zvi, "Hindsight and Foresight: A Conceptual Framework for the Analysis of Surprise Attacks," *World Politics,* April 1976, pp. 381–395.

33 The calculation on growth rate is based on the rule of 72. This handy rule of thumb states that if 72 is divided by the interest rate, the result tells you how long it will take an amount to double in size.

38 Kepner-Tregoe Business Issues Research Group, "Decision Making in the Digital Age."

40 The French-made Exocet missiles are called "fire-and-forget" missiles. The pilot programs the coordinates of the target into the missile's guidance system. The missile is then fired, and the pilot takes his plane away from the scene as the missile rockets toward the general location of its target. At a preset distance from the target, the missile then activates its radar guidance system. Only at this point can the target ship detect a signal of danger. Although there is time to launch chaff to distract the missile, there is little margin for error.

41 The description of Captain Rogers as aggressive and of the *Vincennes* as "Robocruiser" comes from John Bary and Roger Charles, "Sea of Lies," *Newsweek,* July 13, 1992, pp. 29–37.

44 Tom Peters and Robert Waterman, *In Search of Excellence* (New York: Harper & Row, 1982).

45 For the discussion on the Palm Pilot, see Pui-Wing Tam, "Palm Puts Up Its Fists as Microsoft Attacks Hand-Held PC Market," *Wall Street Journal,* August 8, 2000, pp. A1, A14.

47 Diane Vaughan, *The Challenger Launch Decision* (Chicago: University of Chicago Press, 1996).

48 Material on space shuttle *Challenger* comes from Joseph Trento, *Prescription for Disaster* (New York: Crown, 1987).

50 The research on situation analysis and fighter pilots is discussed in Wayne L. Waag and Herbert H. Bell, "Situation Assessment and Decision in Skilled Fighter Pilots," in *Naturalistic Decision Making,* ed. Caroline E. Zsambok and Gary Klein (Mahwah, NJ: Lawrence Erlbaum Associates, 1997).

CHAPTER 3 Find the Causes

54   The Tom Clancy quotation comes from <www.elibron.com/english/sayings>.

60   The syphilis illustration comes from Malcolm Gladwell, *The Tipping Point* (Boston: Little, Brown, 2000).

62   Charles Perrow, *Normal Accidents* (New York: Basic Books, 1984).

64   Cisco World, "Root Cause Analysis and Its Role in Management," <www.ciscoworldmagazine.com/whitepap/smarts.htm>, (October 2000).

65   For the Texas A&M bonfire report, see Special Commission on the 1999 Texas A&M Bonfire, *2000, Final Report* <http://tamu.edu/bonfire-commission/reports>, (October 2000).

67   For Petroski's analysis of the bonfire, see Henry Petroski, "Vanities of the Bonfire," *American Scientist* 88 (November–December 2000): 486–490.

68   Marcia Vickers and Gary Weiss, "Wall Street's Hype Machine," *Business Week,* April 3, 2000, pp. 113–126.

69   Experiments on the illusion of control are discussed in Ellen J. Langer, "The Illusion of Control," *Journal of Personality and Social Psychology* 32 (1975): 311–328.

69   Kathleen Wynn, "15-Year-Old Settles Stock Fraud Charges," *Record-On Line,* <www.bergen.com/news> (September 21, 2000).

71   For statistics on dot-com failures, see <www.webmergers.com> (January 3, 2001). Also see <www.webmergers.com> (March 25, 2001).

72   Frequency of death statistics and availability come from J. Edward Russo and Paul Schoemaker, *Decision Traps* (New York: Doubleday, 1989).

73   Annual report study is based on James Bettman and Barton Weitz, "Attributions in the Board Room: Causal Reasoning in Corporate Annual Reports," *Administrative Science Quarterly* 28 (1983): 165–183.

74   For a discussion of the fundamental attribution error, see Richard Nisbett and Lee Ross, *Human Inference: Strategies and Shortcomings of Social Judgment* (Englewood Cliffs, NJ: Prentice-Hall, 1980).

75   For a review of research on the hindsight bias, see Baruch Fischhoff, "For Those Condemned to Study the Past: Heuristics and Biases in Hindsight," in *Judgment and Decision Making,* ed. Hal Arkes and Kenneth Hammond (London: Cambridge University Press, 1986).

77   These ideas on creativity were gleaned from two sources: Robert J. Weber, *Forks, Phonographs, and Hot Air Balloons: A Field Guide to Inventive Thinking* (New York: Oxford University Press, 1992); and Roger von Oech, *A Whack on the Side of the Head* (New York: Warner Books, 1998).

CHAPTER 4 Evaluate the Risks

83   The John Ciardi quotation comes from <www.elibron.com/english/sayings>.

83   Although this story is true, David Gordon is a pseudonym.

86   The Boeing quote comes from Anthony Ramirez, "Boeing's Happy, Harrowing Times," *Fortune,* July 17, 1989, pp. 40–48.

87   For the new Boeing project, see Ann Marie Squeo, "Boeing Plans to Build Smaller, Faster Jet, *Wall Street Journal,* March 30, 2001, p. A3.

87 For the Boeing and Airbus forecasts, see Charles Bickers, "Tough Take-Off," *Far Eastern Economic Review,* June 22, 2000, pp. 46–47. Also see Jeff Cole, "At Boeing, an Old Hand Provides New Tricks in Battle with Airbus," *Wall Street Journal,* January 10, 2001, pp. A1, A12.

88 Interestingly, from a decision-theory perspective, the tough calls that managers face cannot be described as involving risk. In fact, for most business decisions, at least one of three factors that are necessary for a decision to be made under conditions of risk is missing. First, the outcomes of a decision may be numerous instead of limited. Second, the likelihood of each outcome is usually unknown. Third, the value of each outcome may also be unknown. In sum, tough calls are much harder than decisions made under risk because tough calls are actually made under conditions of uncertainty rather than under conditions of risk (where the conditions are not completely unknown). Rather than attempting to change the vocabulary of millions of managers, however, we will use the term "risk" to describe situations of uncertainty that many managers face.

95 The availability heuristic is discussed in Amos Tversky and Daniel Kahneman, "Availability: A Heuristic for Judging Frequency and Probability," *Cognitive Science* 5 (1973): 207–232.

97 For the research concerning anchoring and adjustment, see David Kahneman and Amos Tversky, "On the Psychology of Prediction," *Psychological Review* 80 (1973): 237–251.

97 Stephen Hoch, "Who Do We Know: Predicting the Interests and Opinions of an American Consumer," *Journal of Consumer Research* 15 (December 1988): 315–324.

97 The real estate study is found in Greg Northcraft and Margaret Neale, "Experts, Amateurs, and Real Estate: An Anchoring-and-Adjustment Perspective on Property Pricing Decisions," *Organizational Behavior and Human Performance* 29 (1987): 228–241.

101 The idea of decreasing marginal effects can be seen in economics in the idea of decreasing marginal utility. In psychology, it is found in Steven's power law and in prospect theory. See Daniel Kahneman and Amos Tversky, "Prospect Theory: An Analysis of Decision Under Risk," *Econometrica* 47 (1979): 263–291.

103 The saving-the-factory study comes from Max H. Bazerman, *Judgment in Managerial Decision Making* (New York: Wiley, 1990).

103 Kiev's quote is from Daniel Kadlec, "Day Trading: It's a Brutal World," *Time,* August 9, 1999, p. 26.

104 The GM chairman's quote comes from Maryann Keller, *Rude Awakening: The Rise, Fall and Struggle for Recovery of General Motors* (New York: William Morrow, 1989).

104 For the discussion on optimum stimulation level, see Marvin Zuckerman, *Sensation Seeking* (New York: Lawrence Erlbaum Associates, 1979), 176.

105 The quote about accident-prone skiers comes from Daniel Goleman, "Why Do People Crave the Experience," *New York Times: Science Times,* August 2, 1988, pp. C1, C13.

105 For the day-trader statistics, see Michael Maiello, "Trading Eldorado," *Forbes,* June 12, 2000, p. 360.

105   The day-trader quote comes from Tia O'Brien, "The Day Trader Blues," *Upside*, January 2000, pp. 182–192.

106   Michael Hammer and James Champy, *Reengineering the Corporation: A Manifesto for Business Revolution* (New York: Harper Collins, 1993).

106   For the GM story, see Keller, *Rude Awakening*, 205.

108   The Warren Buffett story is related in L. J. Davis, "Buffett Takes Stock," *Business World: The New York Times Magazine*, April 1, 1990, pp. 16–18, 62–64.

109   In addition to an interview with Beck Weathers, we also based this story on Jon Krakauer, *Into Thin Air* (New York: Villard, 1997).

113   The Tennessee-Tombigbee waterway project is discussed in Hal Arkes and Nancy Blumer, "The Psychology of Sunk Cost," *Organizational Behavior and Human Decision Processes* 35 (1985): 124–140.

114   Benjamin Graham's rules are found in John Train, *The Money Masters* (New York: Harper and Row, 1980), 105.

CHAPTER 5   Apply Intuition and Emotion

118   The Ernest Hemingway quotation comes from <www.elibron.com/english/sayings>.

118   The auction story is told from the viewpoint of John Mowen, who has observed Keith Murnighan run the game.

122   The material on the biology of emotions and decision-making is taken from Antonio R. Damasio, *Descartes' Error: Emotion, Reason, and the Human Brain* (New York: Avon Books, 1994).

125   The story of the tire plant was told to John Mowen by Greg Nixon, one of the representatives in the Oklahoma delegation.

126   Upton Sinclair, *The Jungle* (New York: Harper, 1951), 98–99.

128   *Challenger* material is taken from William Starbuck and Frances Milliken, "Challenger: Fine-Tuning the Odds until Something Breaks," *Journal of Management Studies*, July 1988, pp. 319–340.

128   George F. Will, *Men at Work* (New York: Macmillan, 1990).

129   Daniel Goleman, *Emotional Intelligence: Why It Can Matter More Than IQ* (New York: Bantam Books, 1995).

129   The model is discussed in John C. Mowen, *The 3M Model of Motivation and Personality* (Boston: Kluwer Academic Press, 2000).

131   The quote concerning rationality comes from Robyn Dawes, *Rational Choice in an Uncertain World* (New York: Harcourt Brace Jovanovich, 1988).

132   For the John Glenn story, see Charles Murray and Catherine Bly Cox, *Apollo: The Race to the Moon* (New York: Simon and Schuster, 1989).

134   The quotations on intuition and executives are taken from Daniel Isenberg, "How Senior Manager's Think," *Harvard Business Review* 62 (1984): 81–90; and Weston H. Agor, "How Top Executives Use Their Intuition to Make Important Decisions," *Business Horizons*, January–February, 1986, pp. 49–53.

135   Herbert Simon material is taken from Herbert Simon, *Reason in Human Affairs* (Stanford, CA: Stanford University Press, 1983).

135 For more information on Klein's work, see Gary A. Klein, Judith Orasanu, Roberta Calderwook, and Caroline E. Zsambok, eds., *Naturalistic Decision Making* (Mahwah, NJ: Lawrence Erlbaum Associates, 1997).

137 For Klein's discussion of the fire-fighting action, see Bill Breen, "What's Your Intuition," *Fast Company*, September 2000, p. 290.

138 The tonsillectomy example is related in J. Edward Russo and Paul Schoemaker, *Decision Traps* (New York: Doubleday, 1989).

139 Judith Orasanu and Terry Connolly, "The Reinvention of Decision Making," in *Naturalistic Decision Making*, ed. Gary A. Klein, Judith Orasanu, Roberta Calderwook, and Caroline E. Zsambok (Mahwah, NJ: Lawrence Erlbaum Associates, 1997).

139 Kathleen L. Mosier, "Myths of Expert Decision Making and Automated Decision Aids," in *Naturalistic Decision Making*, ed. Gary A. Klein, Judith Orasanu, Roberta Calderwook, and Caroline E. Zsambok (Mahwah, NJ: Lawrence Erlbaum Associates, 1997).

140 The Henry Kissinger quote comes from a speech by Kissinger at Oklahoma State University, College of Business Administration, Tulsa Forum, in 1991.

CHAPTER 6 Take Different Perspectives

143 The John Trimble quotation comes from <www.el.ibron.com/english/sayings>.

149 Quotes in the Mustang anecdote are taken from David Halberstam, *The Reckoning* (New York: Avon Books, 1986), 373, 376. Information was also obtained from Lee Iacocca, *Iacocca: An Autobiography* (New York: Bantam Books, 1984).

152 Coca-Cola quotes are taken from Betsey McKay, "To Fix Coca-Cola, Daft Sets Out to Get Relationships Right," *Wall Street Journal*, June 23, 2000, pp. A1, A12.

152 Donald G. Krause, *The Art of War for Executives* (New York: Berkley Publishing Group, 1995).

153 The Coke Classic vignette is adapted from John C. Mowen, *Consumer Behavior* (New York: Macmillan, 1993), 22–23.

155 For Zyman's interview, see Patricia Sellers, "So You Fail, Now Bounce Back," *Fortune*, May 1, 1995.

158 Lee Iacocca, *Lee Iacocca's Talking Straight* (New York: Bantam Books, 1904), 145–146.

160 Quotes on Apollo program come from Charles Murray and Catherine Bly Cox, *Apollo: The Race to the Moon* (New York: Simon and Schuster, 1989), 77, 80, 83.

161 Material on the space station is from William Broad, "How the $8 Billion Space Station Became a $120 Billion Showpiece," *New York Times*, June 10, 1990, pp. 1, 16.

161 John C. Mowen, *Judgment Calls* (New York: Simon and Schuster, 1993).

163 Quotes concerning the space shuttle are taken from Joseph Trento, *Prescription for Disaster* (New York: Crown Publishers, 1987).

164 Thanks to Neil Purdie, a distinguished chemist at Oklahoma State University, for identifying a third liquid (benzene) that does not mix with either oil or water.

164   Amanda Bennett, "Managing," *Wall Street Journal*, April 11, 1991, p. B1.
167   Milton Friedman, "The Social Responsibility of Business Is to Increase Its Profits," *New York Times Magazine*, September 13, 1970.
168   The four ethical rules of thumb are discussed in John C. Mowen and Michael Minor, *Consumer Behavior: A Framework* (Upper Saddle River, NJ: Prentice-Hall, 2001).
169   Donald N. Frey, "The Techies' Challenge to the Bean Counters," *Wall Street Journal*, July 6, 1990, p. A10.

CHAPTER 7   Consider the Time Frame

172   The Rolling Stones' quotation is the title of one of their songs.
174   For the Xerox story, see James Bandler, Daniel Golden, and John Hechinger, "Xerox Seeks to Survive on Tuna Sandwiches, Shared Cubicles, Layoffs," *Wall Street Journal*, December 20, 2000, pp. B1, B4.
174   Margaret Maremont and James Bandler, "Xerox Restates Results from the Past Three Years," *Wall Street Journal*, June 1, 2001, p. A3.
176   Thanks to Dr. Bruce Ackerson in the physics department at Oklahoma State University for his assistance in describing the physicist's view of time.
176   The three views of time are discussed in Robert Graham, "The Role of Perception of Time in Consumer Research," *Journal of Consumer Research* 7 (March 1981): 335–342.
180   The quote from Zeien comes from William M. Bulkeley, "Pushing the Pace: The Latest Big Thing at Many Companies Is Speed, Speed, Speed," *Wall Street Journal*, December 23, 1994, p. A1.
184   Estimates of discount rate are taken from Michael Landsberger, "Consumer Discount Rate and the Horizon: New Evidence," *Journal of Political Economy* 22 (November–December 1971): 1346–1359.
185   Gregory Zuckerman, "How Nasdaq's Mighty Have Fallen," *Wall Street Journal*, March 5, 2001, p. C1.
185   For the University of Arizona study, see Jay Christensen-Szalanski and Gregory Northcraft, "Patient Compliance Behavior: The Effects of Time on Patients' Values of Treatment Regimens," *Social Science Medicine* 21 (1985): 263–273. Also see Mancur Olson and Martin Bailey, "Positive Time Preference," *Journal of Political Economy* 89 (1981): 1–25. As a general statement, the desire to take one's gains in the present is an extremely strong finding. Exceptions to the desire to delay losses, however, can be found. For example, many people who know that they must face a bad experience (e.g., having an elective operation) will choose to have it immediately. A factor of dread appears to be operating in some instances to make people speed up the occurrence of certain types of negative outcomes.
186   The Ford E-Coat story is based on a discussion found in David Halberstam, *The Reckoning* (New York: Avon Books, 1986).
187   Peter F. Drucker, "Marketing 101 for a Fast-Changing Decade," *Wall Street Journal*, November 20, 1990, p. A20.
189   Information on 3M comes from Russell Mitchell, "Masters of Innovation," *Business Week*, April 10, 1989, pp. 58–63.

190 Jeffrey L. Seglin, "Would You Lie to Save Your Company?" *Inc.*, July 1998.

194 This summary is based on our review of the literature on the effects of time pressure on decision-making. Key references that readers may consult include: Ola Svenson and A. John Maule, *Time Pressure and Stress in Human Judgment and Decision Processes* (New York: Plenum Press, 1993); and Itiel E. Dror, Jerome R. Busemeyer, and Beth Basola, "Decision Making under Time Pressure: An Independent Test of Sequential Sampling Models," *Memory and Cognition* 27 (1999): 713–725.

195 The offshore explosion is discussed in Rhona Flin, Keith Stewart, and Georgina Slaven, "Emergency Decision Making in the Offshore Oil and Gas Industry," *Human Factors* 38 (1996): 62–89.

195 A discussion of crisis-management plans is beyond the scope of this book. Readers should note that numerous consulting firms, such as Crisis Management International, specialize in developing crisis plans for corporations.

CHAPTER 8 Solve the Problem

197 The quotation from Gilbert K. Chesterton came from <www. geocities.com >

199 You might be wondering how this is really possible. In truth, we all make split-second decisions with more ease than we might expect. Thus, if we were ever faced with jumping into a huge cauldron of deep liquid to help someone who had fallen in, we would immediately determine two things: (1) Do we swim well enough to be of assistance rather than simply adding to the problem? and (2) Is that liquid something noxious rather than water? If the first answer is "no" or the second answer is "yes," we won't dive in. We will determine this very quickly, just as we would if we heard screams coming from a burning building. If the building is engulfed by fire, regardless of the screams, we would in all likelihood not go in, a decision made almost instantly.

199 Although the outline of the Zephyr story is true, the names and details have been changed.

217 As you may have guessed, it was one of this book's authors, John Mowen, and his wife, Maryanne, who made the $20,000 investment in Zephyr Technology.

CHAPTER 9 The Master Decision-Maker

229 The quotation from Ernest Hemingway comes from <www.elibron.com/ english/sayings>.

230 Ponzi schemes are named after Charles K. Ponzi, who in 1920 collected $9.5 million from 10,000 investors by selling promissory notes offering "fifty per cent profit in forty-five days." In fact, he was using the money invested by later investors to pay his early investors. Needless to say, this scheme cannot continue forever without any investment income. Although he was certainly not the first to use such a scheme, his notoriety led to his name being attached to it.

231 Information for the New Era Fund story comes from Roger Lowenstein, "Why Gurus Weren't Wise to New Era's Wiles, *Wall Street Journal*, May 25, 1995, p. C1; William Power, "Philadelphia Wonders How It Got Fooled By New Era—and What Lies Ahead," *Wall Street Journal*, May 18, 1995, p. B1;

Joye Mercer, "Too Good to Be True," *Chronicle of Higher Education*, May 26, 1995, p. A33; Tony Carnes, "How Could a Little Known Christian Business Executive Defraud Charities of $354 million While Claiming to Do God's Work?" *Christianity Today*, October 27, 1997; and Steve Stecklow, "How New Era's Boss Led Rich and Gullible into a Web of Deceit," *Wall Street Journal*, May 19, 1995, pp. A1, A4.

234   E. S. Browning and Greg Ip, "Here Are Six Myths That Drove the Boom in Technology Stocks," *Wall Street Journal*, October 16, 2000, pp. A1, A14.

234   In the five years prior to 1929, RCA stock went from $11 a share to its September 1929 high of $114 (adjusted for the five-for-one stock split in February), reflecting an appreciation of 936 percent. And all this time they never paid a cash dividend.

235   The Ross Perot quote comes from Maryann Keller, *Rude Awakening*, 185.

236   The flight attendant's monologue is quoted in Kevin Freiberg and Jackie Freiberg, *Nuts* (Austin, TX: Bard Press, 1996), 210.

237   Dale Dauten, *The Max Strategy* (New York, Morrow, 1996).

239   Kelleher is quoted in Freiberg and Freiberg, *Nuts*, 86.

240   Peter Schwartz, *The Art of the Long View* (New York: Doubleday, 1996), 6.

240   This vision is taken from Freiberg and Freiberg, *Nuts*, 48.

242   The Xerox copier story is related in Bruce Nussbaum and Robert Neff, "I Can't Work This Thing," *Business Week*, April 29, 1991, pp. 58–66.

244   For the Aetna story, see Barbara Martinez, "Aetna Tries to Improve Bedside Manner in Bid to Help Bottom Line," *Wall Street Journal*, February 23, 2001, pp. A1, A9.

244   Information on the Hudson Institute and Walker Information study comes from Sue Shellenbarger, "Work and Family," *Wall Street Journal*, January 26, 2000, p. B1.

245   Based upon Jennifer Ordonez, "Burger King's Decision to Develop French Fry Has Been a Whopper," *Wall Street Journal*, January 17, 2001.

247   The Warthog story is taken from John J. Fialka, "A-10 'Warthog,' a Gulf War Hero, Would Fly to Scrap Heap If Air Force Brass Has Its Way," *Wall Street Journal*, March 29, 1991, p. A10.

247   Richard Hoffman, "Keep It Simple, Stupid," *Network Computing* (March 6, 2000). <www.networkcomputing.com/columnists/1104colrich.html>

250   The Nokia/Ericsson story is related in Almar LaTour, "A Fire in Albuquerque Sparks Crisis for European Cell-Phone Giants," *Wall Street Journal Interactive Edition*, <www.wsj.com> (January 29, 2001).

INDEX